LEE DAVID CARTER

living with LISA

ANGEL VISITORS GIVE A YOUNG MAN
THE COURAGE TO CLAIM THE GENDER
HE WAS DENIED AT BIRTH

LEE DAVID CARTER

living with
LISA

ANGEL VISITORS GIVE A YOUNG MAN
THE COURAGE TO CLAIM THE GENDER
HE WAS DENIED AT BIRTH

MEREO
Cirencester

Mereo Books

1A The Wool Market Dyer Street Cirencester Gloucestershire GL7 2PR
An imprint of Memoirs Publishing www.mereobooks.com

Living with Lisa: 978-1-86151-715-9

First published in Great Britain in 2016
by Mereo Books, an imprint of Memoirs Publishing

The address for Memoirs Publishing Group Limited can be found at
www.memoirspublishing.com

The Memoirs Publishing Group Ltd Reg. No. 7834348

The Memoirs Publishing Group supports both The Forest Stewardship Council®
(FSC®) and the PEFC® leading international forest-certification organisations. Our
books carrying both the FSC label and the PEFC® and are printed on FSC®-certified
paper. FSC® is the only forest-certification scheme supported by the leading
environmental organisations including Greenpeace. Our paper procurement policy
can be found at www.memoirspublishing.com/environment

Typeset in 10/14pt Century Schoolbook
by Wiltshire Associates Publisher Services Ltd. Printed and bound in Great Britain
by Marston Book Services Ltd, Oxfordshire

DEDICATED TO THE ANGELS

The ones walking the Earth and the ones
lovingly close by.

Acknowledgements

—∞—

I am indebted to the following people for their help and support:

To my mother Michelle, thank you for standing by me through my struggles and obstacles, on this amazing journey and believing in me. To my father, who passed away 2012, before publication.

To my editor Chris, those connected in the networks, in indulging in this journey of mine, in doing a wonderful job, in standing by me in the publication of the book.

Thank you for all the helpful advice and support in all those who knew me from the start, in what has been a long and challenging journey.

I would like to express my gratitude to all those who saw me through the book, including all friends and associates and those in the network. A very special 'thank you' to you all in supporting me and the encouragement received, and to the angels, in giving me the guidance and strength to see it through, facing all challenges, as well as bringing in a message of hope and love into the world. And to all who have taken the time to read this journal of discovery, may it bring many blessings to others in sharing the light.

Peace, love and light

Namaste

About the author

Lee David Carter was born in London, brought up in England and has also lived in Ireland, Mexico and the USA. He attended the University of Hertfordshire, graduating with a BA degree, and has a deep interest in spirituality and healing as well as celebrating the strangeness and wonders of the universe and of ordinary life with much love. He says:

'I can be seen as a spiritual healer and guide, as well as a motivational speaker, with a strong desire to shine my light, becoming aware of what lies within. This can be seen as meditation using the chakras, sensing inner peace in order to feel those light vibrations, love, joy, happiness, compassion and kindness, being directed from the divine, and recognised as an indigo child within the spiritual networks. I needed to heal myself first, before I could heal others regarding this astonishing story. I have been praised for my warm belly of laughter and humour. I have a tender poignancy in my writing that speaks truth. I have been featured in articles in national newspapers and magazines, as well as broadcasts on national TV. I have also made appearances on radio, both nationally and in the USA. I have now appeared in an international feature film. I am looking forward to my second book as a project regarding the continuation of this story.

The Spacious Firmament on High
Joseph Addison, 1712

The Spacious Firmament on high,
With all the blue Ethereal Sky,
And spangled Heav'ns, a Shining Frame,
Their great Original proclaim:
Th' unwearied Sun, from day to day,
Does his Creator's Pow'r display,
And publishes to every Land
The Work of an Almighty Hand.
Soon as the Evening Shades prevail,
The Moon takes up the wondrous Tale,
And nightly to the list'ning Earth
Repeats the Story of her Birth:
Whilst all the Stars that round her burn,
And all the Planets, in their turn,
Confirm the Tidings as they rowl,
And spread the Truth from Pole to Pole.
What though, in solemn Silence, all
Move round the dark terrestrial Ball?
What tho' nor real Voice nor Sound
Amid their radiant Orbs be found?
In Reason's Ear they all rejoice,
And utter forth a glorious Voice,
For ever singing, as they shine,
The Hand that made us is Divine.

PROLOGUE

Try, for one moment, to imagine a life in which you are condemned to live as an imposter, never being allowed to be true to yourself. For the past forty years I had lived such a life. While everyone else looked upon me and saw a woman, I knew, with absolute certainty, that I was a man.

* * *

8th April, 2012 – Ward 33, St John's Wood Hospital, North London. It is silent, without other patients, without staff. I am left to my own thoughts. And these are coloured by the leap of faith I am about to take. In less than three hours my life will change for ever, or it will end. I am endeavouring to co-create my reality. I am endeavouring to choose life on my own terms – and the gravity of this is overwhelming.

I have come to this point having looked into the darkness of self-loathing and self-denial. I looked into this darkness and it grabbed me and pulled me down, deeper and deeper, into an abyss of hopelessness. By the time I reached the bottom I was living a hellish existence, without purpose, without love, without light. Now the spark of life that I had come into the world with had finally vanished, and with it went my willingness to continue with the futile struggle of life, as I saw it. For, I had become the subject of my childhood nightmares – a member of the living dead. And I wanted out, and I wanted it all to end, and it was right at this moment, just seconds before my departure, that an unseen hand shone a thin beam of light into my darkness, just enough hope to sustain me for another day.

And so my life went for another two decades. Time and time again I stood perilously between life and death until finally, amid the joy of my new-found self-acceptance, a miraculous hand lifted me far into the firmament. Only then, soaring high above the illusion, could I see that the whole world was ablaze with enough hope and love for everyone – even me.

"How are you feeling, Mr Carter?" Ward Sister Beckett said, checking my chart through her red-rimmed glasses. "It won't be long now. Doctor Jennings and his team are almost ready for you."

"Thanks, I'm okay. Feeling excited."

"Let me have your arm now and we'll check your pulse," she said, breaking a little smile, because we both knew that "excited" was patient-speak for terrified.

"I heard there was some excitement on the ward last night. Were you awake for that?" she asked, skilfully pressing for my pulse.

"Yes there was!" I said enthusiastically. "There was this unusual scent, it was very strong."

"Like perfume? Hold still now, one moment."

"More like fresh washing or a flower shop. Janice and Carmel smelt it too and, couldn't make head nor tail of it."

"Nurse Barnes and Nurse Jessop," she said, correcting

me. "Perhaps one of the other patients got their hands on a spray. It wouldn't be the first time a patient misbehaved."

"Maybe, but I don't think so, and to be fair you'd need a bucket load to get rid of the antiseptic in here," I ventured, knowing full well that it hadn't been one of the three sleeping patients, nor either of the two who were awake.

"There's always a logical explanation for everything, you'll find."

"I don't know, I've witnessed some strange things" I continued, testing the water.

"All normal," she said, ignoring my statement. "I'm just going to take your pressure," she continued, taking my arm. "Now, I'm not saying I don't believe you. But in my book, if things seem too good to be true, they are."

"I guess," I said half-heartedly, knowing full well I wasn't going to get anywhere. In my experience, conversations about the supernatural either instantly met a brick wall or went in a long and winding direction – this one was definitely the brick wall.

"You mightn't think it, but I'm as open as the next person, just show me the proof. Okay, you can unclench," she said, peeling the Velcro joins apart and putting the machine aside. "Take last night," she continued, scribbling on my chart, "your mysterious smell could as easily have been imagination, auto-suggestion even or like I suggested, simply a prank. It doesn't do to let the mind wander, especially when you have patients under your care. You know, I once had a junior nurse, many years ago now, who refused to do night duty simply because she thought she saw a ghost."

"Really?" I said, my optimism perking up. Maybe Sister Beckett was more awake to the spiritual realm than I had assumed.

"All I know is that in all my years of nursing I've never seen anything. Best not to get yourself overexcited."

"I won't," I said, inching down on my pillow, feeling suddenly tired. It wasn't that I was disappointed not to be believed, I was used to that. I guess I just enjoyed sharing these wondrous experiences with others. Just like little children playing with the fairies, it's so much more fun that way.

"Anyway, that's my tuppence worth," she said, moving over to straighten the curtains. I could have added my own tuppence worth, but discernment swayed me from it, even though I was certain that the mysterious scent had, in fact, originated from an other-worldly source. I knew this as truth, because I had smelt the very same scent quite a number of times over the past two years. I could even put a name to it, for Ward-Sister Beckett, "Nan Barbara's Washing Scent," And, I would have gladly, if I had thought for one moment she'd believe me – which I didn't.

Sister Beckett had her beliefs, and they were, at this moment, unshakable as cement. No doubt she had developed them over her fifty-something life-span, and that was perfectly understandable. I did wish, however, that I had a magic wand, or the likes, to swirl her foundation just a little, so I could confide to her that the mysterious scent was only the half of it. I would have loved to tell her about the incredible sight of small glowing balls zig-zagging about the ward – for a full ten minutes. And I would have loved to chat with her about my astounding two-and-a-half-year rocket ride with the angels and spirits. Alas, since the mystifying scent went too far, I knew that brick wall wouldn't come down for love nor money. Belief is a strange commodity, especially where angels and spirits are concerned – I guess you either believe or you don't, no half-measures.

"It feels a little warm in here. A bit stuffy. I'll get that checked out for you," Ward Sister Beckett said, coming away from the window.

"No, that's okay. I feel fine," I said, suddenly feeling a little distressed. I was trying so hard to keep my mind from wandering onto my operation, another reason why I had hoped the conversation with Sister Beckett had gone the long and winding path, but all, it seems, I had managed to achieve was to exhaust my defences. I could feel them faltering, and it unnerved me. Becoming suddenly conscious of every bodily motion, I focused in on the flushing of my face, and as I did so my breath began to shorten, and this frightened me – a lot.

"Now you listen to me," I ordered myself, as I watched the door close over, "This is not a panic attack, it's just warm in here," I was praying with all my might that I was correct. "Dear Archangel Michael, please be with me now, and be with me throughout my operation, and give me your peace and your strength," I prayed, making great efforts to lengthen my breath. And as if in answer, almost instantaneously the surge of tightness released from my chest, like an opening fist. The pounding in my heart subsided to a gentle pitter-patter. And my mind, bent out of shape momentarily, snapped back to saneness.

"Thank you, Archangel Michael," I said, clasping my sweating hands in tremendous relief. I had been the victim of panic before and had no intention of giving that terror a door back into my life.

I went to take a sip of water from a glass on the side cabinet, and suddenly noticed that my fingertips were buzzing. I drummed them to make sure I hadn't inadvertently put them to sleep – No, they were working fine, but now the tingle was working its way into my wrist.

As I wriggled both wrists, I felt a distinctive Arctic shiver race up my spine, and I knew instantaneously that I was being visited by the angels. The tingling in both my hands continued for another few seconds before vanishing. Only moments before, I'd been heading towards the barbed-wire gates of panic, and now I was enjoying a paradise called peace. I knew it was the angels, I knew they had come to support me, and I knew they would walk beside the orderlies who would, within the hour, wheel me down the long, narrow corridor towards one of the most pivotal moments of my life.

Ten. Nine. Eight... a mask is put on my face and a large needle is eased into my arm. I close my eyes, trying not to think. I know the anaesthetic will take me down quickly. From beneath my lids I sense the theatre suddenly brighten. It is as if somebody has just switched on a row of blinding spotlights. I breathe deeply, willing calm. I tell myself over and over, I am not alone, and I will not succumb.

Seven. Six... I go further now, beyond the theatre light, down into a curious blue twilight. Just like a beautiful star-filled night. This blue darkness sparkles with substance, with form, but there are no hauntings here, no threats, only the trumpeting energy of transformation, rebirth, life anew. In this shimmering void, I see in full clarity just how wondrous and precious life truly is. I want to cry now. I want to scream. I want to grab onto life. How close I had come to forgoing my sacred birthright – to know thyself and be thyself.

Words reach me from the world back in the operating theatre. But I am too far gone now to acknowledge. For the next three hours I have no choice but to leave my lifeline in the hands of the surgeon. But I have no fear, because I know he won't guide the knife alone. And I know, with all certainty that when those three hours are over, I will come back changed forever.

How had my life transformed so dramatically from such dark despair to such bright happiness? How could a person fall so far and never break? How had I come from a point of self-loathing to where I could look in a mirror and truly love myself, both inside and out? How had the hopeless, the loveless, become so blessed?

There once was a girl who, with the help of the angels, saved her life by becoming a man. His name is Lee David Carter, and he is me. This is the story of how my life was saved by the grace of God and the support of the angels.

CHAPTER 1

$$\bowtie$$

It is September 14, 2009, two and a half years and five operations earlier. It is Sunday lunchtime, and having wanted to get a few bits and pieces for the week ahead, I set off on the short drive to my local supermarket. I am weaving my way through the empty car park with a definite spring in my step. And the reason? Well, exactly six months ago to the day was the momentous occasion when I began my hormone treatment. Momentous, because that was the day my second shot at life started.

Although I didn't need any additional inflation, as I was already as high as a city skyscraper, another contribution to my buoyancy was the fact that I had just started university, and in doing so I fulfilled one of those bucket-list aspirations you so readily hear about these days. Attending university had become one of my major goals, largely because poverty and want had plagued my life for so long. I saw uni as a giant rubber stamp pounding security into my future. And for someone who had ridden the rocky roller-coaster of insecurity for far too long, this was nothing short of miraculous. However, much as it made me jump for joy, by and far the biggest cause of my high spirits this day was the blessed realisation that my torturous decades of being in the wrong body were swiftly coming to an end.

I might well have done a Mary Poppins right up to the supermarket doors, I was so happy with thoughts of my new body. Just imagining the peace of mind I would receive and the wonderful opportunity for finding lasting love, just like everyone else, made me feel I could float all the way to China. I was so happy knowing that the isolation, the vulnerability, the loneliness were all gone forever that I might well have sailed into outer space. I had hope now. I had a future. I had a plan.

Like any good plan, there was a blueprint, and my brand-spanking new one went something like this. In a little over ten months' time, I would have my first operation – a mastectomy. Four others, equally daunting, it has to be said, would follow, over the space of two years, to finally give me the body I had always dreamed of – the body I could identify with, live with and from which I could say, hello world, this is me!

Soon after this momentous, life-changing transformation I would complete university – yippee! And then, with my new business degree emblazoned upon my CV, I would walk into the perfect job, maybe in London, maybe New York. (Why not New York?) Whatever the city, I would get an apartment, nothing too fancy, nothing too big to start with – a bachelor pad. (I could so see myself in that bachelor pad, with the toilet seat eternally up.) Once instated in my city, in my job, in my bachelor pad, I would make new friends, play new sports, eat in new restaurants. My eating would be done alone at first, but soon, maybe very soon, I would walk in to my new favourite restaurant with the perfect partner on my arm and she would be that significant other that I had been dreaming about (but never really expecting) all my life.

Yes, this was my plan, my blueprint. It was my dream and rather naively, at this point in my life, I assumed it was pretty much an outline of everyone's dream. That said, it felt good to me – really good to me. Finally, I was just like everyone else – no limitations. No hindrances. Nothing clipping my wings. I was finally free to be myself. I had a plan and it was a darn good one – or so I thought.

"Don't forget razors," I reminded myself, for the third time since awakening. I can't imagine in the history of people buying razors that there has ever been anyone more ecstatic about the prospect. As a youngster, I had watched my father perform his morning shaving ritual in awe: the white lather going on thick and heavy, the steady razor like a plough banking up snow. If I had made one of those bucket lists at age seven, 'SHAVE' would definitely have been highlighted boldly in red crayon. However, what would not have made an appearance on this list would have been the word 'university'. Not only would I not have been able to spell it at this stage, being a working-class London boy of the 1970s, I wouldn't have had any concept of it. university wasn't exactly something that was automatically pinned to one's horizon in my neighbourhood; being a postman or a soldier, maybe, but never university. It wasn't until much later in my life that my dreams of going to university formed.

Razors, and oh, some more pens, some green ones and maybe another bottle of Tippex, just in case.

I had legally changed my name and my gender a year

ago, which allowed me to make my university registration with both a name and a gender that matched my male identity – what an incredible moment for me. Should I get another folder? I had everything I could possibly need already, but it felt so good buying my little bits and bobs, and after decades of neglect, why on earth would I deny myself?

So up I strolled towards the supermarket entrance feeling a gentle autumnal breeze brush across my face. The rising sun was at my back; it felt warm and cosy, and it made me smile, inside and out.

I was about to float away with my daydreams when, from the corner of my eye, I noticed a woman trying to make eye contact with me. She was in her late forties or early fifties, with bottle-blonde, home-permed shoulder-length hair, outdated round glasses and an oversized smile. I smiled back, thinking maybe she was being kind for no other reason than that she too was smiling on the inside, or maybe she was just being kind because she felt so sorry for me.

I probably would have felt sorry for me too, if I hadn't felt so darn good about myself. Honestly, my looks, at this stage, a couple of months into hormone treatment, were something of an oddity. Well, to be totally honest, for all the world to see, I was a woman with staggeringly bad facial hair – it was a forest, and I loved every curious whisker.

I walked past her smile thinking, "Stare away world! Because you have no idea how good the Amazon on my face makes me feel."

And once I was inside, she wasn't the only one who was gawping. Actually, having so many people stare at me, mostly in pity, made me want to giggle. A year ago, I would have wanted to die if anyone had stared at me in this fashion (that's when I hated myself), but now, being able to truly love myself meant all the staring in the world didn't matter a jot to me.

"Mental check," I said internally, just to make sure. "Yes indeed, no fear of other people's opinions," I passed with flying colours. I was liberated. I was free.

Actually, I could have had some fun by guessing who would stare and who wouldn't, but that would just have been childish. I headed to the nearest checkout.

"Monday tomorrow," a teenage assistant quipped.

"Oh I love Mondays."

"You do?" she asked, surprised.

"I've started uni."

"You have?" she asked, extra surprised.

"I'm a late starter. I'm in my forties."

"You are?"

"Don't look it, do I?" I said, having a laugh.

"No," she said, scanning my items extra quickly. She couldn't tell, but beneath my vegetation I did look reasonably young for my age.

I really did love Mondays, no Monday blues for me. In fact, I couldn't wait to get back through the doors of uni. This was my third go at gaining a higher education. The two previous attempts were upended, at the time, by the darkness in my life. But now, this time around, it was all so different. I had all the hope my new body was bringing and I had good people in my life; yes, the support system was there, so was the determination and so was the belief. I couldn't fail and my life-plan couldn't fail – or so I thought.

As I left the supermarket and headed across the car park, the sun was in fuller glory now, and the wider world was starting to stir.

"Daddy, can I have an ice cream and a chocolate bar?" a small boy shouted, approaching me.

"Beautiful morning," I said, smiling at them both. My voice was still not deep enough yet, so I still passed as a female.

"Daddy, that woman's got a beard!" I heard over my shoulder. The poor boy was shushed up sternly by his mortified father.

"That would so be me at that age," I laughed, digging for my keys.

It was such a beautiful morning, even in the grey of the car park, it was just perfect. I let my mind drift into daydreaming as I opened the boot to store away my groceries. I really was so excited about the prospects my new future held. I had read, in one of the many self-help books I had devoured, that it was really good to visualise the things you wanted in life, and so I got busy seeing my new life: my furniture, my weekends, my sports clubs, my new friends and most importantly my new lover, right there in the midst of it all – what a day-dream. My goal now was simple: I would work the plan I had created diligently, and with a whole heap of determination and hard work, I would achieve it all.

I smiled broadly as I lowered the boot lid, sensing that my dream was finally within reach, and turned right into the face of a smiling woman. Not any woman mind – it was the same blonde fifty-something who had been so eager to make eye-contact with me at the entrance, only now she was standing uncomfortably close to me, still smiling.

"Hello," I said lamely, not knowing what else to say. I really hoped this wasn't going to be one of those awkward situations where you had to inch your way slowly towards your car door for your own safety. Don't get me wrong, I like being nice. And I'd be the first to admit that I am guilty of rubbing every single dog I can get my hands on, and equally guilty of talking to their owners, whether they really want me to or not. But there are limits (are there not?) to how far friendliness with strangers should be taken, and at this moment I'd have to say that the blonde fifty-something was taking it way too far.

"I was sent to speak with you," she said, drawing on a cigarette. "I waited inside and had two coffees, even though I really only wanted the one."

"Okay."

"I was waiting for you."

"Just smile and keep smiling," I told myself, "and by the way, right about now would be the perfect time to start edging your way along the side of the car."

"You know there are spirits and angels all around you. And I'm to tell you that they are supporting you."

"Really?" I said, turning and walking towards my door.

"You don't believe me, do you? Anyway, you're not to worry about university, you're going to be fine."

"How did you know I'm studying?" I asked turning back to her. My immediate thought was that this lady was actually trying to do a number on me, followed by, "I mean, how hard would it be for her to find out details about me?" Followed by, "Not so difficult, you hear of confidence tricksters all the time, don't you?"

"How did I know about university?" she said, obviously pretending to read my mind.

"They told me."

"They?"

"Well, John to be precise. He told me, he's my guide."

"Your guide? Like a guidance counsellor? Does he know me from uni?"

"He knows you, yes, but not from your university. It's because he's a spirit."

"He's dead?" I said, truly wishing I hadn't turned around.

"They usually are," she said laughing," Listen honey, haven't you heard the term Light-Worker before?"

"Should I have?"

"It would make it easier for me if you had. Still, the angels know what they're doing."

"Come on, you're saying there are angels about me now?"

"They're always around us, but in your case, there are quite a number of them. You've had it hard, haven't you?"

"That's a pretty general statement, don't you think?" I said questioningly. "So they're here wings and all?"

"If you like."

"And you can see them?"

"No, but that doesn't change the fact that they've sent me here to wake you up."

"Wake me up?"

"From the illusion, from your forgetfulness, so you can see your truth."

"The angels want me to wake up to who I am?"

"The angels, the helpers, the guides, the higher-beings, the spirits, call them what you want. There are millions of people waking up all across the planet, and today's your day."

"Is that so?"

"I'm here to tell you that you have a unique journey ahead of you. A purpose, if you like. It's why you're here. It's why you were born. In other words, there's work to be done."

"No offence, but you know, it does all sounds just a little far-fetched," That was the politest way I could find of telling her she was nuts.

"Okay, but you've already been receiving signs, haven't you?"

"Signs? How do you figure that? No I don't think so."

"Feathers, scents, dizziness, heavy head – signs."

"Yeah no, nothing special," I said, suddenly feeling a little queasy. "Well, maybe some physical stuff, but that's all perfectly explainable," I said guardedly, not wanting to divulge any more personal information to her.

"Okay, but what about the burning sensation you're having?"

"What…" my question was curtailed by an unexplainable heat erupting across the right side of my chest.

"You're feeling it, aren't you?"

"Yes" was all I managed to get out before my head turned into a spinning-top.

"You okay hun?" she asked, totally unconcerned. "They do that, the burning, to prove to you that I'm not bonkers. You thought I was, didn't you?"

"No, well, yes, okay maybe a little off the tracks," I said, gaining my breath.

"I'm Candy, by the way."

"I'm Lee. Did you know that already?"

"No, I'm only told what I need to know."

"They're not going to bolt me again are they?" I asked, like there was an invisible angel holding an electric cattle-prod beside me.

"Not unless they need to," she said, clearly enjoying herself. "Do they need to?"

"No, no I'm listening."

"Don't worry hun, they're great fun, when you get to know them."

"They are?" I said, sceptically.

"Yes, you'll see, your life will never be the same again."

"Never?"

"Never, isn't it great? So was your life very bad? I'm getting that it was."

"No, not very. Um, what else did they say about me?"

"Just that they're going to help you heal."

"I'm going to have operations, five in all."

"Yes and everything will be fine, they said I can tell you that. But it's not your physical healing I'm talking about, it's your spiritual."

"Spiritual? I'm not even sure I know what that means."

"It means clearing out all the garbage you've accumulated from living a life in darkness and denseness. It means clearing the way so you can realise who you are. You've had a lot of darkness in your life, haven't you?"

"That's all in the past," I said, really hoping, because she was right, that she hadn't been filled in on all the gory details.

"They say you're writing a diary, to help you get to grips with everything, and they want you to know that they're very grateful that you listened."

"I did?"

"You were guided to do that."

"Was I? Actually a friend of mine suggested I do it."

"Yes, but who plunked that idea into her head, it was a her wasn't it?"

"Yes, Sarah, my good friend Sarah."

"Well, Sarah was guided to help you. You see hun, you've probably met countless others who have helped you in one way or another. Anyway, the fact is you've still some way to go. There's still a lot of healing to do first."

"First?"

"First, and then you can get on with what you're supposed to do."

"After uni, I want to get a job."

"No listen," she said, waving me down. "I don't do predictions, but I'll say this, your plans for the future might alter slightly, or greatly."

"Slightly or greatly?" I asked, hoping it was the slightly.

"The biggest challenge you have in front of you at the moment isn't your exams, it isn't even your operations."

"Then what is it?" I asked, almost afraid to ask.

"It's your journey to move from fear to love and, fulfil your life's purpose."

"Purpose?"

"Yes purpose. Do you suppose we're all here just to work and get cars and houses?"

"Well, why not? I mean, if it makes you happy."

"You think it does?"

"Your parents had a house and a car, yes?"

"Yes."

"And were they happy?"

"Sometimes. How much have they told you about me?" I said, feeling the sweat about my collar. I hated talking about my past – too many heartaches, too much sorrow, too many regrets.

"Look hun, we all come into this world having already set out for ourselves a life purpose. For some it might be a series of lessons to help our souls grow, and for others it might be specific work for the planet."

"But I'm not spiritual and, to be honest I haven't a clue what you're on about. You'd have more luck speaking with my friend Sarah, she's into all this stuff. Look, I'm not sure I even believe in God and angels. Well, maybe I believe, with the burning chest and all, but I'm not sure, that's what I'm trying to say."

I was having a really strong suspicion, at this point, that maybe the angels had fingered the wrong person. There had been darkness in my life, so much darkness. I had done things I wished I hadn't. I had seen things no one should see. And I had dealt with things alone, when no one should be alone. I had lived the best part of my life in survival mode, and there had been no place for faith in anything.

"We are all spiritual, whether we believe it or not. And we all make mistakes, especially when we are unhappy, especially when we are forced to be someone we aren't. You know what I'm talking about, don't you?"

Let's see: unhappiness, mistakes, forced to be someone I wasn't, wrong body and all... hell yes, I knew what she was talking about and it unnerved me.

"You okay hun?" she asked, a little more concerned this time.

"Just feeling a little dizzy again," I said, when in truth I felt like something had just come behind me and pushed me off balance – deliberately.

"I'm just a little out of breath," I added. In fact I felt like the air had just rarefied and that gravity was pressing Mount Everest down upon me.

"Okay?"

"No, actually I'm feeling... I don't know how I'm feeling," I said looking about me. I felt excited and exhausted at the same time. I felt clear-headed and confused. I felt perhaps my blueprint was nothing more than a well-packaged dream and that if all this was actually happening to me then, reality was something much more elusive than I had been led to believe.

You do hear of people having profound awakenings in exotic places, don't you? Exotic places like a hidden ashram discovered by the lapping Ganges; like a heavenly high-altitude Tibetan paradise complete with fluttering prayer flags. But, here was in a downscale supermarket car park being asked to accept the fact that I was having my own spiritual awakening. As I said, don't tell me the universe doesn't have a sense of humour.

"You'll get used to it, all the new energies," Candy said, resting against my car. "It's for your own good, for everyone's good. There's a ton of people we need to reach, to help. I shouldn't have worn these shoes, I knew I shouldn't," she digressed, like we were discussing the weather.

Crazy as it all sounded though, the ludicrous thing was, I was finding myself starting to get sucked in by her. This Candy, whoever she was, was starting to have an effect on me. I was starting to see how my life could involve more than a self-centric existence. I was starting to see how I could, through self-love, become a positive addition to the world – maybe even be of use to others. My mind flashed back to my early childhood; I certainly would have put "Helping People" on that hypothetical bucket list. What a departure this way of thinking was from the thoughts I had been having only five minutes ago, that plan that contained so much singularity: my job, my apartment, my car, my sports club, my lover. Thinking of "WE" as a plan, we as in not just me – it was revelatory.

Yes, I dare say going from me to we in five minutes was as profound an awakening as any. And maybe, as short an awakening as any. Because just at the moment when I caught a glimpse of the WE version of life, it was instantly snatched from my new eyes by a multitude of doubts restoring my old vision.

"Here, take my number. We'll have to go for a coffee," Candy said, passing me a pink Post-It note.

We most certainly will, I said to myself, taking the innocuous scrap of paper. "We most certainly will," I continued. "It seems you've just upended my entire life in as short a conversation as I just had with the checkout assistant."

"Call me!" she said, breezing off as happy as you like.

Call me? Is that all I get? My goals, my dreams, as shaky as a sandcastle bracing the approaching tide, and she quips 'call me'! I thought, wide-eyed. And that's pretty much how I stayed, wide-eyed, watching her walk off into the distance. What the hell had just happened? And how in hell did she know those things about me? I was in the midst of a great debate, or maybe a great trauma was closer to the mark.

"Okay, let's look at this logically," I told myself. "The stuff about university, well that was easy enough, all she had to do was follow me and put two and two together. But the bit about the diary, the feathers and the scents – oh that was good, seems no one apart from my mum and my friend Sarah knows about that. Okay, what the hell just happened?"

I have to admit, she had me convinced enough to half-expect to see some angelic manifestation walking beside her. For a second, in her wake, I felt an unbelievable sense of awe. I mean, wow – what the hell had just happened?

And then, as I turned back to my car, I felt an unbelievable sense of panic. "What in God's name are you thinking?" I scolded myself. "Are you mad? Hormonal? Delirious?" I scanned the car park for a moment, half-expecting to see a TV crew filming it all. It had to be the hormones. And she had to be batty.

I slid into my car, and paused inside – I needed to. What the blazes had just happened? I stuck the key in the ignition. And then, this terrifying thought hit me. What if there were angels sitting in the car with me right now? I paused again, keeping my eyes stuck on the windscreen. "Crap, I'm going to have to look," I told myself, knowing that if I didn't I'd be imagining Bigfoot behind me by the time I got home. I glanced back over my shoulder. Nothing there, thank God. But what if they were invisible? It seemed to me that there were two conflicting voices now in my head, one cheering for logic and the other cheering for, well, the angels. Had one of those invisible cattle-prod wielding angels hopped onto my shoulder so they could whisper straight into my head?

But what the hell was I blabbering about?" Boy, that lady had really done a job on me. I looked hard around the car. No angels. I told myself to get a grip.

My journey home turned into a battlefield in my head. One minute I was firmly rooted back on Planet Earth, thinking the woman was completely bonkers. The next I was looking for wings. My plans were torn up and sticky-taped back together so many times in the three-mile drive that I honestly didn't know whether I was going to be wearing a suit in New York or a saffron robe in New Delhi. It felt like my mind was being split in two. And that's when the sirens went off, prompting me to slam down on the brakes.

"Woo! Hold on a minute, slow down there buddy, let's back up here, throw yourself a lifebuoy, hold onto your plans, your dreams," I told myself. I took a deep breath. The dominant voice in my head pushed itself to the fore, taking charge. "Right, we'll have ourselves back on track in a jiffy, right now – what was it? That's right, take a deep breath. Right, there's the job, the apartment, the friends, the furniture, the weekends, the sports club, the sports car (eventually) and the beautiful, adoring wife." I took another deep breath, letting the insanity wash from my system. "Yes there it is, I could get it back," And then, just when I thought I could safely put the whole episode down to a left-over plate of lasagne a small voice whispered in my ear a very sweet, "NO!"

It was such a small, gentle voice; how had that dominant

one allowed it to slip in? Where had this voice come from? Who was being such a poor sport? And then, another chest glow materialised, and I knew in an instant that I was in trouble. I knew it wasn't the voice of an angel or some higher being, which I could go on ignoring. I knew resistance was futile, because that wee, gentle voice with a gut-churning sting to it was in fact me, or a part of me, making us somehow a WE. In all honesty, I didn't know at this point what to make of it all. I just felt now that there were two of us in the driving seat.

If I had pondered spiritual awakening before this (which I can assure you I hadn't), I guess I would have imagined that you would suddenly find yourself a glowing, saintly encyclopaedia – total revelation and total holiness in a snap. Maybe this is how it happens for some.

I pulled over a block from my home. I looked down the avenue of trees. "How can this be an awakening?" I asked myself, not getting it at all. Firstly, I certainly didn't feel knowledgeable. If anything, it felt like I had just been turned upside down and all the knowledge I had acquired over my lifetime had just been spilled into the gutter. And secondly, as to the matter of holiness, let's face it, back in the car park, when I thought the angels might be hitching a ride, had I not been far more concerned with the state of my upholstery than the state of my soul? Awakening? I just didn't get it, and yet, turning the key to make the last block of my journey, I had the uncanny feeling that there were other hands on the steering wheel.

CHAPTER 2

—⟨✕⟩—

Three weeks earlier, all the established hopes and dreams for my future had still been intact. I'd been up a ladder, paintbrush in hand, swishing new magnolia over old magnolia. Below, my mum, Michelle, and my friend Sarah (guider of diary writing), supervised, as self-appointed spotters of bits I had missed. It was hard work, and my face must have shown it.

"It must be the hormones. Lee, it's the hormones. I'm telling you," Mum said, looking up at me with an aromatic cup of fresh coffee clasped within her hands. It was a little over five months since I had started my hormone treatment and the hormones were getting blamed for everything. If I sneezed, it was the hormones. If I didn't spend the entire afternoon up a ladder painting Mum's hall, it was the hormones.

"Bound to be the hormones, when you think about it,"

agreed Sarah. She hadn't known Mum too long, but they got on like fellow conspirators. Sarah had come into my life under extraordinary circumstances, and in a matter of a year, had led me along the thorny path towards my gender transformation. And as if this wasn't enough, straight after that she guided me into third level education.

So you see, it wasn't hard for Mum to adore Sarah. After years of torment, Mum could see the glow of happiness swirling about me. Without doubt, Sarah was one of those bright beacons that shine in your life, whether they are around or not. Meeting Sarah was without doubt a pivotal moment in my life. She turned up at the very moment when I needed a friend. And again, right on cue, she introduced me to someone who, like me, felt they were in the wrong body, only this person was already walking the path of transformation. I had no notion, at this stage of my life, about synchronicity, or I would have instantly recognised meeting Sarah as synchronicity in motion.

"It's not the bloody hormones!" I chided. "Honestly, what are you two like? Get up here for an hour and you'll see what's making me sweat."

"It is the hormones. Look at those arms and that stubble," Mum said, scrutinising my hair growth.

"Yeah, puberty all over," I said, deepening my voice. We all knew that having my chance to go through a puberty of sorts as a male meant everything to me.

"You know you'll have to take a razor to that stubble," Sarah said teasingly. She knew how proud I was of my facial hair.

"No, not yet, I'll wait until its Epping Forest," I said, feeling my face. My periods had stopped four months before, which had a hugely positive psychological effect on me. Whereas before I had hated the mirror, I now found myself enjoying my reflection. I was becoming more masculine by the day – I was finally becoming me.

"Well by the time you've finished it might have grown a couple of millimetres, so don't think you're coming down until you've finished!" Sarah scolded, waving a playful finger at me. She was such a breath of fresh air. I just loved being around her.

"I notice I didn't get a cup," I said, trying to worm my way into a break. It was hard work and I really was sweating – not perspiring, honest to goodness bucketing – manly farmers' aftershave and all – it was fantastic.

"Did he tell you he's finding small white feathers all over the place?" Mum asked Sarah, skilfully ignoring my whingeing.

"It's the cat, it's Felix," I replied, without looking.

"Oh Lee don't! You don't have a cat."

"Well that puts Felix in the clear," I said, stretching into the corner.

"He was like this as a child, a real cheeky sod!" Mum laughed, proudly. She really was happy that important strands of my life were knitting together so perfectly. Finally, at long last, I had a genuine smile upon my face beneath the magnolia. What mother wouldn't be happy?

"All right, which one of you just sprayed me?" I demanded, almost choking on a mouthful of floral scent.

"Ah Lee, don't!" Mum said, looking around cagily.

"What don't?"

"Don't mess like that, you know I don't like it." Mum was superstitious, so anything out of the ordinary immediately stood her hairs on end.

"No, I'm serious. Sarah, let me see your hands," I said, well wise to her antics.

"Look, nothing!" Sarah replied, palms up. "I swear it

wasn't us, was it?" she said, drawing Mum in for backup.

"No Lee, it wasn't," Mum confirmed, shaking her head, then, paused. "Hold on, I'm smelling something too."

"Thank you! Am I right?" I said, feeling vindicated, while eyeing Sarah as the culprit.

"Oh my God Lee, you know what I think it is?"

"I think I know, Sarah!"

"No, it's not me!"

"No it's not her, it's Nan Barbara. Oh good Lord! I think it's Nan Barbara."

"Oh don't be mad! Here grab this Sarah, I'm coming down," I said, holding out the brush.

"No Lee, I'm telling you I'd know that smell anywhere. It's her washing powder."

"Washing powder?"

"Could be," suggested Sarah.

"Oh don't encourage her, Sarah. Next she'll be saying Nan is the one shedding feathers."

"Lee! Don't joke like that about the dead."

"Seriously Mum. Nan Barbara waits twenty years for the moment when I'm up a ladder to put in an appearance – please!"

"No Lee, that could be the angels. That would make sense because of the feathers," Sarah said seriously.

"Look Sarah, come and look at all these feathers," Mum said, going to the drawer. "And that's just since he's been with me."

"Chuck them away. Crikey, I don't know why I said anything."

"No Lee you can't do that!" Mum said, horrified, "What will your Nan think?"

"Even worse, what will the angels think?" Sarah added, stirring the pot.

"Spirits and angels? You're having a laugh," I said, not believing a word of it. "What would Nan say? What would the angels say?" Not very much, I thought, leaving them to their madness.

* * *

"Now who's the mad one?" I thought, glancing over my shoulder as I pulled up outside my apartment. Maybe if I hadn't been such a cocky little sod, and actually listened to what Sarah and Mum were trying to tell me, the other side might have gone easy on me. I turned off the ignition. Maybe they of the Celestial Realm had been trying to get my attention for a very long time, and maybe the ladder incident was the final straw. And maybe they were simply sick of being ignored. Feathers and scents were nice, subtle, elegant prods, but now instead of subtle, I'm dealing with a 100-ton in-your-face explosion called Candy. Why didn't I listen?

Instead of being up a ladder, I now found myself out on a ledge. And, I of all people, knew only too well that a ledge is a very lonely place to be. I had fought tooth and nail to get my life back on track. Against all the odds, I had finally gathered up the pieces necessary to take me to a good life, an accomplished life. And now what did I have? What plan did I have for my future? Nothing. Nada. Zilch. There was only this elusive path signposted by feathers, scents and invisible angels. It was a journey without guidelines into the unknown, into the unimaginable, into the inconceivable. I was asking myself to put all my trust, all my faith in the navigational skills of an invisible force which, to be honest, I wasn't at all sure existed –

and even if it did exist, could I be 100% certain that it

was benevolent? And even if it was benevolent, how on earth could I be certain what it truly wanted with me? What if it wanted to redirect me one way, and I made a mistake and went the other, as I inevitably I would some time? What then – would it get annoyed and leave me? What if it all got too much for me and I wanted to call a halt? What if I couldn't? What if I just had to carry on down a path that was obscure and unsettling? Would I have the courage to handle it, to keep going? What about my own wants and wishes? Was I still free to choose? What if this and what if that? There were just too many what ifs. And suddenly, that ledge touched the stratosphere.

* * *

I went to bed later that night having exhausted myself getting on and off that ledge. Was there anything in my past that signalled this might happen? I pulled the razor from its package and placed it beside the sink for the morning. The dreams I had for my life had been very much upscale versions of the dreams I enjoyed growing up. Like most people I know, the dreams I conjured in my formative years were very much moulded by my family circumstances. And the circumstances of my birth in April 1968 placed me in a working class family, whose motto, inherited from my mother's side of the family, went along the lines of, 'Don't expect too much out of life, because you won't get it'. Living hand to mouth, in one of the poorest suburbs of North London, I guess the motto fitted perfectly. Yet despite these humble beginnings and that depressing motto, I must point out that by and large my earliest memories were coloured brightly by happiness.

I was born into a world in turmoil. Martin Luther King

Jr. had just been gunned down in Memphis, the prolonged Vietnam War showed no signs of resolution and the movie-going population were happy leaving for *Planet of the Apes* whilst heading off with Stanley Kubrick on a grand Space Odyssey. And into all of this oddity, came me; Lisa Keepence, a seven-pound pink bundle of confusion. For all intents and purposes, if you consider the body the be-all and end-all of our identity, then I guess the blanket they wrapped around me was appropriate. My body was that of a girl, but my psyche, my mind, my personality, call it what you will, was always male. This may be hard to fathom if you haven't had to live with such a mismatch, as I have. Try to imagine, for one moment, that you have never seen your reflection. You could, I'm sure, still very easily sense your masculine or feminine identity. For me, no matter what my reflection said, or what people said, I just couldn't feel anything but masculine. I felt 100% that I was male, and nothing on this planet could ever convince me otherwise.

Feeling this way so strongly created quite a dilemma for that little bundle in pink. From day one, when I started to get a sense of my identity, I gravitated to all things boyish – and footballs in particular. I could dare anyone to find a picture of me, from the age of one onwards, that didn't contain a ball of some description. The pinks and the frills were part of my wardrobe until my opinion became vocal, around the age of five, and from this point forward the cotton dresses were kicked to the kerb, to be replaced by dungarees, baseball caps and T-shirts. Luckily for me, it was the seventies, and the "tomboy" look was everywhere. Twiggy, the original supermodel, had started the ball rolling in the 1960s, making the look the height of fashion. Now the look ditched the tailoring in preference for a more casual "American Heartland" feel, which of course was manna from heaven for me. I could dress and act as I liked – salad days if ever there were.

The freedom to express my male identity, under the cover of my tomboy label, cleared the way for my father and me to become best buddies. And, as far as buddies went, I couldn't have imagined a better one than Dad. He was an ex-army man, so in my eyes he was a real hero. And whenever I played with my bag of plastic green soldiers, at maybe six or seven, I always had my Dad leading the charge. Until his married life began, the army was all my father knew. He signed up, at the tender age of 15, alongside his brother Gerry, who was a year older. Their older brother, Raymond, was already stationed in Italy when the boys donned their uniforms for the first time. It really was no surprise to anyone that the three Keepence boys entered the service. You see, their father, a naval officer, was tragically killed during the Second World War in North Africa serving his country. So you can understand why the military meant so much to my father and his brothers – their father being immortalised when they were all still in short trousers.

Like millions of other British children, my father was an evacuee. Weeks before his seventh birthday, he found himself miles away from his mother and all that he knew. Unlike other children who were reunited with their families straight after the war in 1945, my father, having lost his father, had to remain in care. He was in care, in fact, right up to the day he signed up for the army. His military career consisted of tours stationed in Italy and then Germany. He probably would have remained a career soldier had it not been for a tragic car accident during his second tour in Germany, in which his older brother and his best friend died. Traumatised by the accident, my father resigned his post and returned to Britain. Back in civilian life, he moved to the London Borough of Enfield, bought a small three-bedroom semi-detached, married my mother and took up a job in Ferguson, the television maker, as a supervisor. And it wasn't long after this that the second bedroom in the house to be wallpapered was occupied by me – all 7Ibs of me.

Not long after my arrival my mother started working full-time on the assembly line at Ferguson. Female employment rose steadily in the 1970s owing largely to an increase in the divorce rate. But at this time, it was still very unusual for a married woman such as my mother to work full-time, especially with her husband being so gainfully employed. I never questioned why my mother had to work long night shifts as well as raise her growing family.

Within four years, there were three of us: me aged four, Karen, two, and baby Gavin. I suppose alarm bells should have gone off at some stage, but I guess there are lots of things you should notice as a kid and thankfully don't.

By the time I was six, the configuration of our family was well established. In the words of Nan Barbara, going from bottom to top, 'there was a proper boy, a proper girl and a proper tomboy'. And this labelling suited me just fine.

Now at this stage, me being six or seven, the only feathers in my life were the ones you stick in your head whilst running up and down the street pretending to be a barefoot running brave, or occasionally, Robin Hood, who was enjoying something of a resurgence at this time. As for angels, apart from Christmas, and the occasional throwaway mention of a guardian angel, they really didn't figure too strongly in things. Spirituality in general, in all honesty, was on the vague side. Whilst my father presented us with a curious philosophical mixture of the bible and science, it really didn't go anywhere. If anything, for me it was the science that stood head and shoulders above everything my father discussed with me, everything apart from football, which was king for me. Still, science was a comfortable second, mainly because it allowed my fertile imagination to stir with the most wondrous imaginings of off-world places. I loved the idea that there were other worlds out there, stuffed with other civilisations. But, as for the Bible, in truth, with the exception of Nan Barbara, none of us had much use for it – even at Christmas. (Which maybe is one of the reasons why I found it so hard to buy the revelation, from Candy, that spirituality had been earmarked for me.)

I can imagine Nan Barbara having some satisfaction at the turn out of events, because, God bless her, she never gave up with her Bible preaching, no matter how wild and wayward we became. With my mother working full-time, we were often left in her care, which, at the time, scared the living daylights out of us. Oh, she was a good woman all right, a religious person who walked the talk, you could say. If she wasn't kneeling in prayer, she was scavenging through the house for things she could donate to the Salvation Army. I guess her overt show of holiness never gelled with us. It just seemed too formal, too restrictive, too dangerous (the hell bit) for youngsters to relate to. By and large, we left the state of our immortal souls safe in the hands of Nan Barbara, preferring to have nothing to do with religion until the 25th of December came around. And even then, it was the pomp, not the ceremony, that made Christmas the highlight of our year.

Those early Christmases when Santa was still stuffing himself down the chimney were especially happy times for me. Ah, the days of magic when wonderment was still thick in the air! I may have looked like a girl, but believe me, all my adventures were boy stories. I sailed the high seas avoiding scurvy-ridden sea-dogs. I fought fearsome dragons with my trusty sword and shield. I went off to Neverland, dirty-faced and ragged just like all the lost boys. And when the happy occasion of losing a tooth came around, I, like any boy, eagerly awaited the arrival of my good pal the Tooth Fairy. But this was not any Tooth Fairy; mine came with bow and arrow ready to protect his loot. And at seven, I was glad of that, otherwise some greedy vagabond might magic himself up to rob it, and then where would I be? I wouldn't have been able to buy a bag of penny sweets in the morning.

To my mind it was obvious that the Tooth Fairy had to be a boy because gathering teeth was something only a boy would do. What he did with all those teeth I couldn't imagine, but I was sure he took them all back to his home, which I'd imagine, from all the interstellar stories my Dad had begun to tell me, was definitely somewhere in the stars.

Whilst I firmly believed in Santa and the Tooth Fairy, my belief in my elusive guardian angel and the whole notion of God was at best wavy and unstructured. Many would say I was living a thoroughly godless life; be that as it may, all I know is that my young heart still soared eagerly every morning to the rising sun and the chirping birds.

* * *

Still in the time-frame when my teeth were very lucrative, I was busy one fine summer's day out the back, kicking a ball. I had, in the space of twenty minutes, walloped the window a couple of times, so when my father's mother, Nan Ethel, stuck her stern expression out the window I expected quite the tongue-lashing to commence.

She was a frail woman, Nan Ethel, but her tongue could

peel the skin from you. Karen and Gavin were terrified of her. As for me, I didn't mind her so much. You see, I had a secret weapon. It drove my siblings crazy when she would pull me aside just to compliment me for my red hair and pale complexion. They reminded her of her own mother. So you could say she had a soft spot for me – which, by the look at her flailing nostrils, might be the difference between life and death for me.

"Lisa! Come on in here for a second," she called. Not exactly the skinning I had expected. But maybe she just wanted me inside first. Maybe I should make a run for it.

"Lisa, inside!" she hollered, "and leave that ball there!" She knew me too well.

"I'm in for it now," I told myself, sulking into the kitchen. At best I could expect a right old telling off, at worse, a grounding. I raised my head, steely myself for the inevitable. Where in blazes had she gone? I looked about the kitchen. And more importantly, what was she up to?

Five-year-old Karen was sitting at the table playing with her dolls. I ignored her, as I always did when she was playing with dolls, and went straight for the hall door. Peering outside, extra covertly, I spotted Nan Ethel bent over rummaging in a draw. Surely she wasn't looking for something to wallop me with? No she wouldn't, Mum wouldn't stand for it, I tried to convince myself. Although my Nan was always civil enough to her daughter-in-law, even a seven-year-old could tell there was no love lost between them.

And then the thought flew into my head, "Oh no, please God not on a fine day like this, let her be searching for a bible." Whereas Nan Barbara's preaching was mostly soft and warm like her, Nan Ethel's was more on the traditional side; hell and brimstone.

Getting a second wind, I cagily slipped my head back into the hall just as my grandmother straightened. Within seconds she was back in, hiding something behind her back.

"Yeah, must be the bible," I said, preparing myself.

"Sit down there for a moment," she said, pointing to the stool beside Karen. I did as I was told, as cagily as a lion tamer, keeping both eyes on her. She stood over me until my chair was dragged under the table. And only then did she take her arm from her back.

"Ah Nan!" I hollered, spotting the gigantic scissors dangling from her hand. This was even worse than the Bible. "I don't need another trim," I protested sternly, "I just had one a couple of months ago. Give Karen one, she never minds. Do you, Karen?"

"Oh stop your moaning. It'll only take a minute, then you can go back out and play."

"I'll have my hair trimmed, Nan," Karen said, shoving a shoe onto her Sindy doll.

"After this one," Nan told her, grabbing my hair back into a ponytail. At this stage my hair went halfway down my back, not as long as Karen's waist-length hair but long enough for my mother to be proud of it. "Stay still will you? You're like someone with ants in their pants!" she snapped, taking a brush to it, over and over and over.

At this stage even Karen put down her doll, probably thinking the same as I was thinking; "What on earth is this crazy woman trying to do to me?" For Karen to stop playing, Nan must have been doing a pretty darn good impression of a Nan possessed; Letting my hair go, then sweeping it back up, letting it go, sweeping it back up. At one stage she yanked my hair so hard I thought she was trying to pull it straight off.

"Nan, you're hurting me!" I cried, wriggling to break free.

"Sit still, will you!" Nan shouted back in a panic. Before I could say another word my head flew forward and Karen sprang to her feet and raced to the door screaming, "You're not doing that to me, I'm telling, I'm telling!"

Nan dropped the scissors in fright and ran after her with my lovely pony tail dangling from her hand. The whole ordeal had left me flummoxed. I just couldn't understand the way the females in this family behaved – any of them. And that was why I did my level best to avoid shopping, hairdressers and beauty parlours at all costs.

Upstairs, I could hear Nan banging on Karen's door. I got up from the table and took myself out to the hall mirror. Now, this should have been the moment when my head exploded or something. It should have been the moment I accused Nan of totally ruining my life, as any little girl would. But, as I was, let's say, not your typical little girl, I looked in the mirror and smiled profusely, as any little boy would.

The aftermath of my shearing had Karen locked in her room and refusing to come out until Mum got home, and my poor Nan calming her nerves with one powerful cup of tea after another. My mother had never let my hair go above my shoulder blades, so my new short crop was a bright curiosity to me.

"Why did Mum let you cut my hair, Nan?" I asked picking off bread crusts from my jam sandwich.

"Don't speak with your mouth full!" Nan snapped, looking me over cautiously. I think, maybe, she was having second thoughts, because she left long before Mum could get her hands on her.

I still don't know why Nan decided to cut my hair that day. By the way she sulked about the kitchen for the rest of the afternoon, I don't think she understood herself. Maybe she looked out and pitied me struggling to play football with this mass of tangled hair. Or maybe Nan's intuition told her that I needed to be treated as a boy. And for once, she simply let her reason stand aside for her to act on impulse.

Now obviously my mother didn't see it that way. She absolutely hated my hair. She thought either Nan had gone stark raving mad or de-cloaked into the wicked witch she had always suspected she was. Mum seethed for a couple of days, while Dad just shrugged off the incident. "Her hair is fine, I don't know why you're making such a big deal about it," he said.

"Well you would say that, anything for a peaceful life."

"Anything. I'm off to meet Tom and Jerry."

Hearing my father say this always made me laugh, but not too loudly, especially when Mum was in a mood. Thankfully, her mood ran its course quickly enough and Hairgate was forgotten about temporarily. Mum might have hated my hair but I, on the contrary, loved it. I loved it so much that I swore, even if it meant taking scissors to my head, that I would never let it grow long again. From there on in, there was a race between me and Karen as to who was having their hair trimmed first. And every time this happened, Hairgate was revisited, and my mother spent the next ten minutes blaming my Nan. (My hair never did grow long after that – Nan in heaven, I don't know what drove you, but I'm grateful anyway.)

In addition to football and hair-trims, stargazing was another of my great passions at this time. Santa being the wise old man that he is, gave me the perfect gift, age eight – a telescope. And my father and I immediately took every advantage of it. I'd look up at my father pointing out the various constellations, talking about the great expanse of the universe and all about the teeny tiny atoms and I thought to myself that he was more than a father, he was like a wizard, a genius even. Searching for the stars through my tiny telescope, dunking Rich Tea biscuits into cups of tea and hearing about the wonders of the galaxy filled my head with wonder. My dreams were good in those days, travelling to exotic places inhabited by the most exotic beings. My mother meanwhile filled us with practicality, often saying, "Life is hard, so you've got to be grateful for what you've got". My father would countermand this by telling us to reach for the stars. Now, who do you think an eight-year-old is going to go with?

The remainder of my salad days were spent out on the streets of London. Having no interest in girl things, all my friends were boys. My mother often worried about what we got up to, and little wonder with the 70s being the era of stunt sensation Evel Knievel. There wasn't a boy on my street who didn't want to be the next Evel, and I was no different. The fact that Evel Knievel was frequently in and out of hospital with life-threatening traumas which typically involved an arm or a leg hanging off made us love him all the more. The stunts we concocted would have turned my mother cold had she been around to witness them.

The fact that our house was such a den of danger didn't ease our mother's weary mind. She worried a lot. She especially worried about the array of deadly weapons my father insisted on displaying. It was the 70s after-all, and don't ask me why, but somehow it became the zenith of fashion to have lethal force ornamenting your walls. My father's collection included seven Indian swords, which were especially perilous. As soon as we were left to our own devices, which as we got older was often, my brother and I, spurred on by the BBC series Monkey, took down a sword each to follow the elaborate sword fights. How we kept our heads and how mum kept her furniture, I will never know.

Keeping out of trouble wasn't always easy. There were the usual cases of smashed windows, broken toys and the occasional tale of a fist fight I had won – typically my parents never heard from other parents about the ones I lost. All in all, these minor indiscretions never kept me in the bad books for long.

In the April of 1979, I must have been a glowing example of a model child, because that was the year of my 11th birthday, and the celebratory year when I unwrapped the most spectacular present a child had ever received, a brand new yellow Raleigh Chopper – coolness on wheels.

Now as I said, money in our house, in spite of two wages, was never fluid. And in 1979, this was especially true. Every person in working-class Britain, it seemed, was either moaning about the union strikes or the bad weather or both. January had witnessed the largest one-day strike since 1926, which in reality didn't mean a whole lot to me other than the fact that I had to listen to my dad and his friends rail about it. And so, I naturally assumed this pessimism, which was still lingering in April, would rub off on my birthday present, and boy was I wrong.

Five minutes after the wrapping was torn away, I was the envy of every boy for miles. There wasn't a bike in the area that could match mine in either street cred or speed. I remember whizzing around the neighbourhood with a posse of lads chasing me without a care in the world. I was eleven and I had a brand new yellow Chopper. Salad days indeed.

CHAPTER 3

—✕—

Eight months after my new supercharged dream machine
and I became inseparable, a dreary December morning
found me out on our street looking up and down for someone
to race. Two lads swerved and skidded away, having come
up with a pathetic list of excuses for not racing me.

A thought struck me. "Chicken!" I shouted after them
knowingly. Granted, their Grifters were the acknowledged
little brothers of my Chopper, but still I knew their
cowardliness had nothing to do with inferior hardware.
Even with all the bra burning which typified the feminine
revolution of the 70s, females were still very much
considered the inferior sex – at least by men. And that
meant for me that it didn't matter how I dressed, what bike
I rode, how many races I won; to the boys on the street, I
was still a girl, and this meant that losing to me might make
their head explode or something.

There aren't many obvious blessings that come with being locked inside the wrong body, but, one I can think of, probably the only one, was that it gave me a unique insight into the way a male-dominated society treated women. I could have been the inspiration for Mel Gibson's character in *What Women Want*.

Moving back to my racing dilemma, I soon got fed up waiting and decided to ride down to the river. I paused to take one final look, and that's when I spotted this girl. Now as a rule, I never went anywhere where dolls and tiaras reigned, so that ruled out every girl I knew, but this girl was peculiar; there was definitely something different about her. I paused, trying to figure out why in the hell I was looking at her in the first place. She was about my age, I guessed, although in truth, it was hard to tell with her body dangled over her gate. She had just moved in to the house across from us. I had seen the van, the boxes. But I hadn't got a good look at her, or her father or little sister from my lookout point behind our curtains.

"You've just moved in haven't you?" I shouted over, curiosity getting the better of me.

She pulled her blonde head up slowly, gave me a "sod you" look and went on swinging. I knew there was something different about her, I told myself, riding over for a closer look.

"You got a bike?" I asked randomly.

"I'm too old for bikes," she snapped, head down, still swinging.

"So you've just moved in?"

"Why do you repeat yourself?"

"I don't, I don't," I replied cheekily.

"It's all we could afford. My parents got divorced" she said, not bothering to look up.

"Rebecca, get in here, it's starting to rain!" came an irritable male voice from a window.

"Who's that?" I asked.

"My dad. They drew lots and we had to come with him. Are your parents together?" she asked, still swinging defiantly.

"Yeah, but they fight."

"What about?"

"Oh, money and a washing machine mainly."

"A washing machine, that's a funny thing to fight over."

"Not when you don't have one. My dad won't buy one."

"Why not?"

"I guess he thinks it's a waste of money."

"You smoke?"

"Do you?" I countered. It wasn't a question I had been asked before, so I wasn't sure what to say.

"No, but I'm nearly eleven so I'm thinking about it."

"Me too."

"Thinking about it or eleven?"

"Both," I said flatly.

"You want to come over later when he's gone? We could listen to Another Brick in The Wall, I got it yesterday."

"Yeah, all right," I said, surprising myself – she was a girl after all.

"I'll come over and get you when the coast is clear. Oh, and you can call me Becky. I hate Rebecca," she said rebelliously.

"All right, see you later Becky" I said, astounding myself. I had never had the slightest interest in hanging around with girls before. But there again, I hadn't ever met any girl like Becky before.

What came as no surprise was that Becky's Pink Floyd single spun rebellion from every groove. I had never heard anything like it. And I had never seen anyone with so much anger in their eyes as Becky – well anyone our age that is. She was angry on so many levels; she was angry that her family broke up, that she had to leave her nice big house, her nice school, her friends. She was angry that the council hadn't helped her mother, and that the mother had left anyway. She was angry that her father had taken her and her sister without having the slightest clue how to raise them, and worse still, she was angry at him for not having the slightest intention of learning. There was so much angst going on behind those blue eyes of hers you couldn't help but notice. But it wasn't pity that attracted me to Becky in the first place; on the contrary it was admiration. I admired her strength and her spirit, which I imagined would be indomitable forever.

* * *

My friendship with Becky budded over the next two years, and by the time we reached the milepost of thirteen, we had all the hallmarks of true best friends. With our teenage crash helmets barely strapped to our heads came the raw compulsion to hurtle through the teenage rite of passage at top speed. And for us, this meant smoking and drinking.

Our first dip into the dark pool of adulthood was by and large a sporadic affair to begin with. The occasional nips of Bailey's or brandy and the occasional fag down some back alley provided us with enough resistance to quiet the rising flow of discontentment. We were getting older, our minds and our bodies were changing and we were beginning to question everything, the authorities, the restrictions, the rules – everything that got in the way of our own self-expression.

By the summer of 1981, we were veteran teenagers of a couple of months and had pushed watering down our father's booze to the max. All it would take was for one of our parents to have a drink while sober and our number would be up – and we knew it. And so, having a greater understanding of our own mortality by now, we decided to look further afield for our alcohol. That meant that we had to widen our circle of friends to include those with access to older teenagers who were happy to take financial bribes. And as it happens, with the wider circle came the opportunity of parties, which in turn brought about the opportunity of sex – to whatever extent you wished to experience it.

While this new world widened Becky's eyes considerably, on me it had absolutely no impact. I was still as tomboyish as ever. My periods were still a year away. I had no concept of the peculiar eruptions that were moving Becky to wear make-up and look sexy. Which, I suppose, was a blessing, because it gave me another year of not having to deal with the horrible complexities of being sexually activated in the wrong body.

My close friendship with Becky had meant that she had become a regular in our home. I continued to spend weekends hanging out with my Dad or playing football, but weekdays I spent with Becky. Totally oblivious to the marauding Huns thundering down from the north, I went about my happy business utterly ignorant of major life-changes smouldering underfoot. For, unknown to me, Becky's mascara-laden strides into womanhood were starting to become markers by which my parents would judge me. Becky was starting to wear make-up, and I was not. Becky was starting to style her hair, and I was not. Becky was starting to wear sexy clothes, and I most certainly was not. Becky was starting to chat up boys, right on our street, right in front of my parents, and I was still happy in my dungarees and playing ball. I didn't know that all these contrasts were being tallied by my parents, but they were. And like a dam riddled with bullet holes, my sanctuary was about to collapse.

"It's not that we think there's something wrong with the way you look, it's just time for you to grow up. Look at Becky," Mum explained gently after my shock at having my father criticise the way I dressed for the very first time. Now, while other teenagers might take this intervention as an act of open aggression and immediately declare war, I, on the other hand, wanted to please my parents – they were my pillars, and I loved them and wanted them to be proud of me.

Another major reason for wanting to make them happy was that I had noticed them arguing more of late. In truth, you'd have to be on another continent not to notice, and I just didn't want to do anything to add to the burden. And so, in an attempt to smooth the ways, I devised a plan.

It was a Sunday afternoon. Blue skies and a rising thermometer had opened front doors all along our street. My father was already out, sitting in his favourite blue-striped deck-chair with his suit trousers rolled up, busy tuning in his transistor. As for my mother, she was a little away from him, lying on a blanket exposing as much skin as was appropriate. Although we always considered our parents to be old, the fact was my mother had barely left her twenties, whilst my father had just entered his forties.

"Hi Mum, Hi Dad, this is Richard, we're going over to Becky's, okay?" I said, catching them off guard. I knew my parents' eyes would follow us across the road to Becky's house. I knew also, that when Richard went in for a kiss, as

I had planned he would, their eyes would be there too. I had never given any daylight to imagining what a kiss would feel like – I was still not sexually developed, so why would I?

"Maybe it wouldn't be so bad, maybe I'll even like it," I told myself, as I prepared myself for what I knew was coming. I had spent the entire morning chatting Richard up, to the point where he was now fully confident of his powers. I closed my eyes, for the moment had arrived. Our lips touched, his tongue sought entry and I felt an overwhelming urge to vomit. It was so strong that I pulled away immediately, fighting the impulse to kick him in the privates. And I might have, except that I knew my parents' eyes were still upon us. I sincerely hoped my scam had done the job, because there was nothing on earth that was going to make me go through that horror again.

Inside Becky's, I immediately distanced myself from Richard's subsequent advances. I had no idea kissing a boy would feel so disgusting. You see at this stage I hadn't come to the realisation that I was a male trapped in the wrong body. I know that might be hard to figure, but without the issue of sexuality there really wasn't much for me to consider about myself. It isn't until puberty that you start worrying about yourself – and I certainly was no different.

Holding off Richard's advances wasn't easy. I had revved him up and he was all set to go. Which was an awkward situation to be in because my stomach wasn't even up to looking at him at this stage.

"What's wrong, I thought you liked him?" Becky whispered, pulling me aside.

"I don't want to kiss him again."

"Isn't he good?"

"I just don't want to do that again."

Kissing Richard had been reduced to "that", which didn't

go down too well with him at all. He left the house in disgust.

"He's going to go about telling everyone you're frigid."

"So? I don't care," I said, because honestly if it meant I had to kiss a boy again that was fine with me. In the haze of my prepubescence, I still couldn't understand why kissing a boy had caused me so much repulsion. I certainly never considered I was gay or otherwise. Those thoughts never dawned on me. I was still a child who didn't have any compulsion to kiss anyone – boy or girl.

The need to please my parents had not diminished in light of the Richard debacle. After it I just decided to please them in other ways – and one stellar way was to keep away from drugs. I don't know if it was because we had untied our mother's apron strings and ventured out, but it seemed to me that literally overnight the neighbourhood seemed awash with drugs. Suddenly they were overtaking drinking and smoking and even sex as the number one rite of passage. And Becky and I were seeing it first-hand; drugs of all sorts had started to filter into our own circle. Which meant that there was now a choice to be made.

"I'll stick to the fags and the drink if you will," Becky said, setting the ground rules for our next party.

"I'm never going to take drugs."

"So no matter who offers them, we say no, right?"

"Right," I agreed, translating what Becky really meant, which was no matter how good-looking the boy was, she was going to say no.

It wouldn't be until years later that we would realise just how poignant memories of this conversation would be, for both of us.

CHAPTER 4

—∞—

The friendship between Becky and me strengthened in the winter of 1981. I don't know if I was ever labelled frigid, but Britain certainly should have been, for its stellar impression of Lapland. It was a novelty at first, for a country that rarely experienced more than a flutter of snow, but by January 1982 a freezing nation collectively agreed that we had had more than enough of the Arctic experiment. I for one never liked frost one bit, nor the extra effort of cleaning and lighting fires, which I was pretty much forced to do with my parents both out working. The only good thing, I suppose, about the hibernal conditions was that they kept us indoor and safe.

As we approached our fourteenth birthdays, having our "say no to drugs" pact (which quickly caught on in the US, I might add) became even more imperative, especially for Becky, who was becoming more rebellious by the day. Three years of living with her father meant that her behaviour now followed a familiar pattern – the more he neglected her, the more she rebelled. Like most men of his generation, her father's duties ended with his pay packet, and divorce or no divorce, as long as he continued to put food on the table, he couldn't imagine anything else being expected of him. This stance of course denied Becky the rooting and nurturing that she so desperately needed. And sadly, she wasn't alone. It seemed a mysterious plague had hit our street, and families were falling like flies.

Whilst Becky's relationship with her father was one of cold detachment, her relationship with her mother was hazardous at best. How hazardous largely depended on the nature of the boyfriend who was around at any given time. It certainly wasn't the healthy environment Becky needed – far from it. And so, not too surprisingly, not finding the love she needed at home, she turned to the next obvious choice – boys. From the saucepan into the frying pan.

What of me? Well by this time, the occasional parental tiffs in our household had turned into frequent fighting, with no one keeping score. While I still clung to the last vestiges of my youth in the form of my football friends, when it came to a shoulder to cry on, I turned to Becky.

"At it again?" she asked, applying some lipstick, even before my sorry behind could hit the bed.

"Mum thinks Dad is having an affair."

"Is he?"

"Don't think so. He said she's off her head."

"You think they'll split?"

"No, it's seasonal. January to June they slag each other off, then we go on holidays, then come September they're at it again until Christmas."

"Move out, and only come back for Christmas and the summer."

"I should."

"Hey, what do you think?" Becky asked, pulling down her top to show off her new red bra.

"Nice," I said, mustering some false enthusiasm. I hated it when she did things like that. It was just too weird. It was venturing into territory I just didn't want to go. If the kiss misadventure taught me anything, it was that I was perfectly happy the way I was. I didn't want to change and I certainly didn't want to grow up, if kissing and the likes came in the bargain.

"Would you move out?"

"Maybe I'll have to, if they keep it up," I said, making big of it, although I certainly hadn't the slightest intention of doing anything of the sort. Yes, my parents fought, but so did every other parent I knew. For Sarah it was different; she had gone from a broken home to a neglected home, and my home was neither.

"We could go to Islington and squat for a night."

"What, stay out all night?"

"Why not? I'll say I'm staying with Bev, and you say you're coming with me." Bev was Becky's mother, her title having gone with the divorce, or abandonment, as Becky called it.

"Only drink and smokes?" I asked, nervously.

Becky's mother had moved to Islington, which was about an hour's bus ride from us. And there, she soon swapped her parenting responsibilities for drugs and alcohol. Becky would knock on her door, never really knowing the reception she would receive, or the potential danger she would be in. I guess, to a naive, rebellious fourteen-year-old this arrangement could seem advantageous.

As it turned out, it didn't take much to set Becky's cogs spinning. She had spent the previous weekend in Islington and met a guy named Jeff in a record store. He was a couple of years older, 17 maybe 18, but this didn't stop him from sharing Becky's fish and chips at a local café, nor did it prevent him from inviting her back to his friend's squat for "a laugh". It was only because she was too mortified to tell him about her time of the month that she turned him down. After a long passionate snog, Becky reluctantly said goodbye, but not before promising to return in a week or two with a friend – me.

"I promise, only drinks and smokes," she said, still scheming.

"Okay," I said, reluctantly, sensing it probably wasn't one of the better ideas I'd gone along with. Still, that's what best friends do.

"Wait till you see him. He's got a motorbike jacket and hair to his shoulders. He plays guitar. He's the lead. He's the one."

"No."

"Yes," she said trying to be mature but then giggling.

* * *

A cold and dreary evening in February 1982 found Becky and me on the upper deck of a London bus headed for Islington. The air stank with an unusual concoction of cigarette smoke and mildew rising from steaming duffel coats, a popular fashion staple borrowed from that famous Peruvian bear Paddington. A ludicrous item really, which in the absence of the sub-zero temperatures most teenagers had to contend with while out wandering the streets out of sheer boredom.

On the top of the bus, smoking was still considered good for your health. A little less accepted was the obligatory drinking or cavorting that was conducted at the back of the bus.

"Smoke?" Becky asked as the bus jolted to a halt.

"Thanks" I said, turning to the window. "No drugs," I whispered, turning back, having watched a spiky group of punks pile on.

"No drugs," she agreed, straightening beside me. We were both so nervous and excited about our first night of freedom.

The squat, when we arrived like two drowned rats, was everything the imagination could threaten: dank, dingy and reeking worse than the bus. The primary squatter, Dave, once the rightful tenant, had fallen foul of the new sentiment of greed descending upon the capital. With no hope of making the revised rent, he simply gave up and turned squatter. What we also learned later, was that he, a nice enough guy in reality, had run away from home after trying to kill his father, after finding him abusing his younger sister. Angry and confused, he had arrived in London without a shilling, and was saved from becoming one of Islington's first beggars by his talented involvement in the underground London band scene.

"Hi!" we said, like the schoolkids we were. To which Dave, tall, scrawny, old by our standards at eighteen, instantly turned away, leaving the door wide open.

"Do you think he wants us to come in?" whispered Becky, not having the chance to launch into the rehearsed history of Jeff and me. After a moment's deliberation, which was worthy of a couple of seven-year-olds, we walked into what I can only assume was at one time called a sitting room. Our confidence was battered instantly by the presence of an older teenage girl in tight leopardskin jeans. It recovered somewhat when we saw that she was reading a paperback novel by torchlight.

"Hi, is Jeff around?" Becky asked cautiously.

"He's gigging, he should be back later," offered the girl, turning a page. She was probably a year or two older, definitely pretty and definitely not Jeff's girlfriend, we deduced, to be giving this information away so casually.

"You got some stuff?" asked Dave, lounging in a brown tatty recliner, which had obviously been dragged off the street when the bin-men had refused it.

I looked around at the anarchy against tidiness and shuddered. My own home was always spotless. Mum cleaned and Dad fixed. I had in all honesty, never in my life seen anything that resembled a garbage bin so closely. It wasn't just last year's dishes, it was the mould, the scratching mice, the condemned electrics, it was everything. I just couldn't imagine it being remotely habitable, even when he had been the tenant. Which was spot on, because Dave confirmed later, after a bottle of our brandy, that nothing much had changed about the place apart from the lack of electrics.

"Weed, pills, anything?" Dave continued, picking up drumsticks to drum the holes in his knees.

"We've brought a bottle of brandy and half a bottle of gin," Becky said almost throwing the bag at him, she was so eager to please.

"Got any smokes?" Dave asked, after helping himself to a large portion of the brandy. Seemingly, there was no place for bashfulness in squatting. Nevertheless, sharing our booze with Dave gave us an exulted legitimacy which we enjoyed for at least the first five minutes. There never was any issue about us being kicked out. Between supplying Dave and taking turns to answer the door, we were as welcome intruders as anyone.

However, about two hours in, I really wished we could go home. My head was spinning and my bones were starting to feel the lack of carpeting, but Becky was adamant. She was in love, and a herd of rampaging rhinos wouldn't have moved her.

The two hours that followed didn't improve the experience. Mostly, we whispered amongst ourselves. The girl in leopardskin had disappeared hours ago, her bottle-green armchair now occupied by a cloud of weed. Luckily the stuff must have been in short supply because the joint stayed between the two armchairs in the room. I was glad of this. It meant the carefully constructed persona Becky had so diligently worked on remained intact. Becky was a virgin and this was to be the night. Now that she'd found Mr Right, the sense of waiting for her fifteenth birthday easily disappeared.

Eventually, another hour gone by, a clearly drunk Mr Right staggered through the door with a groupie wrapped tightly around his torso. It was Jeff. This I could tell by the diamonds in Becky's eyes. And before we knew anything, he had acknowledged Becky by taking two smokes from her before stumbling upstairs.

This, my first taste of marginalised life, didn't come close to the blue-skied glamour I had heard of – mostly from Becky. Just because something has a roof doesn't mean it's not a hovel, was the very first conclusion I drew passing the clanking milkmen on the way up the street. The second was that there wasn't much glam to alcoholic poisoning either. I was sick. I was tired. And all the way home I had to consider the enormous price I might have to pay for the pleasure.

As for Becky, her eyes were red raw by the time she slipped upstairs to have yet another cry. She had dreams, big dreams, mostly of escaping the loneliness she endured at home. She went searching for a prince and came home lacking even a kiss from a toad.

My own sulky arrival home was filled with the anticipation of condemnation. And it was my father's condemnation that I feared most of all. I thought the world of my father and despite my youthful dalliance with waywardness, the last thing I wanted was to disappoint him. So in I tiptoed, mercifully finding the house still. I went up to my room, collapsed on my bed, vowed never to drink or smoke again and ran straight for the bathroom. The gleaming riotousness of teenage living had worn itself dull in just one night. (I only wish I hadn't after this lost my memory.)

When the house finally filled with the living, a couple of hours later, it barely reached a whisper. I lay with my head buried in my pillow, smiling broadly inside and out. My headache had disappeared. My stomach had settled and my mother must have either forgiven the affair or acknowledged the pitfalls of an overripe imagination. Either-way, peace (and sobriety on my part) reigned throughout February and March, leading me happily towards my fourteenth birthday.

* * *

And then, like a thief of dreams, came April 1982. Right at the time when aisles of Easter eggs taunted children across the nation, Argentine troops invaded the Falklands. On 5 April, the British Government, led by Margaret Thatcher, dispatched a naval response, and so began the Falklands War. In an instant, every TV channel, every newspaper, every mouth was speaking of nothing else – the country was at war, over a place most of us had never heard of.

Meanwhile on home soil, an unseen enemy was moving with stealth from one impoverished town to another, sowing the seeds for a full-blown heroin epidemic. Before the 1980s heroin was rarely seen in the UK, and then only in the capital among affluent users, and crack was unheard of. When the new decade commenced estimates placed the number of heroin user at no more than 25,000 and no fewer than 10,000. By the end of the decade the estimates were in the hundreds of thousands. And these hundreds of thousands were in the main young, working-class and unemployed. Friend to friend, family member to family member, directly or indirectly, the evil drug would devastate the most vulnerable lives – including my own. Totally ignorant of the enemy at the gate, all eyes, including father and all his ex-army buddies, were on the war in the South Atlantic Ocean. Naturally, as children, being more interested in chocolate than war or drugs, our minds were largely unburdened by the waves of worry depressing our elders.

It was right in the midst of this national crisis that we were summoned out of our beds by our mother and without explanation ordered to gather quickly in the kitchen. Still yawning, I was the first to arrive. I could hear the complaints of my younger siblings winding their way down the staircase. I went to the window to inspect the weather and was happy to find a beautiful Saturday morning smiling back at me. The street outside was quiet. An early morning shower had washed the paths clean and they were now glistening in anticipation of the early risers, who were undoubtedly gulping down toast and cereal, right at this very moment. Normally, I would be one of the first out the door because sunny Saturday mornings meant only one thing – football. But on this sunny morn, normality had been suspended by my mother.

Upstairs, I can still hear Mum hurrying Karen. At eleven, Saturday normality meant, for Karen, spending at least an hour deciding which of the three Pineapple Studio T-shirts she would wear later to dance lessons. Pineapple was the dance studio. Located in Covent Garden, it had benefited enormously from Fame, the fictional series about students at the New York City High School for the Performing Arts. It had launched itself into every living room in the country and instantly captured the imagination of every girl under the age of 15. Wanting to be a famous dancer was the new dream, and Pineapple Studios instantly became the 'starmaker' for hundreds of little girls just like Karen.

At this age, summing up our family life was easy; shopping and dancing were the meaning of life for Karen, just as football and hanging out with friends was for Gavin, and just like football and hanging out with Dad was for me. Our lives were by and large ordered and we were by and large happy.

Hanging out with Dad was in truth a major part of my life. No wonder then that on this beautiful sunny morning a major complaint still seethed at the back of my mind. It had been lodged only the previous night upon discovering that Dad was leaving for an archery tournament in the morning and that I wasn't going. Apparently, there wasn't enough room, or it was too far or it was too early; a concoction of why nots which, no matter how many times they were said, still came out as pretty lame.

"He must have slipped out while it was still dark," I grumbled, pouring myself a glass of milk. Although I looked forward to a good game of football, when the toss came between football and excursions with Dad, Dad always won.

To be fair, if he could have taken me he would have, I reflected, standing over the toaster waiting for it to pop. There were lots of these little skills that made a boy feel like Dirty Harry, and snatching the toast mid-air was a good one.

Retrieving the butter from the fridge, I give myself a slap on the back. I was thinking that there were far worse things to do on a Saturday than football. This seemed to work, because with the first bit of my hot buttered toast my father's tournament slipped completely out of my mind.

Taking a second bite, I glance out of the window. No one was on the street yet. I could still be the first. Then Karen and Gavin walked in, both still puffy-eyed from the unnatural awakening.

"Any toast?" Gavin asked, slumping at the table.

"There's bread in the cupboard," I said, a polite way of telling him to get it himself. At nine, he still wanted everything done for him.

"Where's Mum?" I asked, impatiently.

"She says she'll be down in a second," Karen replied, going to the cupboard for a bowl.

Five minutes later and there we still were, the three of us sitting around the table poker-faced.

"Where is she?" this time it was Gavin who asked.

"She said she's on her way," I said, having received this answer down the stairs.

"What's up?" Gavin asked, sensing something wasn't right.

"Must be bad news," I concluded.

Instantly our shoulders rounded, taking on the solemnity of kids fully expecting to hear that another relative has died. Most likely someone from abroad, I told myself, as it was my mother delivering the bad news. Most likely someone I hadn't heard of. Mum had family in Malta. Most likely a cousin of a cousin, as my mum had lots of those. But there was also the possibility, although remote, that someone we knew had died in the war. Another good reason for not going and shouting up at her again, I concluded.

Quite frankly, all this talk of war had made vivid my worst nightmares. It had let a great big monster out of the cupboard to remind everyone just how turbulent the world was. It seemed there was no good news anywhere. The cold war between the US and The Soviet Union was still apocalyptic as far as the news anchors were concerned. My father had, rightly or wrongly, exposed us to the news from an early age, so war, and especially the threat of nuclear war, felt like a dangling noose over my head. What if this war in the Pacific was the start of World War Three? What if it went nuclear? At thirteen, I rightly thought I was far too young to die.

I was so glad Dad was too old to be called up, was the thought that went racing through my mind as I continued scanning the window for signs of life. I turned away suddenly, for a great thud had sounded from above. And then came another. We all looked up automatically.

"What's she up to?" Gavin huffed, slumping in his seat. "I'm going out, just call me."

"No, wait there," I said, keeping him in check.

"No!" he said, seething with all the war-like indignation of a nine-year-old. As good an example as I was putting on, I too wished that I could make a bolt for it. The morning was inching on and I was itching to get on with it. I had arranged everything with the five Irish lads from across the street, the Burkes; the teams were picked, the prestigious captain's position had been fought over, the ball had been pumped, trainers cleaned and we were all set for the kick-off.

I glanced out of the window again thinking, "Any minute now the lads will be banging down the door and I'll have my escape and..."

My daydream was cut short by Mum walking in through the door. "All right Mum?" I said brightly. To this she said nothing. She looked pale and fidgety, not at all her usual bubbly self.

"Flippin' hell, it must be worse than a second cousin," I thought as I watched her take a seat opposite me. Her face assumed the position of a smile, but I sensed something was wrong because this smile didn't reach right inside me and work its warning magic. This one tightened up my insides, and I didn't like it.

"Now I want you to stay quite while I get this out," she said. "This is very hard for me," she went on, avoiding eye contact. "What I need to tell you," she continued, stumbling on the words, "is, well... your father and I have decided it's time for us to go our own ways."

"Divorce!" I said, barely believing it.

"Your father and I have decided to separate."

"Divorce?" I The blood rushed to my feet. This was not expected. Tell us about a relative dying, not this. There must be some mistake. How could this be? It was impossible.

"Yes, probably, yes eventually," she said as gently as she could.

"But you can't. You can't!"

"Lisa, you're all big now. Things like this happen all the time, nowadays. People don't have to stay together. Look at Becky's parents..."

"Becky hated them divorcing. This is why I know."

"But in our case there is nothing to worry about, nothing

at all," she added quickly.

"Don't you love Dad any more?" Karen asked.

"Your dad and I have been together for a very long time. People change, and I just don't want to spend the rest of my life with him."

"But what about us, Mum?" Gavin cut in, squeezing the worried look from his face. He was trying so hard not to be the kid he was. But in truth he was very much a kid. Nine, eleven and thirteen, we were all kids.

"Well, you can either stay here or you can come with me," Mum said, answering Gavin's question gently.

"Where are you going, where would we live?" I asked as calmly as possible. Being the oldest, I had always been expected to set an example, although in the past that example had totally been ignored by the others. But this was different. In this moment I knew I was needed.

"We would have to stay with Nan Ethel and Granddad. We'd have to share a room."

"All of us in one room?" I yelled, dropping the good example. How could I remain calm? The thought of this was unimaginable. Since meeting Becky my life had taken on a strange duality; when I was with her I became a teenager, tentatively testing out the world beyond my doorstep, and when I wasn't with her, when I was at home, I left the complicated teenager outside and went straight back to being myself. I was walking a transitional tightrope and it was high and scary, and divorce just couldn't be allowed to come and knock me off. This can't be happening! I screamed inside.

"We'll have to share, for now, until I can get a place of my own."

"But four of us in a box room mum?"

"If you want to stay here you can..."

"Until you get us a new house," Gavin asked, cutting in again.

"That's right, you can stay with your dad until I get myself fixed up. How does that sound?"

"What about Pineapple, Mum?" Karen asked, emotion rising in her voice. "I have to go today!"

"Not today Karen, we'll sort it out for next-week, okay?"

"But Mum!"

"It's just for today love."

"What about the shops? I need new trainers and so does he" she said, bringing Gavin into it. "You promised!"

"Please, just leave it till next week and I'll sort it all out. I know I promised, but please…"

"But…"

"When are you leaving?" I interjected, feeling Mum's distress strike my own chest.

"I thought I'd head off soon."

"Today?" I asked, feeling the tightening rise into my throat.

"Yes, today."

And with that short address, the news of our family breakup was delivered. One by one, like little lost souls, we followed Mum into the hallway. Seeing her suitcases stacked at the doorway told us this was final. We had never actually said we weren't going too. But I suppose the fact that none of our suitcases were there beside hers spoke volumes. I looked at my mother. I did not know what to say or how to act, so I acted like nothing was happening. I just smiled and shoved my hands into my pockets.

"I'll call by tomorrow," she said, scrabbling in her handbag.

Just then the sound of an elephant stampede arrived at

the door. "I'll get it," I said, already on my way. As I opened the door, five eager Burke faces pushed in.

"Come on! Let's go!" said five voices in unison. I looked at my mother and saw the mountain of worry which she couldn't disguise.

"You go, go on and play," she said, fixing her scarf on her head.

Normally I wouldn't have needed telling twice. But no matter how matter-of-fact Mum tried to make it all sound, my instincts told me different. It just wasn't normal to hear your parents are splitting up one minute and be out playing football the next. It wasn't normal for Mum to have her suitcases packed and none of ours beside hers. So, totally out of character, I made up some lame excuse. It didn't go down too well with the Burkes.

"What about you Gavin, are you a sissy too?" they jeered in unison. I might have looked like a girl at this point, but inside there was a boy who wanted to go out and punch the living daylights out of all of them. Instead I hung back, leaving Gavin to answer.

"I'm getting my breakfast first," Gavin replied. Young as he was, he still knew what family loyalty meant.

The Burkes left the doorstep, colourfully cursing our betrayal. I turned and smiled at my mum. "Fancy a cup of tea, Mum?" I asked, suddenly hoping she would.

"I think I'll get on, Lisa," she said, picking up her cases.

It was still very early, so no one, apart from the Burkes, would witness her slipping away from our world. With all the talk of women's equality, it was still taboo for a woman to leave her husband, and unthinkable for her to leave her kids. If any of the street curtains had twitched and one of the neighbours had seen Mum, the news would have shot to every breakfast table, knocking the war off everyone's lips. I think this was why Mum was so eager to slip away into the pale yellow light.

"Bye Mum," we called, waving her off just like she was heading to work.

CHAPTER 5

———⊰⊱———

After waving Mum off, we all stood in the hall looking past one another. It was like one of those movie scenes where everything freezes for a moment, then carries on. For us this put Karen upstairs washing her hair, Gavin in the kitchen with a bowl of cornflakes and a UB40 album dropping down upon the turntable with me beside it. Everyone was carrying on like it was any other day – but it wasn't. I had barely got through one song and I became restless. Something ominous was filtering into my mind, and despite my best efforts it was making me feel very uncomfortable. I went to the turntable and tried another album, this time, Pink Floyd. Only a few bars in, the same thing. I put the record back, thinking maybe music wasn't the brightest idea right now. What if I lost it and started crying, then where would we all be? Music, of any description, just wasn't the same without Mum. I really wished my Dad would come home, because I now felt the burden of my younger siblings, and I wasn't sure how much longer I could hold up. No, music wasn't a good thing right at that moment because it reminded me too much of her. Having married at 17, Mum was still only 31. A veteran to us, but in reality still a very young woman.

My association between Mum and music was strong. All through my childhood, memories were stored of the impromptu lounge dances we would have. With Michael Jackson blasting she'd pull my friends over one by one, saying, "Come on, come on, have a dance," And they'd go along with her, saying to me, "Your Mum is off her head," but this was always meant in a good way. She was like one big happy meter, until the meter ran out.

My mother walking out with her suitcases less than ten minutes ago was nothing short of surreal. Slipping Dark Side of The Moon back into my record collection, the thought dawned on me that maybe the best thing after all was to go out and play football. If nothing else it would keep my mind occupied for an hour or so.

In truth, I didn't want to stay put, nor wanted to go out, however as a third option failed me I went for my jacket just as Karen walked in, spiritedly wearing her navy 'I Love Pineapple' T-shirt.

"I'll still get my new trainers, won't I?" she asked, sitting on the sofa.

"You heard her. Nothing is changing. When Dad gets home, he'll explain it all to us. I'm not worried anyway, are you?"

"No, I just want to make sure I can get my new trainers before dancing next week. Is Mum going to take me to Pineapple?"

"Yeah, why not?"

"What if she can't? Who will take me?"

"There's a bunch who go off the road isn't there?"

"Yeah."

"Well then, we just have to sort it with one of the women off the road. But Mum will take you."

"Do you think it'll be funny Mum not being here tonight?"

"It's not like we need her to tuck us in any more, do we?"

"No."

"Well, once you can still go shopping and dancing with her, it'll be pretty much the same, won't it?"

"I suppose," she said, standing. "I'm going up to practise for next week."

And so Karen went off happy in the knowledge that nothing major was about to change. All very sensible. All very calm. Too sensible. Too calm. Maybe it would have been better for us if there had been floods of tears, screams of anger. If there had been a heart-wrenching scene of children locked around their mother begging her not to leave. Perhaps then we could have started dealing emotionally with the reality of our situation. Instead we acted sensibly, and we acted calm. I suppose this was because, unknown to us, our survival instinct had already kicked in to make sure our feet were firmly planted in the safer world of make-believe.

A moment later a thought flashed through my mind on my way to the kitchen. I was glad that we didn't have an upmarket life to lose, like Becky. It would take a little getting used to, for sure, but I couldn't for the life of me see any reason why this new arrangement wouldn't iron itself out soon enough.

"What do you think will happen to us?" Gavin asked upon my entry.

"Mum and Dad still loved us and the only difference now that I can see is that Mum is sleeping under a different roof."

And just like magic, the day went back to being just another ordinary day; Karen stayed in her room all afternoon practising, Gavin and I eventually got to play football after a mouthful of abuse and a spell on the sidelines. The accusations of betrayal long forgotten, we played into the twilight, until one by one the other players deserted us for their dinner. Gavin and I stayed out for a little while longer, kicking the ball against a wall, neither of us daring to go back into the reality of our empty home.

About a half an hour later, the hunger got the better of us and we went in to our spreadable cheese sandwiches. Stomachs filled, all three of us settled ourselves in front of the TV, awaiting our father's return.

Ten o'clock, then eleven, and still no key in the door.

"Why do you think Dad's so late?" Gavin asked, yawning his words.

"Maybe he's met Mum and they're talking," Karen suggested optimistically.

"He probably won the tournament and they're just celebrating," I said, tucking a blanket under my chin. It was late and my body was feeling the chill of the early hours.

"Do you think he wanted Mum to leave?" Karen asked innocently.

It was the most valid question of the night and I don't think any of us up to that moment had considered Dad's feelings. Just how was he feeling about it all, I wondered, followed in rapid succession by oh my´ God, did he even know? What if he didn't know, would we have to tell him?

"She would have told him, wouldn't she?"

"Yeah," said Karen, curling herself up in her own blanket.

No of course he knew, but how was he feeling? I turned away from Karen. Was he feeling sad? Was he out late because he was feeling sad? Question after question swirled through my head.

"Oh blimey, I really hope he knows and he's okay and he's just out celebrating his victory," I murmured, worrying myself.

"He probably didn't want her to leave but I'm sure he's okay with it," Gavin said after a moment.

"But why did she leave, didn't she love him anymore?" Karen pressed, turning away from the TV, as we all did. Right at the time when the country was coming together in a swell of national pride, our family was breaking up. In truth, none of us had a clue why our mother had left. Sure, they fought, but we were used to that.

"Maybe it was the age gap," I said. Twelve years between them - it was as good an explanation as any to pluck from the air.

"Yeah, maybe she wants some fun before it's too late," Karen said, running with the idea.

"What about your birthday?" Gavin said, straining to hold open his lids.

"What about it? I'll still have it obviously, won't I?" My birthday was less than two weeks away and I really hoped to get a more powerful telescope, so Dad and I could up the ante on our stargazing.

"Yeah, will you ask for a chocolate cake, not a sponge, this time?" Gavin said, not bothering to open his eyes.

By the time the key eventually turned in the door both Karen and Gavin had fallen asleep. I must have dozed off myself, on and off, because I had no clue as to the plot of the old black and white horror that was coming to a climax. I sat up straight, rubbed the sleep from my eyes and waited for the door to open. There was no sound I loved more than hearing the turn that said one of my parents was coming home.

"Hi Dad, you all right?" I said as normally as I could. I didn't want him to think we were upset or anything. I naturally assumed he would be worried about us. I smiled again, waiting for his answer as he went to the TV and turned over the channel. Instead of answering he barely glanced at me as he sat in his chair.

I could feel my chest tightening. I had never seen my father act this way, and it scared me. Why didn't he answer? Why didn't he reassure me? Why was he just sitting there? Their mother has just left, surely the first thing you think of doing is reassuring your children?

I glanced over at him, not sure if I should speak again. His eyes caught mine.

"Make me a sandwich, will you?" His voice, stern and cold, woke Karen and Gavin.

"Hi Dad," They said, one after another, sleepily.

"You two, up to bed," he said, lashing out at them.

Half asleep, they went off to bed submissively. I went out quietly too. I could feel my cheeks flush as I pressed the slices of bread together. I put the sandwich on a plate and returned with my stomach on tumble.

"Ham and tomatoes," I said, offering the plate and a glass of milk to him.

"Put it there," he snapped, pointing at the side table, "and get to bed."

Timidly, I did as I was instructed.

"And Lisa, I never want to hear your mother's name in this house again, is that understood?"

I left the room without answering, biting back the tears. Closing the door softly behind me, I stood for a moment in the hall and looked back at the door between us. It wasn't the words so much that had cut me it was the way he'd looked through me as if I meant nothing. There was a stranger sitting in my father's chair and it scared me and confused me. I felt a dangerous compulsion to rush back inside and to demand an explanation. What the hell was he thinking? What the hell was he playing at? But I was too afraid to act on the impulse, so instead I took myself up to the loneliness of my pillow, where I knew I would lie holding back the weight of the world. My dad wasn't one for punishment, one for shouting, one for smacking, he was my hero, my idol, my pillar and my rock.

As I walked into my bedroom a thought overtook me. Maybe he was just devastated that Mum had left and he was trying not to fall apart, not to break down in front of me? It was a good explanation to pluck out of the air, and as I did so a plunging wave of pity for my father overran me. I wanted, instantly, to go back down and hug him. I wanted to tell him I loved him and reassure him that everything would be all right. Convincing myself that this was the only course of action to take, I went quietly down the stairs.

"Dad," I said softly from the door, "can I come in?"

"Get out! Get out!" he shouted, so loudly that my heart jumped to my mouth. I closed the door instantly. I wiped a rolling tear from my cheek as I took the bottom stairs. His eyes contained no sorrow, no heartbreak; they were consumed by a black anger. It was palpable. It was like a dense darkness had descended upon him.

I took the rest of the stairs as quietly as I could, almost afraid to breath. "It's just the hurt making him act this way," I told myself as I climbed into bed. I needed to hold onto something, it was all I had.

I closed my eyes, but sleep wouldn't take me. My stomach hurt and all about me felt heavy and unfamiliar. It was as if the same heaviness I had felt downstairs had worked its way up and was now all about me.

"It's going to be all right. He'll be better in the morning, back to himself," I told myself. I wanted so much to feel better. In that moment I would have done or said anything to convince myself.

My father was, in every sense, the epitome of a man's man. I could see why he would find it so difficult to talk about his feelings. Men just didn't wear their hearts on their sleeves, it just wasn't the done thing. Men were Dirty Harry. Men were tough. Maybe in a couple of days, when he was over it, he would open up and talk about it to me. My father was so wise, so knowledgeable. I trusted he would know exactly how to fix this.

I put my head on the pillow and stared into the darkness. I began to feel really sorry for my dad again. How horrible it must be to have someone you love leave you. I really wished I could erase all memory of today, or even better, go back in time and prevent it all happening to begin with. Knowing that I couldn't, I instead told myself that the best thing we could all do was to make every effort to make him happy. We would all have to do our bit; clean the house, do the dinners, look after him, show him how much we loved him, until he got back to himself.

And then, as I was feeling decidedly better, another thought landed. Hold on a moment – if Dad was so cut up about Mum leaving, that meant he really, really loved her. And if he really, really loved her, that meant he would take her back. I took a deep breath, knowing I was really onto something. Mum didn't make all that much money, so she wouldn't be able to afford a house big enough for all of us. And according to Becky, the only reason her mum had stayed with her dad so long was because the council man had told her that single mothers go to the bottom of the pile. Which, Becky said, was his way of saying it would be a cold day in hell before she could expect help from them. So that meant Mum wouldn't get any help either.

Okay, so she would probably end up staying with Nan Ethel for a good while, but let's face it, what woman in her thirties wants to stay with their parents? And Granddad, he wouldn't make it easy. He would tell her to get back around to her husband and kids. They were bound to fight, a lot, and she was bound to get fed up soon, very soon. And then she would want to come home, and Dad loving her so much would obviously take her back. Yes, that was good, very good, and pretty soon, everything would be forgotten and our family would be right back on track. I closed my eyes, the smile back on my face. My mother was coming home; it was only a matter of time.

The next couple of days went by without any major upset. We got ourselves to and fro from school, the only big difference being that we now had to completely fend for ourselves, but we managed. We hardly saw Dad for the entire week, which was not in itself entirely unusual. Easter was only a week or so away, and Dad always did overtime in the run-up to holidays.

Much as I understood why we had to walk on eggshells, much as the self-chatter continued to tell me to do my best, it didn't make me like it. It all felt so unnatural, so strange. And then there was the blaring fact of our mother's absence to content with. Although she had never been around all that much, especially during the week because she worked so much, her presence at the end of the day was all-encompassing. And that's what I missed the most; the sound of her voice calling up the stairs; the touch of her hand moving the hair out of your eyes, the sweet smell of her perfume as she bent down to say goodnight. This is what I missed, what we all missed.

As the week drew to a close, our anticipation mounted that Saturday would be the day when we would at last see our mother. It would also be the day when we would all sit down and iron out the details of the "separation". In my mind, almost a week in, we were still the family, the good family, the happy family we had always been. This separation was only a bump, a glitch, a minor snag in the fabric of our family life. There was no notion of us doing anything other than quickly getting back together. I was more convinced than ever that Mum would return, and maybe Saturday would be that day.

* * *

At last Saturday arrived, and it found us all sitting down to breakfast. I had made a really nice breakfast, bacon, eggs, tomatoes. "A good fry up, nothing better to set you up for the day," as Mrs Burke, the mother of the Irish lads I played with, was famous for saying. I certainly hoped she was right and that this breakfast would set Dad up for smoothing the ways to take Mum back. They were bound to really miss each other by now, I told myself, slipping a second fried egg onto his plate. And after everything was made up, there was the snooker tournament. No better way to celebrate. I put a fried tomato beside the egg, for good measure. I really wanted to go to that tournament – everyone was going.

Now normally the thought of not participating down the sports hall wouldn't even enter my mind. But these last couple of days, walking on eggshells seemed a prerequisite to keeping your head. Dad was moody and distant. He was off in his own private world, and any pull back into ours was met with hostility. We learnt this the second day, and hence the eggshells. "Just stay out of his way," I had told Gavin and Karen, when they came complaining bitterly to me.

I left these negative thoughts behind and passed some toast to Dad. There was still a definite stiffness to his demeanour, a coldness even. He lacked the usual warmth we were so used to him radiating. Still, he hadn't complained once about the breakfast, which was a really good sign, I thought. I swallowed my toast and checked my watch, nearly ten. I could feel the anticipation rising in me, because I figured Mum would be around any minute now.

Karen's eyes were upon me as she sucked up some pink milk through her straw. She must have been thinking the same thing, because a moment later she turned to Dad.

"What time is Mum coming to collect me?"

Taking his time, Dad continued chewing. Another pause, to wipe his mouth. We all hung for the answer.

"She's not," came the ever-so-casual bombshell.

"But I have dance. I'm not missing it again!" Karen cried, smashing a couple of dozen eggshells.

"You're not going and that'll be the end of it. Now finish your breakfast or get upstairs!" he said, reddening with every word.

Karen sank shell-shocked into her chair. Gavin glared across at me;, I knew his instincts were calling for action, as mine were. I knew he wanted me to say something, to stick up for Karen, to stick up for all of us, but the angst in my stomach said otherwise.

Ignoring its good advice, I waited a moment, until I couldn't wait any longer.

"When are we going to see Mum?"

"She's not your mother any more, she wants nothing more to do with you."

"But that's not what she told us. She said she'd see us all the time."

"Well she would, she wouldn't have wanted a scene, would she?"

"But..."

"But what? She left, end of story, get used to it," he said, rising to get his snooker cue from the corner of the room. We watched him silently, one as confused as the other. "I'll be back late," he said, pulling on his jacket. "I don't want any of you up when I get home."

"Um, Lisa was thinking of heading down to the club too," Gavin said bravely, paving the way for both of us to go.

"No."

"But everyone..."

"No one's going anywhere! There's washing to be done. And you can get a bag of coal while you're at it. There's money on the table. I'm out working, so who do you think is going to do it?"

"But Mum will be back, she's not gone for good. I don't believe it!" I blurted out in sheer desperation.

"I'll never let her back, you hear, never, believe that!" he said, with such venom that my face dropped to my shoes. I just couldn't look at him.

"Maybe if you'd helped out more she's still be here. Did you ever think of that? Go on, hang your head, you've no one to blame but your bloody self."

The cruelty of these words went straight into my heart, as intended. And in that moment, for the first time in my life, I felt a real dislike for my father. There were many things racing through my mind, demanding to be heard. But instead, I buried them. I let the resentment go deep inside, planting the explosive seeds in dark and unreachable places.

With all my hurt and my anger turned down to a silent simmer, I watched my father walk out of the door. And when he was gone, we looked to each other, sharing each other's dejection. It wasn't until we heard the door slam that we dared to speak, and even then it was in whispers.

"Why can't I go to Pineapple?" Karen said, bursting into tears. Deep down what she was really asking was what was wrong with her Dad. Karen may not have spent all the time I did with my Dad, but she was still very inch a Dad's girl. She loved him, and this new one-way street was hurtful to her, to all of us.

"Dad's sad at the moment, Karen," I said, trying my best not to cry alongside her. "And that's what's making him angry. He's not angry with us."

"Well it looks like it," said Gavin, defiantly.

"No, he's just hurt."

"When will she come around though?" Karen asked, drying her eyes with her sleeve.

"Look, Easter is next week and then it's my birthday. It can't go on too long."

And with that we all drifted to different parts of the house. Karen went upstairs. Gavin went into the lounge to watch the Saturday cartoons. I went out the back and sat on the step. A football was only a few feet away, but I just couldn't muster the enthusiastic for anything. We had all been given a hell of a shaking and the knot in my stomach was still twisting.

I sat on the step for a moment longer, picking up small weeds from the concrete. But what I was really picking through was my utter dismay. At the moment when I most needed my father to turn up and be the hero I believed him to be, he was absent. Instead of racing to our rescue, he had turned and abandoned us. Maybe he was right, maybe our mother had abandoned us, but wasn't he doing a terrific job of copying her!

I moved my hands from the weeds and placed them on my lap. The step I was sitting on was cold, our house was cold, our father was cold; suddenly everything about my life seemed cold. Whatever was going on with my father was stone-cold serious, I got that now. Exhausted in so many ways, I closed my eyes and let the tears fall. There was no more denying, no more convincing; our father was not himself. He was clearly angry and he was clearly pained. The coldness, the anger, the accusations, the cruelty would all go on for another while, and we would just have to put up with it. What else could we do but wait?

I looked over at my football, with even less enthusiasm then when I first came out. Knowing not what else to do, I went back inside to face a houseful of cleaning. I would just have to get on with it. I was the oldest and it was now up to me to do everything I could to speed up Dad's recovery. The rationale was simple; once he got better, everything would get better. What else could I do?

With less patience and sympathy than before, I told the others that we would all just have to put up with things the way they were, for now anyway.

* * *

Later that night lying in bed I prayed, probably for the first time in my life, a real honest to goodness prayer, that my father's recovery wouldn't take too long, because above all I desperately needed my dad. As I looked up at the ceiling, random thoughts swirled through my head: I was born on the 16th of April 1968, Louis Armstrong's *Wonderful World* was playing on the radio, everyone had gone to the moon, bangers and mash was the culinary favourite on every working-class plate. Men carried twenty cigarettes in their pockets and enough change for a quick one or four after work. Woman wore their hair big and their skirts long. They dreamed of adventure and careers, but mostly they ended up dishing out the mash. Children ran wild, with no fear on their doorsteps. Our house was like the next; kids running in and out, friends dropping in at weekends, music blearing out the windows. A perfect dream until the dream ended and the "separation" began.

CHAPTER 6

———✖———

Two weeks on, our father's behaviour had not improved. He was moody and withdrawn whenever he was in the house, which wasn't very often. There had been absolutely no contact from Mum. Karen had missed yet another week of dance. The father who would fetch a blanket for his sleeping child had become the man you avoided. It was confusing and it was disturbing, a constant reason for tears, and none of us escaped its consequences. But what could we do? Nothing, except go about avoiding him as best we could.

Easter came and went without the passing of even one piece of chocolate between our lips. But it was not the chocolate that we missed. It was a very lonely day for us all – the first major sign that our family was in serious trouble. We complained amongst ourselves, sharing the same bitter pit in our sandwich-filled stomachs, but again we said nothing. Our father was becoming more unapproachable by the day, and by the day the neglect was growing.

A couple of days after Easter came my fourteenth birthday, the second major opportunity of the month for my father to redeem himself. 16th of April 1982, a Friday. I closed the front door and went off to school thinking, "Not even a bloody card". I arrived home to find the situation hadn't improved. I waited until my father came home after closing, hoping against hope. When he finally made his appearance he was ruddy from beer and smelling from pub smoke. Without a word, he went straight for the TV, then slumped down in front of it.

Another night of watching a zoned-out father. No thanks, not this night. I took myself off to cry my eyes out. "Not even a bloody card. Not even from Mum," I grumbled through the tears. I put sadness, anger and frustration all in a pot and shook it up until it was frothing. "I want my old life back!" I sobbed into the darkness. I wanted my Mum to come back and say sorry. I wanted my father to tell her he still loved her and I wanted them to get back to being parents. And wanting these things so badly made everything so much worse.

* * *

Summer came and went without any of the youthful happiness I was so accustomed to. My father spent more of his free time away from home, either with mates or in the bookies. After Mum left, I suppose, he must have felt in many ways that his masculinity had been compromised. Men left women, not the other way around. In the world he lived in, Mum's departure was an embarrassment. It wounded his pride. Her name rarely passed his lips, but when it did, we tried to close our ears to the poison that rolled with it. But with no word from Mum in such a long while, this form of self-defence started to falter.

Finding ourselves back at school in the September of 1982 without the make-believe of things getting better was very difficult for us. Doing everything for yourself was difficult; getting up, getting to school, getting home from school. It was especially difficult doing the walk for home knowing there was only bricks and mortar waiting for you – no hugs, no welcome home, no dinner, none of the simple things to tell you that you are loved. It was difficult.

Feeling unloved took its toll on every aspect of our lives, and everything suffered. Even feeding ourselves became a signpost that screamed unloved. More times than not, food amounted to a slapped-together sandwich or a pile of greasy chips, if we had the money. Sometimes, when fortune smiled upon us, Mrs Burke would treat us to some of her home cooking. The Burkes, a big family by any standards and potless by any standards were by far the happiest people I had ever met – if you could believe my judgement, which I was having serious questions about.

Sitting around their table, half-expecting the doggy chair to give way at any moment, put some warmth into my heart – at least while I was with them – until I closed their door and looked across the street. Yes, even a basic thing like feeding yourself had become a chore for us. My father was always tight with money, which only got worse with no one around to pry it from him. Asking him for house-money was soon transformed into something you had to be apologetic for. There were no more home cooked meals, no more sitting around the table and for all intents and purposes, no more family. Instead of us all clinging together to soften the tragedy of our mother leaving, taking the lead from my father, we allowed ourselves to be spun off into very separate lives.

For me, at this time, my life felt like I was wading through immovable mud. The mundaneness of my day-to-day was stifling. The frivolity of my youth that been short-changed for responsibilities and cleaning. I guess somewhere in the recesses hope resided, tempting me with the notion that one day the father I mourned would show up. Playing into his dream, I continued to make everything perfect for his evening arrivals.

"Again? You scrubbed that yesterday," Gavin said, annoyed that I was trying to hold him out of the kitchen.

"You want him to kick off?"

"I'm starving! And the lads are waiting for me," he said, rubbing the sweat from his brow.

"What about your homework?"

"I'll do it in the morning."

"Did you even go to school today?"

"You can sign me a note."

"No I won't."

"Fine, I'll do it myself. Now can I get a sandwich?" he said, walking in anyway.

The hardness that comes with hurt was encrusting all of us. And chip by chip, the functional life that we knew was crumbling.

* * *

By the winter of 1982, nearly all the chores in the house were lumped on my shoulders. Karen and Gavin had quickly seen that Dad fought with me, not them, when something wasn't up to standard. With no incentive, good or bad, what angry ten or twelve-year-old is going to sit around and do chores? I didn't blame them. I blamed my dad. I blamed my mum. Didn't they realise I was still in school, still only fourteen? Didn't they care? The way my father looked at me sometimes left me cold. The more he pulled away from me, the more I cleaned, the more I studied, anything to try and get him to love me again.

With the arrival of the cold season a new burden was added to my list of responsibilities. I now had to go to the end of the street, to a corner shop, and collect a bag of coal in a trolley.

"I'll do my back in and that will be football out the window for a while," I told myself, lugging the 40kg bag out of the shopping trolley and in through the front-door.

"Where are you going?" I asked Karen as she raced out past me.

"To a friend's!" she shouted, still running. Karen was growing up faster than she should, and by now friends meant boys. With Dad giving both Karen and Gavin a virtual free rein, how in the hell was I going to be able to control them? The answer was simple: I wasn't.

Even at weekends the work would continue.

"Off to do the washing, Lisa?" one or another of the women in the road would say as I passed then on a Saturday. "Tell that father of yours to buy a machine, him with a car and a manager's job."

"Yeah, maybe if he had, my mother wouldn't have left," was what I wanted to say, but instead I said, "I will!"

Stepping into my mother's shoes, as I was forced to do, gave me a unique appreciation of just how hard her life must have been. Lurching between anger and loss, I felt moments of great pity for her. Whilst my childhood eyes only saw what they wanted to see, my growing adult eyes witnessed the harsh reality that my father was a compulsive gambler.

In moments of sheer frustration, I spat at the hypocrisy of how he used to tell me that the world was far too occupied with fighting over money, when it seems that's all he ever did himself.

In truth, there was always a duality about my father. He was a contradiction, a man at war with himself, though I couldn't see it clearly while my mother was around. Nothing, I suppose, is ever hidden completely; if we care to look, we can catch glimpses. I never questioned why my mother was absent so much. I never questioned why money was so scarce. I never questioned and I never saw. To me, the father of my youth was a wise, placid man who inspired us by encouraging us to look to the stars. This was the father I knew and loved, the father I was so desperate to get back. This was the father I created and my mother supported. To her credit she could have so easily pulled him down, but she didn't, to her credit, because she loved us.

* * *

November had proved to be an especially bleak month for all of us. We were all increasingly fed up by our father's behaviour. With each passing day our disillusion with our situation grew – and still no sign of our mother.

The weather had turned cold and nasty, echoing our surroundings. A particularly vicious flu laid me low for a couple of days, with running nose, coughing and spluttering. If a truck had levelled my bedroom I mightn't have minded too much. At a time when I needed a cuddle more than any medicine, I had no one. Yes, November was a black month for me and I might have given up all hope of happiness ever returning to our house if it hadn't been for the Christmas cheer arriving in abundance come December. As the shops filled with tinsel and the airwaves blasted one cheery tune after another, my heart began to lift to the idea of a Christmas miracle.

Christmas had always been such a happy time for our family. Less than twelve months before, I had received a spectacular Timex watch. How many times had I stared at its face since April, just to remind myself of what my father was really like! Less than twelve months, a lifetime ago now that sadness was our prevailing wind.

Still, if miracles can happen, they can certainly happen at Christmas. Three weeks to go, and this was the type of sentiment I locked firmly in my mind. If there was ever going to be a turning point for our family, the arrival of the big fella was going to be it. No one, not even my dad, could wipe away all those special memories. Our Christmas tradition was textbook; Dad getting up early to do a great big fry-up; Mum joining him later in the kitchen, sharing a drink, sharing a laugh, working together, pulling together an amazing feast; church songs playing in the background; all together on the couch, waiting for the Queen's speech at three o'clock. So much happiness, so many reasons to put the breakup behind us and move on as best we could, together. Even if it was just for one day, it would be the start. Darkness had lodged for far too long in our house. Now it was time to bring in bring back the light.

Two weeks to go now. I am still optimistic but less so. The main reason for the sliding scale is that I can't see any evidence of the usual planning that goes into making a great Christmas. Still two weeks is fine, though three would have been better. I had wanted to broach the subject with Dad a lot earlier than this, but hadn't found the appropriate moment. Even the mere mention of Mum lately had sent him ballistic, so I was treading safely.

"If I leave it any longer, we won't get a turkey or a ham for that matter," I reasoned with myself. It was a Saturday morning and I could see Dad reading his paper in the lounge.

"Oh to hell with it," I tell myself, thinking, "Now or never!"

I paused at the door, steeling myself.

"Will Mum be here at Christmas?" I blurted out.

"What, and have her eat everything? Don't you remember how much she ate?" He replied, not even bothering to look up.

"No, I just wondered, would we see her?"

After a pause he lowered his paper, which was not a good sign. My stomach somersaulted, waiting for it.

"Why would you want to see someone who abandoned you? You think that's normal for a mother to do that?"

"No," I said, knowing anything else would only fuel him.

"She's no good. I gave her everything. How many times do I have to tell you lot?" he said, rising to the mantelpiece to get his cigarettes. "Now go on, bugger off and don't mention her again."

I lowered my head and turned.

"Oh and Lisa," he called, "You can make yourself useful by getting that washing down to the laundry."

I turned again, my cheeks flushing. I left the room silently fighting the urge to turn around and scream at him, "Gave her everything? You didn't give her a bloody washing machine for starters!" I was so sick of his bloody moods. What did I care if we didn't have a bloody Christmas? To hell with it, to hell with it all. I dropped myself down like an empty sack. I was done. I had had enough. I was over my grief, and I was on to full-blown anger. Grief, hurt and anger empowered me – or so it felt. I bit into my lip. I was far too angry to water it down with tears.

I shook my head. I was truly sick of it all. I was sick of being criticised for every little thing I didn't do and never thanked for all the things I did do. And I was sick of being confused about my feelings for my mother. There were days when I was so angry at her; I was so angry at her for leaving us. I was so angry at her for ruining our family. But, there were days too, when I missed her so terribly much. On those days I didn't blame her. I could see the turrets Dad had created around himself and I didn't doubt that any attempt to enter back into our lives, in whatever form, would have been met with bitter resistance.

I knew only too well that he was systematically waging a campaign of words to poison our memory of our mother. And when this poison spilled out onto us, I gained a little clarity, a little perspective and I didn't blame her. And today was one of those crystal clear days when I too wanted to escape. Today, I wanted to run a million miles away from him, from everything.

With these thoughts and more, I shivered, feeling the cold for the first time since coming out. It was near freezing, and in my distress I had left without a coat. I looked up at the sky pulling a blanket of thick cloud over itself and I wondered if we were to have a Christmas at all. Much as I really wanted to vanish into a puff of smoke, I soon took myself back in, wondering if we would have any sort of Christmas at all.

My father came into the kitchen as I was gathering up the laundry.

"I need some money for food and for the washing," I said, unable to keep the shimmering resentment from my voice. To this he said nothing. He walked back into the lounge, to return a moment later with some money which he laid on the table.

"What are we going to do for Christmas?" I asked, taking the money.

"As far as I'm concerned it's just another day. So if you're thinking you're getting any extra, think again."

"I'll do the dishes when I get back, it'll be busy today," I said, picking up the heavy laundry bag as if it was filled with feathers and walking slowly past him. It wasn't until I was out of his sight that I let my shoulders reflect the weight of both the bag and my heart. "Why is he doing this to us?" I asked, holding back the tears with all my might.

"Hey Lisa, wait up!" The call came from across the road. I dropped the bag and looked over. It was Becky coming out of her door. "Wait up, I'll come with you," she shouted, throwing on her denim jacket. "Everything all right?" she asked, pulling her hair from under her collar.

I thanked God for Becky. She knew only too well what I was going through.

"I've just been told we're not having Christmas," I said.

"What do you mean? How can you not have Christmas? Even we have Christmas. Ah he's just talking shite," she said, making light of it.

"No, he's serious. We won't be having Christmas. He's getting worse Becky."

"Then what will you do?"

"What will I do? Keep it together, for God's sake!" I'm asking and telling myself this at the same time.

It's the 25th of December 1982, and I'm sitting next to Becky and everyone is staring at me, thinking, "poor sod" no doubt. I've an orange paper crown on my head and a giant lump in my throat that won't disappear, no matter how much I tell Becky's Nana Marcy that I'm okay.

"Where's your brother and sister? What are they doing?"

"With friends."

"And your Dad, wouldn't he like to come over and join us?"

"He's not at home. I don't know where he is," I said, not bothering to veil anything.

"Would you like some gravy, son?" she said, skilfully backtracking.

Much as I tried to dig into the spirit of the day, I just couldn't ignore the fact that D-Day had arrived and my family remained on the shore in tatters. I went to bed that night with the cold realisation that we had been abandoned not by one parent but by two. It had taken me nine months of hard growing up to finally accept that the break-up was never going to be reversed.

When Big Ben chimed into 1983, the New Year found my eyes coloured by cynicism. Christmas had yank the proverbial wool aside and I was seeing my family situation clearly for the first time. With my new 20-20 vision, I saw myself as the sole custodian of my happiness. Which meant, or at least I convinced myself it meant, freedom from the pain that loving my father had caused me. Bolstered by anger and immaturity, I easily fooled myself into believing love was like a tap which you could turn on and off at will without drowning. I was in fact looking forward to moving on with the idea of emotional independence when puberty dumped a forty-floor building upon my naivety.

"I can't have them, I don't want them," I said, looking at my growing breasts in absolute horror. "This isn't right. I hate it. I hate them!" I slumped back on my bed. I was on the way to becoming a girl, but it was the wrong way. My body had taken the wrong turning, and I had no idea how to get it back on track.

"What is going to happen to me?" I groaned, looking around my bedroom. The football posters, the dirty socks, the half-eaten sandwich under the bed, all testified to the fact that I wasn't a girl. I paused, landing on no place in particular. Although I didn't understand it and I certainly couldn't explain it, I just knew as much as I knew I needed air that I wasn't a girl – I was a boy. There were the breasts, the curves and the menstruation, there was all this and yet I knew. It was too weird, too unbelievable – yet I knew.

I stood up and went over to the mirror again to examine how bad things really were. If I wore a baggy top maybe no one would notice. Something must have gone wrong with me, maybe on conception, maybe in the womb, maybe at birth, somewhere, somehow I had got trapped in the wrong body.

That was the moment when the forty-floor building crashed down upon me, splattering my emotional body into a thousand pieces. From that moment on, my life was never to be the same. For added to those cynical eyes I wore were fear and desperation. I was so frightened what my future might hold, and so desperate for none of it to be true. It was the stuff of nightmares, and I wanted so desperately to wake up. One of the biggest complaints you are likely to hear from teenagers is that no one gets them, no one understands. Largely unfounded, many would say, but in my case, a boy stuck inside a female body, that perspective kinda had gravity. And to make matters worse, who could I tell? Becky was the only candidate. She was my only friend. But instead of running to her for help, I let fear take a hand and convince me that this was even too big for Becky. She wouldn't understand – she would reject me. The more I listened, the more my demons grew.

By far the worst thing about the change were the breasts. Everything else I could hide. And to my absolute horror, once they appeared they just seemed to get bigger by the day. I'd spent the vast majority of my life in tracksuits. I'd kick a ball as well as anyone, ride a bike as well as anyone, climb a tree as well as anyone, and I could run as well as anyone too until my breasts arrived – now they just got in the way. It got to the stage where I was getting teased in school for not getting a bra.

"Lisa, you seriously need to buy a bra, they are enormous." The words coming from Becky's mouth made me physically sick. "I'll come with you, we'll go Saturday."

"I'm playing football Saturday."

"What's with you? You have to get a bra."

It's cold, it's grey, it's February, in my estimation one of the most miserable months, and I'm staring at rows upon rows of women's underwear. The glow from my cheeks is enough to light a small suburb of London, or at least bright enough to call for help.

"Can I help you love?" a kindly assistant asked. A robust woman, older than my mother, closer to my Dad's age, probably mid-forties. "Do you need to be fitted?"

"Fitted?" I repeated, absolutely clueless.

"What size are you wearing?" she asked, trying to solve the problem herself.

"Size... um..."

"You haven't worn a bra before?" she asked, raising her eyebrow and checking my volume at the same time.

"No," I said looking to the floor for a great hole.

"Is your mum with you?"

"No... I'm on my own."

"That's all right sweetie," she said, her maternal nature oozing out. "You come with me and we'll get you fixed up in no time." She rubbed my arm. "Lots of girls come in on their own," she added out of kindness. She smiled, giving me the signal, then we moved off together to the changing rooms. Having installed me in one of the cubicles, she yanked across the curtains and stuck her head in the side.

"Right, you slip off your top there and we'll take a look."

"You want me to take off my top?"

"Oh don't worry, we're all girls, and I've seen every shape and size under the sun, so you've nothing to worry about," she assured me. "Right, you slip it off and I'll get my measuring tape."

She had only gone a moment when a cold panic overcame me. I couldn't do this. I stuck my head out the cubicle. There was no sign of her, so I took my chance. I ran straight out of the dressing rooms, straight out of the department, straight out of the shop and straight out of any notion of ever wearing a bra.

By the time I got home, my determination had risen like a wall. I raced through the front door with only one thing on my mind – to get to the bathroom as quickly as humanly possible. Once inside, I knew exactly where I was going and what I was looking for. I opened the cupboard above the sink and pulled out an old bandage from the back. I had used it before for a knee injury, so I was confident it would do the job.

I yanked off my top, and without looking at my reflection, I wound the cloth around my chest, tugging as tightly as I could. I sucked out all of the air from my body and lungs and bound myself over and over until I ran out of bandage, and air.

I took a deep breath, secured the ends with a safety pin and stood up straight. I looked at my handiwork in the mirror and didn't know whether to laugh or cry. I could feel the cloth constricting my air passages. I could feel the pain and the discomfort. I knew this was by no means a natural thing to do – to inflict pain upon yourself. I knew these bandages would set up a whole shadowy life of hiding, of self-deception. I knew all this, yet I didn't care. I could laugh in the face of all of this because these horribly painful bindings gave me my old chest back, and in so doing I felt like a little bit of me had come back.

I went from the bathroom straight to my bedroom and found one of the old football shirts that I had been forced to set aside because of my breasts. I slipped the fabric over my head and pulled it into place. I went to my mirror and examined myself from all sides, and then a minor miracle happened; for the first time in such a long time, I smiled. As far as anyone could tell I had my old chest back and it was just like the chest of every other boy my age – flat.

Maybe if I had had someone to confide in I wouldn't have had to resort to such drastic methods. Maybe, I would have, early on, discovered the nature of Gender Identity Disorder. Maybe I could have been spared the torments of confusion and loneliness. Maybe I wouldn't have locked everything inside and carried on like everything was fine and dandy. And maybe I wouldn't have established the fertile ground for a lifetime of fear and self-loathing.

With both of my parents absent from my world, my one and only ally continued to be Becky. There were so many times I was on the verge of telling her about the "boy inside", but the same old fears quickly choked the courage from me. When it came to it, I just couldn't find the words. In a world ignorant of gender identity disorder, how do you tell someone, especially someone your own age, especially someone you care about, that you are a boy trapped inside the wrong body? How do you say these words? How?

Becky was my last connection to kindness, and I truly believed that if I severed that artery it would be the end of me. And so, early on, way before I could understand the terrible ramifications of my actions, I made a pact with my fear to keep the truth of my identity hidden beneath a false persona which that I would project to the world. What exactly that persona was going to be, I didn't know. I guessed I would carry on as Lisa, the tomboy, for as long as humanly possible. And after that, then we would just have to see.

* * *

By the time the first anniversary of my mother's departure fell upon us, our family life had degraded beyond recognition. I had by now come to the conclusion that no matter how much washing and cleaning I did, no matter how little I asked for to pay for housekeeping, no matter what any of us did or didn't do, the father we loved wasn't coming back. On the contrary, the stranger in his place seemed hell bent on vanquishing any love we still held for him.

And what better opportunity to do some vanquishing then one of those moments that you know really matter. And so, another birthday came and went, without even a bloody birthday card! Hurt and angry, I took my washing gloves off and went into full-scale rebellion. And I wasn't alone. Karen started dating boys, at an age when there was no hope of discernment. Gavin's waywardness ratcheted up a notch, at an age when there was no hope of avoiding trouble. And I went from the responsible one to the leader of the pack, at an age when there was no hope of ever turning back.

In many ways we were mirroring what we saw in our father. And what I saw was a man in self-destruct mode. The addiction and the depression were by now in total control, and the truth was, bad as everything was, we all felt that it was only going to get worse. And none of us had any stomach left for sampling that.

"He's not the same and he's never going to be, now cope!" I told myself, in the midst of giving up all hope in him. Not only was he, at this stage, picking on me for just about everything, but he had also started to latch onto the way I dressed. Given my silent struggle with puberty, this added pressure was such a burden it pushed me from him like nothing could. The truth was, my father was never going to accept my truth, and I was never going to be able to change it. This was an impasse that was only ever going to be used as a weapon against me should I let it. There were to be no negotiations, no truce, only a full-on assault if I put myself in harm's way. So I did all that I could to avoid this – I stayed away and I avoided him as best I could. It had come to this.

One of the quotes my father used to recite to me as a young child went, "Our task must be to free ourselves from this prison by widening our circle of compassion, to embrace all loving creatures and the whole of nature and its beauty". How far my father had fallen from the ideals of his hero, Albert Einstein!

Now up to this point the safest haven I could think of was up in Becky's bedroom. But even there, of late, an uneasiness had entered to disturb our relationship. Or at least, it disturbed me, Becky, on the other hand, was, I hoped, totally oblivious. And as to the source of the disturbance? Well in a word – hormones. With the advance of puberty I found myself viewing Becky in the same way as any hormone-fuelled fifteen-year old boy would – as extremely hot.

The fact that Becky couldn't see the boy inside me, no more than anyone would, gave me my first horrifying insight into how impossible finding love was going to be for me. I had, as I saw it, had virtually all the love inside me bled out by my parents, and now I was standing alone facing the cold reality that I might never be able to replace it.

It was a horrifying realisation that shook me to the core. For the first time, I contemplated just how bleak my future was likely to be. While many, I knew, didn't wind up finding happiness, at least they had their fair shot at it, I told myself. Whereas I wasn't even going to get that shot. It just wasn't fair.

I was only fifteen, and it seemed to me that my future had already been cruelly taken from me. If I went ahead and opened up to everyone, if I told them about my true nature, I would, I believed, be condemned to a loveless life. Now, to save myself, not only did I have to avoid my father, I had to avoid myself – my true self. I could see now the absolute necessity of having my false persona. I would just have to go on being Lisa the tomboy for as long as I could. And after that? Well, I would just have to wait and see. What was my alternative? If I didn't hide within, I would have to face my future head on. But alone, at fifteen, this was not something I was capable of doing.

* * *

I was hardening now to the realities of my plight, and the first thing my new persona and I did was to stop looking back to bygone days. All I had ever wanted was my parents' approval, and by now it was painfully clear that hell might freeze over before that happened.

The end of April was fast approaching, and the disappointment of my fifteenth birthday was still very raw with me. I was by now doing only the chores that were absolutely necessary to offset a full-scale war between me and my father. I came down to breakfast one day. It was the last Saturday of the month and early enough to have everyone still under the same roof. Gavin was already at the table, eating cereal, and Dad was reading his paper in the living room, as he usually did, mainly, I think, so he wouldn't have to talk to us.

"Pass us the milk," I asked Gavin, sitting opposite. "Is Karen home?"

A knock interrupted the answer. We looked at Dad, knowing he would answer it, like the sentry he was. Dad put down his paper, letting us know that he would do exactly that. I went on spooning my breakfast into my face as fast as it would go. I felt the pit in my stomach much more these days whenever Dad was around, and I was doing my level best to hurry myself out into the medicine of the street.

I was just about to stand up when I saw who had come into the house. I felt it had to be a hallucination. It was Mum.

"Mum!" I said, hardly believing the words were falling from my mouth.

"Mum!" Gavin said, obviously having the same feeling.

"I wanted to let you know..." she said, breaking off to wipe her eyes. They were red. She looked like she had gone through a pretty bad night. Just as she went to continue, my father walked in behind her, making his heavy presence felt by everyone. Without saying a word he took up prime position directly opposite her, folding his arms and staring coldly at her. It was a wonder she didn't turn on her heels and run straight out of the door. Instead she composed herself bravely, enough to speak, even though we could clearly see she was shaking like a little leaf.

"I wanted to come and let you know that your Nan Barbara passed away silently last night."

Our estranged mother standing there in the middle of our kitchen, delivering the very speech we had expected this time a year ago, was so shocking, so surreal, I didn't know whether to leap up and hug her or scream at her to get out. I just couldn't fathom how to act.

"Well I just thought you should know," she said, wading through the silence.

"When is the funeral?" I asked, not enjoying the tension any more than she was.

"We haven't got that far. I'll let you know, okay?"

"Okay."

"Is Karen about?"

"She's out with her boyfriend," Gavin said, finding his voice.

"Well, you'll tell her, won't you?"

"Yes," Gavin and I said in unison.

"Okay. Well I'll be in touch," she said, steeling herself for her walk out of the kitchen and back out the door. We watched her leave, much as she had a year before, without any fanfare at all.

We never did hear about my grandmother's funeral and I didn't see my mother for another four years. I often wondered why she had come that day, only to disappoint us further. Walking out of the house that morning, it seemed that she had firmly closed the door on that chapter of her life.

How does a mother leave her family, her children? This was a question we had heard so often that it rattled around in all our brains as the week past and it became obvious that there wasn't going to be any funeral, for us anyway.

A year on, and the battle my father waged against my mother's standing was all but over. He had won. He was victorious. The anger we felt at the lack of any follow-up visit or call was too much for any of our weary hearts to bear. We succumbed to our father's wishes; we succumbed to the anger. She might as well have been buried with my grandmother for all I cared, I had succumbed, love had been beaten.

My mother's presence back in the house even for the briefest of moments was like a red rag to a bull. Dad became moodier – if that was possible – and it was me who suffered the brunt. Maybe it was because I had spoken to her first, maybe he just didn't need an excuse. Whatever the reason, I was really getting sick of living like this. And that's when my fantasies of leaving home began.

Soon the fantasy of breaking free from our chains was all Becky and I seemed to talk about. Summer had arrived, and for us the air seemed filled with the possibilities of something better away from home.

CHAPTER 7

———⌾———

A month on, and I had all my proverbial bags packed when my father arrived home on a beautiful May evening and unpacked them all again with two words – 'family holiday'. Dad had been in the betting shop all afternoon, we hardly expected to see him until all the races were over, and then it was just to get ready to go back out again. So when he walked into the lounge, with what could almost be described as a sunny disposition, Gavin and I were caught off guard, to say the least.

"Spain," he said.

"Spain?" I repeated, hardly believing it.

"We're flying out next month, so you'll need to get passports organised. We're staying in an apartment in a hotel resort."

"Will there be a pool, Dad?" Gavin asked.

"A couple of them, Gavin. Where's your sister?"

"Upstairs getting ready," I ventured lightly. It was the first time in over a year that I had felt the light returning into the house, and I was almost giddy with it.

"Can Craig come?" Karen asked a moment later, running a towel over her wet hair.

"No, it's a family holiday."

"Well then I'm not going."

"Up to you, stay if you want."

I was shocked to hear this, given Karen was only thirteen. Craig was her eighteen-year-old boyfriend. Gavin and I disliked him, but Dad tolerated him because of the way he was. I knew in my heart that he would never have allowed Karen such a reckless amount of freedom had he been "right".

Still, the holiday in itself was an absolute miracle. I counted my blessings and stayed quiet. Passports, planes, apartments, pools – this was the first nice thing our father had done since the break-up. Contemplating it all later that night brought a glimmer of hope to the surface. Maybe the holiday was the start of it, maybe it would provide the healing that Dad so desperately needed. I was not in the habit, at this time, of praying to or even believing in a mighty force that could make drastic alterations to your life upon request, but hedging my bets, so to speak, I had a little word, just in case. I could feel tiny bubbles of excitement erupting in my stomach. The return of family happiness – was it too much to hope for?

The next morning Gavin and I sailed about the kitchen. We were both ecstatic about our forthcoming holiday. We marked it on the calendar, and boy those red marks couldn't come quick enough. I secretly wished Karen was going, but she was so besotted with Craig that a holiday in outer space wouldn't have changed her mind. And so there was no point starting any trouble over it. In fact, until all those calendar squares turned red, there was to be no trouble of any sort. Of this I was determined.

And so, after the great countdown that had almost turned me grey, I was at long last flying high above the clouds, stuck to the little aircraft window, feeling something my heart hadn't known for a long time – happiness. I had all these visions of family bliss racing through my head, going so fast my heart had to beat faster just to keep up. As the wheels pumped onto the tarmac I had to grip the armrests to let go of some of my energy, I was so excited.

As soon as we hit the resort there was a natural separation between adults and kids, which to be honest, suited everyone just fine. The adults widened their domain to take in every local bar that celebrated a happy hour, whilst we were happy to dominate the hotel complex. I didn't care that Dad was going off doing his thing, I was happy for him He had a smile on his face and so did we, and that was all that mattered.

One week in, and everything to my immense relief was going swimmingly. We all still wore smiles, which led me to believe that my "little word" had been listened to. I wandered through the hotel lobby finding myself separated from everyone, and found myself amongst the glittering reflections of the hotel lounge. The music instantly hooked me. On stage a colourful band of Eastern musicians played exotic instruments with a vibrant beat. I couldn't help but move with the sways of the beautiful belly-dancer as I made my way to the bar. Even though I was only fifteen, I knew I looked just that bit older to get me served without too much hassle.

And I was right. I bought myself a beer and turned, choosing my table. The room was three-quarters full, everyone was happy, everyone was enjoying the music. I took my seat and allowed my eyes to wander and that's when I noticed a girl leaning over the bar in her shorts and belly-top chatting to the middle-aged barman. By the look of her bronzed figure I surmised that her holiday, like ours, was probably into its second week.

As my pint went down, as quickly as I could, I rotated my gaze between the dancer and the girl, but it was the girl who held all my interest. She was beautiful, a goddess even, older than me, maybe eighteen, maybe older, I didn't know; all I knew was that she was a vision my eyes couldn't get enough of.

I was by now certain that I was a boy trapped in the wrong body. Even though I had that pact and was never going to speak of this, it didn't mean that in the privacy of my own mind I couldn't acknowledge my feelings. What was the point of denying it to myself? It wouldn't have made a blind bit of difference anyway, as my hormones were a torrent that just couldn't be suppressed. I was a boy and I like girls, I liked them a lot, and in the privacy of my own mind, that was perfectly acceptable, even encouraged.

I had never been so happy to get to the end of my pint, because it gave me a chance to get close to the object of my infatuation. To my absolute joy, she smiled as I came up beside her. She had her back to the bar, and like everyone else she was swept up in the entertainment. A moment passed as the barman busied himself watching the belly-dancer.

Noticing my invisibility, the girl turned to me and smiled again. "What you having?" she asked, totally confident of her powers.

"A beer," I said lamely.

"A beer and a bottle of your best brandy, Lucas," she called, over the music.

"Anything for you princess," Lucas smiled, leaping into action.

"You can run a tab, pay at the end of the night," she said, seeing me producing some cash. "My name's Rachel. And this one's on me," she smiled, turning her back to the bar. "Do you think I could do that?" she asked, shaping her hip in a figure of eight as best she could still seated.

She was gorgeous, she was over-brimming with life. Sure she could do that - she could do anything.

"My very best brandy, only for you Rachel."

"Where you sitting?" she said, hopping off her seat.

"Over there," I said, lamely.

"Okay, grab the tray."

I could not believe my luck. A beautiful woman was not only drinking with me, she was, to all intents and purposes, flirting with me. My mind was in turbocharge, trying to figure out what was happening. *Your chest is bound, your hair is long, and long-haired men are in hot demand. She thinks you're a man. Well, I am a man, so no harm there.*

"So what's your name?" came the six-million dollar question, as soon as Rachel sat down.

"Um... um...," I paused, feeling the enormity of my answer pinning me to the wall, "Um, Lee," I said, ignoring the wails screeching in my head. I was enjoying myself, my hormones were enjoying themselves, Rachel was enjoying herself and after a bottle of brandy the whole world would be enjoying themselves. And just as I predicted, a bottle on, the whole universe was congratulating me for saying, "Lee" and egging me on to say yes to Rachel as she linked her arms in mine, saying, "You want to get another bottle and go back to yours?"

"Yes," I said singing it from the hilltops – YES, YES, YES! Such a simple word, it was so easy to slip it out without the slightest worry over the catastrophe to unfold when Rachel took me under the covers.

With the moon looking down, we walked arm in arm towards the holiday apartment block. Inside, we stole into the darkness of the small apartment with the giddiness of eloping lovers.

"Here we are," I said fumbling for the light. I switched the light on and turned around. "Rachel?" She was nowhere to be seen. "Rachel?" I said again, stumbling my way to the bathroom. "Rachel, you in there?" I said, opening the door slowly.

She wasn't in the bathroom or on the balcony. I came back in from the air feeling my head spin that little faster. No, she couldn't be in the bedroom?

I walked in. "Oh my," I said catching her flesh with a beam of light. It was the most incredible thing, a beautiful woman in my bed. I was so giddy, so excited, so naïve, so virginal and my brain was so soaked with brandy I just couldn't compute what would happen the moment she discovered she wasn't going to get what she expected.

"Well?" she said, laughing.

I stood there smiling. I was just about to make the biggest mistake of my life when my father burst into the room, with more alcohol inside him than even I had.

"Who the fuck is that?" he slurred.

"A friend."

"Well tell her to sling her hook."

Before I could reply, shouts rose from the corridor. A couple in the opposite room screamed abuse at each other.

"Ah, I'm going to bed," my father said stumbling for the door.

"Let me help you," I said fearing he wouldn't.

"Get off, I can do it," he said, wobbling out the door. I

followed him out and down the corridor and took the keys for him, to get him in the door. As I turned back the alcohol seemed to evaporate from my brain and the full realisation of Rachel hit me. I could feel my legs weaken as I stepped back inside my bedroom.

I stood and looked at the bed. It was empty – she was nowhere to be seen. I had had a lucky escape, and I was so grateful for that, because all my wonderful memories of that night with Rachel could remain pristine and intact. Although nothing happened between us, not even a kiss, the feelings, the attraction, the raw excitement told me everything I needed to know – I was 100% male.

* * *

We arrived home from the glory of our holiday laden with goodwill and cheer. Even my father seemed to have a happy hangover, as we collected our bags and caught a taxi home. I was only in the door and I was heading over to see Becky. I hoped we could go to a disco. I was in such a good mood I never wanted the feeling to end.

"Hold on a minute, what are you doing?" Dad said, catching me halfway out the door.

"I'm going to a disco with Beck," I said happily, raring to go.

"Not like that you're not!" he said coming to the door, "get back inside."

"Why?" I said, taken aback.

"Get up them stairs and get changed if you want to get out of this house."

"It's just a disco, down the community centre," I said quietly.

"Get up them bloody stairs and put a dress on!" he said,

grabbing me by the collar and hauling me in. "I'm sick to death of your sloppiness. Have you no pride?"

"But this is me."

"Not any more it isn't. This is my house and you'll do as I say. Now get up them stairs or I swear I'll drag you up myself," he said, pushing me towards the stairs. I took the stairs, shaking all over. "Is it any wonder your mother left?" he shouted up at me, as I reached the landing.

Biting back the tears, I waited, leaning against the wall, listening for his whereabouts. I could hear him entering the living room and turning on the TV. Heart pounding, I crept back down the stairs and slipped out the back door, totally done with him. There was no going back. Whatever bridge I'd imagined had been built while on holiday was now well and truly smashed. I was totally done with him – it was over.

"How the hell did I ever think he was a good father? Why can't he just let me be, if I don't like dresses what is it to him?" I asked Becky, through floods of tears.

"Ah they're all assholes, I wouldn't worry about it," she said, glossing her lips. "You know, we should stop talking about it and really get the feck out of here."

"Where would we go?"

"Who cares, any place is better than this dump," Becky said, thickening her lashes. "Do you think I'd get away with eighteen?"

"Probably."

"Do you want to go to the Cockerel instead?" The Cockerel was a pub about a couple of miles away that was known to serve minors.

"Do you think we'd get served?"

"What do you think, does it look like an engagement

ring?" Becky asked sticking out the blue crystal ring she had got down the market.

"Yeah."

"If we're stopped, I'll flash the ring and say I'm engaged."

"Might work."

"We could walk up smoking. You got some?"

"Yeah, but they're Spanish," I said, pulling out the pack.

"Yeah but they're twenty!"

Back then, a pack of twenty cigarettes was real adult. Mostly teenagers who could afford it would have ten packs, and the ones who couldn't would either resort to nicking one here and there or finding a shop that sold singles under the counter.

"You know you could be a singer, you're good enough." Said Becky. "If we left you could get paid. I'd do it, only I can't sing."

"You can dance."

"Yeah, you sing and I dance and we could get a small flat to begin with."

"You think?"

"Yeah, we could make it big, why not?"

"Maybe."

"Look at it this way, what's there for us? Why don't we? Both our fathers are assholes, mine doesn't want me here, does yours?"

"No."

"No, so why don't we?"

"Maybe."

"Once he's laid his hands on you, it won't stop, trust me. We'll waste our lives if we stay here."

"I know."

"Well what do you think?" Becky asked, all glammed up.

"Totally Madonna," I said, a little embarrassed. She was

gorgeous, growing into her womanhood with vengeance. Any boy would be lucky to have her within ten feet. And here I was in such close proximity that it made every cell of my body spark. I couldn't help the thoughts floating around my brain any more than I could help the stirrings in my loins. I didn't welcome any of it, and yet I was powerless to prevent it.

An hour later we were jumping off the bus, preparing our entrance into the Cockerel as eighteen-year-olds. I wondered, for a moment, what had happened when Dad had found me gone. Probably cursed the ground I walked on until he reminded himself that he didn't give a crap about me, I told myself in that moment of wasted time, thinking about my father.

"Right, give us a light, and remember, let me do the talking," Becky said, pulling me back into reality.

Regardless of the fact that neither of us looked anywhere near eighteen, we sailed through the door in a cloud of smoke without a second look from the bouncer, who was energetically chatting up a leggy brunette. Inside, the pub's low lights masked its jaundiced walls but did nothing to hide the heavy odour of ale and tobacco. Contributing as we were, to the grey contrails billowing out from all directions, we hardly minded the lack of oxygen.

The table we choose was a safe one tucked away into a corner filled with even less light. This we didn't mind. We were happy to fall into the darkness, we had fooled the doorman, yes, but would we fool the barman? He was after all an arms-folded fifty-something with eyes firmly fixed upon his customers.

After a momentary debate, to gain some bottle, it was unanimously decided that Becky would be the one to decide our fate. And so up she went bolder than brass, looking every day the eighteen-year-old.

"Two glasses of Malibu. Will there be music here later?" she asked, taking a seat at the bar.

"No, but there's a jukebox on the wall, you want change?"

"Yeah, go on," Becky replied, handing over the cash. "Two Malibu," she said slipping in beside me.

"Cheers" we said, raising our glasses in victory.

No more back-alley drinking for us. We had arrived; we were in the big league now.

The uncollected empties gathering on our table made us feel instantly older, instantly free. We talked how we could feel like this all the time if we didn't have to live at home. It was a very powerful argument, sitting there, drinking until closing and feeling oh so very free.

It wasn't until the fresh air hit that I began to feel the effects of all the Malibus. Still, it wasn't a particularly bad feeling being so merry, I thought as I stumbled off the bus and rounded onto our road, arm in arm with Becky.

"I'll see you tomorrow," I said, giggling outside her door.

"Shssh... keep it down! Right, see you tomorrow. You going to be okay?"

"Oh yeah, he doesn't scare me."

"You have your key?"

"What key?"

"Your key to get in."

"Oh, no!"

"You want to stay with me?"

"Nah, someone will be up."

"Yeah, what if its him?"

"Oh, he doesn't scare me," I said, stumbling out of the gate. By the time I arrived on my street I realised that I was a little more than merry, a lot more, in truth. But at that moment, I didn't care. "He doesn't care about me, so I'm not going to care about him!" I told myself, pulling together the words with greatest of difficulty.

After a moment of composing myself, which amounted to me leaning up against the porch wall and belly breathing, I rang the doorbell. I was too drunk to truly imagine anything bad happening. Almost immediately I saw the light spill down from the top bedroom. I looked up to catch the curtains pulling across. What I expected was the window to open and a torrent of abuse to be hurled my way, but instead the light was instantly put out. Why I would be surprised by this, I don't know, but I waited in vain hope all the same. I waited and I waited. And then, not knowing what else to do, I hunkered down in the porch for the long haul. Sitting on the cold porch did a wonderful job of advancing my sobriety. In the cold advancing night, I truly had never felt so alone.

An hour on, I was really starting to feel the cold clinging to the lightness of my cotton shirt. "You have two choices," I told myself sternly, "cry, or grow up." Growing up, just a little, I concluded that Becky was right, we would be better off on our own, as both fathers had as much hope of coming back to life as a pair of pebbles. It was time, high time, to drop the illusion and acknowledge the enemy in our midst.

With battle-lines drawn, I laid my head back against the inhospitable concrete wall and closed my eyes as the first few drops of rain started to fall. After a time, enough to feel the stickiness of the cotton against my flesh, out came the alarm of distant footsteps. Straightening my spine and quietening my breath I listened into the darkness.

"Sweet Mother of God, is that you Lisa?" It was my Irish neighbour, Mrs Burke.

"He won't let me in," I whispered, staring up into his perplexed expression.

"Well you'll catch your death. Come on over to ours. The

missus will sort ye out on the sofa."

"Thanks," I said, picking myself up like a soggy alleycat.

"Not a bother, we were turning in, so we were, when I spotted something outside yours. I thought it might be a stray dog of something."

"No, just me."

"You fancy a cuppa? Never know, we might even get a cuppa outta her."

There was never any question of a pot of tea appearing on the table complete with knitted cosy, strainer and a side plate of whatever home-made delicacies Mrs Burke had hid in her cupboard. These heart-given refreshments went as far as they could in cheering me up, as did the dry T-shirt and the makeshift bed Mrs Burke fussed over while Mr Burke and I finished off the last of her blackberry tart.

"It's not Buckingham Palace, but it's the best I can do," she said.

"Thanks Mrs Burke."

"It's not easy pet, but in a couple of years your legs will be strong, then you can decide where you want to go. Look at me, I came from Ireland as green as a blade of grass, got a little job in a shop and then I met Gerry and well, we have our ups and downs but we were happy, and you will be too."

"Why did you leave Ireland, if you don't mind me asking?"

"I don't. It was my father, he was a mean drunk."

"I'm sorry for asking."

"Sure wasn't I the one who brought it up. Has it got that way with you, over there?"

"No... no."

"Well love, that's a blessin'. Now you get some sleep. God bless son."

"Night, Mrs Burke."

"Goodnight son."

My eyes followed Mrs Burke to the light switch, knowing there would be a smile for me before the darkness came. Feeling as I did, I was eager to acknowledge every blessing that came my way. "Night Mrs Burke," I whispered into the darkness as the light was extinguished.

Tucking the last layer of blanket under my chin, I let out a small sigh. I was wide awake, not a condition I wanted to be in. Out of fear of being left with my own demons, I concentrated my mind fully on the sounds drifting down from up above. I could hear the landing footsteps crossing one another out of the bathroom. I could hear the bedsprings creak under the weight of the first body, then the second. I could hear the gentle mumbling of voices, imagining they were talking about my sorry plight. I listened until the house no longer harboured any distractions to keep my thoughts at bay. And then, with my eyes still fixed on the flaky yellowing ceiling the tears came. The fact was, there just weren't enough distractions in the world to hold back the truth; that I was alone.

After the sobbing came the tossing and turning, until mental and physical exhaustion finally put me to sleep. I woke up to see some of the younger Burke heads peering through the door, only to be quickly swatted away by their mother. Although I could have slept on for at least half of the day, I knew my occupation of the largest room was a major inconvenience in a three-bed terraced house filled with two adults and eight spirited children.

After a hearty breakfast I reluctantly took myself back across the street. Mr Burke and his van had left hours ago to start his vegetable round, which in reality included everything from toilet paper to Tupperware. I wished I had been up early enough to catch him leave, because I would have asked to tag along – anything to delay my homecoming.

Sucking in enough metal to face the inevitable, I headed across the road. I could feel my heart sink with the squeak of the small black rusting gate that was meant to protect me from the rest of the world. Who was there to protect me from what waited within?

Before I was able to knock, the door opened and I was never so happy in my life to see Gavin.

"Is Dad inside?" I asked, walking in gingerly.

"Nope," Gavin said, munching on one half of a jam sandwich, the other still in his hand. "Won't be back until tonight."

"He say anything about me?"

"Nope. Why, what you do?"

"Nothing, just wondering," I said, brushing it aside, for now.

I felt relief that day, having dogged the painful disdain I knew would be painted all over my father's stony face. But that relief didn't last long. To make matters worse, not only did I have my father to worry about, I now had something stirring inside me that was wreaking havoc with my level-headedness. I was becoming increasingly aware that something other than my luggage had come back from Spain with me. It sounds like a disease, but it wasn't; an infliction maybe, but not a disease. For you see I now had what I can only describe as an intense burning to be in a relationship. For anyone else, this was a problem that in all likelihood could be remedied easily enough, but for me it was a definite infliction – a Pandora's Box that I just wasn't in any state of mind to go meddling with. Before Spain, I really hadn't cared one way or another about relationships, about sex, but now, after Rachel slid the lid, it was all I could do to keep the female form from my mind.

Now when you become fixated on something you don't have it's annoying, stressful even, but when everyone except you is enjoying it, well that's torture. And on cue, it seemed, everyone around me suddenly was in the throes of their first passionate romance. Everywhere I looked, friends were hooking up. Becky had so many offers it was hard at times to keep track. It was an epidemic of teenage sexual exploration, and I was the only one stuck at home with my finger in the dam. I so wanted to pull it out and be like all my other friends, but I was terrified. I mean, how the hell do you find a heterosexual female partner when you are trapped in a female body? For all I knew, I would be left in limbo for the whole of my life trying to figure that one out. I was fifteen, I was alone, and I was living under extremely challenging circumstance. I just didn't have the necessary mental stability or maturity to deal with the whole hot potato of the transgender thing.

When I wasn't at home trying to make myself invisible, I was out with friends taking on the unwanted mantle of the proverbial gooseberry. And I hated it. I hated the loneliness, the isolation, the differentiation. But mostly I hated the hopelessness. The way I saw it, with my "complications", the chance of me ever having a girlfriend was not a wager even my father would take.

To make those matters far worse, this was 1984 and we were right in the middle of the heyday of the local disco. And a weekend without disco was a weekend you weren't living, according to just about everyone. So despite my growing aversion to all things gooseberry my choice was simple – disco or die.

With the arrival of the long summer evenings, Becky had taken disco to the realms of religion. Come Thursday she went in prep mode for Saturday. There were so many choices for her: what to wear, how to do her hair, what colour makeup to use, who to snog. All this was sorted out well in advance. As for me, what did I have to think about? Trousers and a T-shirt and that was me done. Anyway it wasn't like I was going to snog anyone in a hurry.

Watching Becky prepare with such excitement was hard in many ways; I was happy for her, but sad, I guess, for me. Unwittingly, I had become a chaperone, of sorts, to Becky and the girls we knocked about with. Every Saturday we'd all go together, and by the end of the night some would have "scored" and some wouldn't. The unlucky ones would inevitably walk home with me – in floods of tears. Oh, there were countless times I felt just like they did, but I never showed it – I couldn't. I wouldn't let them see, because I couldn't explain why I was unhappy yet refused ever boy that came near me – not that there were many, but there were some.

By the end of the summer I knew perfectly well what a season of hunting must feel like for a fox. For the first time in my entire school life I was ecstatic that September had arrived and I was once more on my way back to class. Dogging one skirmish after another had taken all the summer promised away from me. I was glad to see the back of it. I didn't even care that keeping up my grades would be tough, very tough, given the deteriorating circumstances of my home life. I was determined to knuckle down and do my level best.

It was the final run up, one year to go to the finishing

line. And it was a way out for me – a very real one. I was bright, there wasn't a teacher to contradict that. And I was popular and funny and good at sports. And that put me firmly, on paper at least, on the likely-to-succeed list. All I had to do was keep my head for one more year and that would get me into university, I was sure of it, and university would get me out of this.

The truth was, I had never contemplated the notion of "me and university" before, but I was desperate. I was in need of a grand escape and I saw no surer avenue away from my father than jumping a class or two. I had seen working class jobs come and go; even Mr Burke's vegetable run had fallen foul of the failing economy by the end of the summer, such was the precariousness of blue-collar employment, and that was the reason why I had set my sights on such a lofty aspiration as university.

My growing desperation at this time was in no short measure caused by the realisation that hardening one's heart to a loved one was a lot harder than I had ever imagined. I wanted to be immune. I even wanted to hate my father. But no matter how much invisible armour I coated myself, his assaults always found their mark. The more I stood up for myself, especially concerning my dress and boyish mannerism, the more scathing his attack became. It wasn't physical, as Mrs Burke had feared; it didn't have to be. His emotional abuse, all focused on destroying my self-worth, did the job. He wanted me submissive, obedient, voiceless, and when I was forced to be around him, he got just that.

Now the obvious result of this carry-on was that I found myself escaping more and more to Becky's. By the end of my first month in school the situation had not changed and my constant need to take flight was putting my aspirations of university under pressure. Much as I wanted to work, much as I needed to succeed, I was finding it increasingly difficult to keep teetering on the edge of depression. I just couldn't keep my mind concentrated on anything.

In reality, it didn't take much convincing on Becky's part to tease me away from my books come Saturday night. Much as I didn't relish the slow dances, the rest of the night was passable, especially when lifted by alcohol. Having an extra one or two than normal, I soon learned, made the night even enjoyable for a spell. And as for the slow dances, these soon presented the perfect opportunity to slip to the bathroom to have a nip of whatever spirit was hidden in my jacket.

It was on one such excursion to the bathroom that I came face to face with Helen, the most wonderful girl I had ever seen. Oh, there were other girls as pretty, others with the same blonde hair, blue eyes, others with the same waifish figure, but there were none that looked at me the way Helen did. I looked at her dumbfounded as I tried to find my feet to take me out of her way, and she just stepped aside gracefully and smiled. I moved on, feeling a strange squidgyness in my stomach. Before going down to the bathroom I paused to look into the hall, and there she was smiling at me again. There was no mistake, no doubt, she was smiling at me.

"Oh shit!" I said to myself, knocking back some vodka, "It's the hair, she thinks I'm a boy. Oh shit!"

Back inside, it didn't take long for me to locate Helen. She was dancing at the opposite end of the hall from Becky and the gang, but by the beginning of the next slow set she was right opposite me. Now any boy worth his salt would have walked over and started to talk to the beautiful girl smiling over at him. But I just stared at the floor, hating my very existence.

After that point the night's end couldn't come quick enough. With ten minutes still to go, I went out to get the coats, and that's when I met Helen again.

"Hi," she said giving me the same intoxicating smile.

"Hi." At this stage parroting was all I could muster.

"Um, I have to go now, my dad's waiting outside for me." I nodded.

"So maybe we could meet next week?"

"Um… you know I'm a girl." It killed me to say it, but what choice did I have?

"But you like me, I saw the way you looked at me?"

This was probably the biggest shock by far of my young life, and with my heart banging on my chest I opened my mouth to say, "Yes, I like you."

"Cool, so see you next week, okay?"

And she was gone. I stood looking at the door close after her. She was gone. "Wow, you know what just happened?" I whispered to myself, grinning from ear to ear.

Such was the elation of my joy that I waited at Becky's door until she was done snogging to tell her all about Helen.

"You mean you're a lesbian?"

Now this was probably the second biggest shock of my young life. I could see her point. But until I actually heard the words, I never considered having to wear another false label.

"No, actually I'm a boy trapped inside a girl's body. So that makes me heterosexual," was what I wanted to tell her, but instead, I said, "Yes".

"Cool. I did suspect you didn't like boys."

Her assumption was correct. I didn't like boys, but I wasn't a lesbian either. I wanted to correct this misunderstanding. I should have jumped all over it. I should have cleared the ways for honesty and truth, but instead I dug a foundation, filled it with cement, built up high walls, put barbed wire around them and flung myself right into the middle of it, all in the name of fear.

The week leading up to meeting Helen was one of the most thrilling and terrifying periods of my life. I was for the first time participating in the hormone-powered rocket-ride of first love. Flushed cheeks, raging heartbeat, sweaty palms, I had it all and more – I also had the gnawing buzzing sensation that Helen might find me out.

Now, I wasn't at all sure how a lesbian relationship was meant to work. I wasn't at all sure how a heterosexual relationship was meant to work, come to that. And I sure as hell wasn't sure how this relationship was going to work. I did also have the burning pit as to whether I was in some way deceiving Helen, but that cleared up pretty sharpish. I was in love after all, and it didn't take long for my heart to kick my mind out to the side. Firmness was required on my heart's side, because it really didn't give a damn about rules and regulations, it didn't care how love was meant to be conducted, it only cared for what it felt, and what it felt was love. And I was totally on board with that. To hell with my mind, I was sticking with my heart, I told myself as I took the long walk up to the Town Hall doors.

When I finally found myself in touching distance of Helen, my heart pushed my blood so hard about my body I thought I would faint. We had sneaked out of the disco, around the back, preparing, although neither of us said it, for the momentous occasion of our first kiss. I could hardly find a footing, but God in Heaven, finally, against all the odds, there I was wrapping my hands around her waist, pulling her closer, looking into her eyes, moving my head to the side, placing my lips upon her, parting the ways with my tongue. God had given me the miracle of miracles – love.

Finally, after soaring to another place, another time, our lips parted and we came back down. I straightened my head and looked into her eyes for a reaction. There it was, that smile. She smiled and the breath of life returned to my limbs and expanded my heart. I was in love, and all was right with the world. Even visions of my father would have had darling cherubs floating around it, had he entered my mind. Which he didn't. Why would he? I didn't have time for all that. In the scheme of things all his bluster was nonsense – I was in love. God be praised, I was in love. The impact sent quivers through my very core, rewriting biochemistry books. The planet spun, the stars came down and every member of the company of Heaven rejoiced the fact that my heart now had a population of two – I was in love.

As our arms let go and our bodies separated, spontaneous giggles erupted from us. The whole way round the building, my face wore the largest smile ever recorded in cosmic history.

"We can't let anyone know about us," Helen said, as we walked towards the door. "For now anyhow, my parents wouldn't get it."

"I know," I said. What did I care? I had a girlfriend. "Anyway a secret love affair is so cool," I said after, to myself. Although the outskirts of London weren't quite Verona, they might as well have been for we were secret lovers just like Romeo and Juliet.

"Is this your first time, I mean, in a lesbian relationship?" Helen whispered as we walked through the doors.

I looked at her and smiled, "Yes, first time," I said, still smiling, even though my heart was sinking just a little. It was the second time this label had been placed upon me, and it wasn't any easier hearing it this time around, especially not from Helen. My stomach fluttered a little.

What was I getting myself into? But I just couldn't face the reality. And wasn't I good at living in the world of illusions? Pretending to be a lesbian should be a walk in the park. I'd been pretending all my life, so why stop now?

"Is it your first time?" I asked her.

"Yes, I thought I might be bi, but yeah my first."

"Wow," I said to myself, my mind doing cartwheels. This revelation had me thinking that maybe it wouldn't be so hard to tell Helen, a little while into the future, that she was, in fact, one half of a heterosexual relationship – an unorthodox one granted, but heterosexual none the less.

As we walked back into the dim hall the music slowed and the last slow set of the evening began.

"You want to sit on the stage?" Helen suggested.

Yet another slow set, sitting it out, but for the first time it didn't matter. It didn't matter one iota that I had Helen sitting close beside me, so close I could decode every nuance of her silky bare legs brushing off mine. It was exhilarating. The excitement I had felt with Rachel instantly paled into a tryst of little substance, for I was with a goddess and her name was Helen.

I lay in bed later that night looking up at the starscape that now blanketed my ceiling. I recognised none of it. I was looking into a galaxy beyond recognition, for my world had changed emphatically. After two years of bottomless sadness I was happy – no, I was ecstatic.

The chirping of the morning found me slumbering heavily. And before I could even raise my eyelids I had a smile upon my face, because Helen was my first waking thought. What a departure it was to wake up happy to be in the world. What a departure to be in a hurry to place my feet upon the earth. What a departure to fling away the dimness and look upon the world with applause, regardless of the shade of the day. And what a glorious departure to be in love.

Leaping to the bathroom, I glanced at my watch. The only blemish to this perfect picture was the fact that there was another seven hours to go until my next kiss. I couldn't wait to see Helen, to hold her again, to feel the softness of her lips again and to drink deep of their sweetness. There was nothing in the world that could steady me, I was besotted.

We had exchanged numbers, and had arranged to meet at the local cinema. As it was the first venture into uncharted territory for both of us, Helen felt it wise to go with a crowd. Having sworn Becky to stay tight lipped about her knowledge of our "gay" relationship, I asked her and a few friends along. Helen, being happy with that, decided to come alone.

"You really fancy her don't you?" Becky teased as we hopped off the bus together.

"Yeah, she's gorgeous."

"Didn't you ever fancy me?"

"Behave would ya? We're like..."

"What?"

"Family." Actually, brother and sister would have been accurate. Actually, yes would have been more accurate, but "family" would have to do.

"Or best friends," Becky suggested.

"Yeah definitely, best friends."

I sideglanced Becky as she checked herself in her hand mirror. Was it just me, or was Becky acting weird? I knew her so well that I could answer with all assurance that yes, she was acting strangely.

"But are you sure this is what you want, I mean a lesbian relationship?" Becky continued, applying lip gloss.

"Yeah, I want Helen."

"What about your dad, are you going to tell him?"

"My dad? Come on, seriously, what does he care?"

"Sure. When we get our own place you can see who you like."

"That's right," I said, keeping our dream going, mainly for Becky's sake.

"I suppose you're going to spend all your time with her now?"

"Can't we all knock around? You're going to really like her, just you wait."

"Anyway, I knew you weren't into boys all along."

"Do you think I look like a boy?" I said, skirting on thin ice.

"I've seen a lot of girls look at you."

"Really?"

"Yeah, if I didn't know you, yeah, I might think you were a boy. Until you opened your gob anyway." She laughed.

"I'll give you that," I said, laughing back.

"You remember now, you don't know, okay?"

"Not much of a relationship if you have to sneak about, I mean with friends."

"Once she meets you I'm sure it will be okay. I'll tell her it's okay."

"So what? You're the butch one?"

"Um..."

"You know butch, femme."

"I know, um, I guess so," I said smiling, but behind it hid sadness. I was genuinely happy, ecstatic, but still, deep down, there lingered the pain of my lie. My best friend and my new love. I longed to be honest, I longed to delve into the truth of myself, but I couldn't, out of fear of losing them. In the midst of my pure and innocent love there loomed an insidious fear that expertly manipulated my feelings for its own nourishment, and the more I loved the more it enslaved me. My reality, it seemed, was to live a life trapped in torturous duality. There were no locks, no doors in this prison, yet what security did it need when the prisoners were all willing participants in their own torture?

Ricocheting back from the dark side of duality, I resigned myself to the notion that we'd solve the problem in time. After all, I was blissfully optimistic that we'd be together forever.

After our little heart-to-heart Becky went ahead to meet the others while I went to meet Helen off her bus. As it pulled in, I wished I could have held a bunch of flowers behind my back and popped them out as she fell into my arms. Impossible as I knew this was, I couldn't stop myself from wishing.

Helen got off the bus and smiled. It was a beautiful smile that made my wishing all the more profound. We didn't kiss or even hold hands, we didn't have any physical contact at all. I kept telling myself that this was all part of the allure, that there was so much fun playing the illusion, but nevertheless, my wishing continued.

As we approached the cinema I looked for Becky. Staying Alive was playing, all the girls had come for John Travolta. I had come solely for Helen.

I spotted Becky in the foyer, chatting with a cleaner we knew from the road.

"Helen, this is my friend Becky."

"Hi Becky, Lisa told me all about you."

"Did she? Great. Here's your ticket, Lisa."

"Didn't you get two?"

"Yeah."

"I mean, one for Helen too."

"You didn't say."

"That okay, I..."

"No I'll get it," I said, walking over to the box office. Becky was definitely acting strange. It just wasn't like her. When I looked back, Becky had joined our other friends, leaving Helen standing alone in the middle of the foyer. No, it just wasn't like Becky at all.

"You all right?" I said, rejoining Helen.

"Sure," she said brushing it off with a hint of amusement.

Becky's behaviour in the cinema made a reality out of her prediction that I would spend most of my free time with Helen. We were having fun, experimenting as teenagers do. And for us, gaining access to one another's bedrooms was easy. As far as everyone knew we were just friends. The only one who knew any different was Becky, and to her credit she never told a soul.

* * *

As the months went by, the bond between Helen and me only got stronger. There wasn't a day that went by that didn't find us wrapped around each other, usually in stitches. We were young and we were living every minute of it. The fact that we still weren't public really didn't bother me by now. I was used to meeting in secret and 'fooling the world' - that's what we told ourselves anyway.

I knew my relationship with Helen was hard on Becky, so I saw her when I could. Christmas as usual was spent amongst Becky's family. It was decidedly sunny that year, which was noted by everyone. Helen made me happy and Becky having a new boyfriend made her happy. So for the first time in a long time, Becky and I found ourselves with something good in common – happiness.

Or at least we did until the New Year. Come January, Becky got two-timed and dumped. Resilient as she pretended to be, I knew she was hurting. I tried to comfort her as best I could, but it was just another footnote to add to the already expanded litany of letdowns. Witnessing Becky's heartache made me appreciate all the more what I had with Helen. Juggling my final year in school with an affair and a broken-hearted best friend wasn't easy, impossible when my father's antics were added into the mix. Still, I held onto my dreams of getting a university qualification. My home life was that never-ending battlefield that I had all but deserted. I needed a qualification because I needed escape.

For now, my escape was with Helen. After school, I'd rush home do what homework was required, then go over to Helen's. Like Becky her finals were a year away, which meant there was no real pressure upon them in that regard. As for me, I doubt my father even knew what year I was in. I could have missed the entire year and he wouldn't have batted an eyelid.

January 1984 was another cold one. I raced this particular evening over to Helen's, firstly because I was dying to see her and secondly because I was freezing. I needed a new coat but put up with it – I wouldn't give me father the satisfaction of saying no.

After ringing the buzzer I blew into my fingers. "Hi Mrs Cartwright, is Helen home?"

"Go on upstairs Lisa, she's in her bedroom. Only an hour, she's homework to do."

"Hiya!" I said, entering with the same level of enthusiasm as always.

"Hi," Helen answered sullenly.

"What's happened now?" I asked, suspecting Helen and her mum had been at it over one thing or another. I took off my coat while I waited for the answer. Helen was stalling.

"You okay?" I asked softly.

"Um, I don't think we can go on seeing each other."

"But why?" I blurted out, feeling the blood drain from my brain.

"I think we've got too serious."

"We can slow down, whatever you want. I don't have to come around so often."

"I think I just want to break up."

"But I don't understand. We can't, we love each other. Don't we? I thought you were happy?"

"I am but, it's just not enough. I'm sorry, I'm just not a lesbian any more."

But neither am I! I'm heterosexual, you're heterosexual, and what does it matter anyway? We're happy, isn't it just fantastic? is what I should have said, but I didn't. I might have been straight, but I knew I couldn't give her what she wanted. She wanted what every other girl in her class was whispering about. Instead I just lowered my head, wanting to die.

Just like Romeo and Juliet our relationship had ended in tragedy. Romeo was in the wrong family, and I was in the wrong body. I might not have really died that day like him. But losing your first love, how can you tell the difference?

It's a universal truth that if getting over your first love is a ten, being hung, drawn and quartered is an easy seven. Nothing could have prepared me for the pain of an emptied heart. No matter what anyone said or did, I just couldn't stop the pain. Bad as my family's disintegration had been, losing Helen was an ache than never ceased. I just couldn't stop thinking of her and missing her. Her smile, her smells, her touch – everything was imprinted upon my brain and set to re-run. My heart just didn't want to go on without Helen.

The gaping hole in my heart kept my mind occupied 24/7. Everything suffered; my health, my confidence, my joy, for what Helen had given me she had taken away. Contributing, in no small part, to my misery was a recurring thought that disturbingly had a mocking underbelly to it: "You'll never be able to find love again," it taunted, "How is anyone going to be happy with a male without parts?"

This question cut to the quick of things as the picture of my future rolled out in front of me, and it wasn't pretty. It was grey and dismal and full of lies and deception. I would have to look for scraps of love here and there, in the full knowledge that nothing pure or lasting could ever come of it. Born of a lie, how could I expect anything else? And yet, what choice was there? If I told the truth I would deny myself even the scraps. That's what my fear told me, and this was the darkness I foolishly hoped would heal my heart.

I missed Helen so much that some days I thought I might not be able to bear it. There were days I couldn't face getting out of bed. Yes, everything suffered, especially my studies. Missing school and giving up on study altogether put all my dreams of university in the garbage bin, along with all the ancillary hopes and dreams that went along with it.

A month later, I wasn't feeling any better, I was actually feeling a hell of a lot worse. The initial shock, I suppose, had shielded me somewhat from the horror but now, with the passing of four weeks, all the sedation had worn off and I was feeling the pain full on. I was also seeing the reality of my situation full on and, in many ways, this was a bigger shock then losing Helen.

"Why the hell has this happened to me?" I begged of my reflection one evening. I had spent the last ten minutes staring into the mirror and trying to understand how something so impossible could have happened. I knew there should have been a reflection of a male staring back at me, but there wasn't, and as far as I knew at this time, there never would be.

This sense of hopeless entrapment sent a wave of panic coursing through my veins. My heart pounded and perspiration broke out all over my body. Suddenly my head spun and my heart raced, and I dropped to my knees, thinking I was having a heart attack. I grasped the edge of the bedding, fearing I could fall over altogether. I hadn't been eating or sleeping properly, so I wasn't in any fit state for my emotions to be overwhelmed so violently.

The truth was, I had no idea how to deal with any of it; losing Helen, being trapped in the wrong body, having no support, having to deal with neglect and abuse. I had been starved of affection for over a year, so it was the hugs and kisses I missed the most. How was I going to survive without Helen? How was I going to survive in this body? How was I going to survive without love?

Two months on, I had turned my pain and hopelessness in on myself. I felt totally betrayed, not by Helen but by my own conspiratorial body. And I hated it for that. I hated it so much that I vowed every encounter from now on would be hostile. My bindings would be tightened. My hair would be shortened. My nails would be shortened. My dress would be overtly masculine. My body had cost me Helen and it would, as far as I was concerned, cost me everyone else I had the misfortune of loving. If I stared at this body at all, it was only to scream the same question at it: "Why the hell have you happened to me?"

All I wanted was what every teenager wants, to be the same, to have the same opportunities in life. It wasn't fair that this had happened to me. It wasn't fair that I was to be so hampered in life. It just wasn't fair.

Three months on, my dreams of attending university lay in tatters, as did my confidence and hopefulness for the future. My mental health wasn't faring too well either. The war of intimidation my father continued to wage against me left me with the conclusion that he wanted me gone. By now the shouting, the bullying, the put-downs, the manipulation and the disdain were a constant in my life. All these trademarks of emotional abuse that he flung left me frightened and confused. I wasn't even sure if come my final exams I would even have a roof over my head. I was still only fifteen. Was this even legal? I wasn't sure. The level of stress my poor mind was under was such that I thought I'd be lucky to remember my name come exam day.

* * *

My enthusiasm for life had not returned by the time my sixteenth birthday was casting its shadow upon the horizon. Instead of cheery birthday cards flooding through the letterbox came divorce papers. This act of open warfare, as my father took it, ignited his anger anew. And as usual, being unable to point his cannon at my mother, he unleashed his fire upon me.

I really was a pitiful sight. My dejection was a thunderstorm that was even starting to overwhelm Becky. Sick of being waist-high in misery, she grabbed a lifebuoy and christened my 16th party 'the party to end all parties'. In bygone days my family were infamous for our parties and I guess nostalgia getting the better of them, everyone seemed to get caught up in the fervour. It didn't take much to get the word about. And it didn't take much for my father to agree – he liked to keep his public face smiling, especially with the neighbours.

As for me, I went along with the front, mainly because I was tired of feeling so downtrodden that I welcomed the opportunity of swimming in alcohol for a while.

The day quickly arrived, and the party kicked off in earnest with the arrival of DJ Andre, who provided the sound system to end all sound systems. His speakers were so enormous it became a point of pride for a number of fathers on the road to be the first to figure out just how to get them through the doors. From across the street, Abigail and Tanya ferried over tray after tray of Jamaica's finest jerk chicken drumsticks. Mrs Burke, not to be outdone, brought mountains of ham and cheese sandwiches. My father, also not to be outdone, chipped in money for soft drinks and nibbles. On the face of it, he was a proud father doing all he could to make sure his child had a wonderful birthday. On the face of it, I'm sure he even looked like a hard-done-by Dad making the most of it. On the face of it, I probably looked like the same adoring child, but things had changed so much that I doubt either of us would recognise the other if they miraculously appeared.

As it turned out, one hundred people crammed into our tiny house, one heck of an affair – on the face of it. But in reality, it was just another party, another occasion full of pomp and no ceremony. A hollow shell decorated to look like happiness. The truth was, my mother had made no contact, and I was feeling that. And my father's public display, despite the bottles of cheap fizzy pop, didn't include anything resembling sentiment; no card, no cake, no hug, no kiss, and I was feeling that too. So when Becky arrived with a bottle of Malibu hidden in her rucksack, I didn't have to be asked twice to spike my drink with a double measure of liquid happiness. Oh, I knew I'd be feeling the effects in the morning, I knew the momentary happiness it provided was as false as my father's smile, but I didn't give a damn. I was tired of feeling sad, I was tired of feeling angry, I was tired of feeling one way or another, I was just so tired of feeling.

"Come on upstairs," I said to Becky, meaning that was where we'd fill our cups.

"Hold on a minute, I want you to meet Jen."

Becky had already filled me in about Jen, a girl who was so awesome she was destined to wind up being a pop star or movie star, at least. She had met her whilst visiting her mum in Islington, and couldn't get over how cool she was. And she wasn't lying. As soon as I clapped eyes on Jen, I understood fully why Becky was so star-struck with her. Jen was a grand contradiction of carefreeness and wildness. She had an irresistible meld of beauty and cynicism. Although she tried to hide it, it was obvious that she didn't belong to the same social class. She came from money, and lots of it. She was the youngest of seven sisters. Her parents had made their money in the casino business and each of them had benefited. Some were actors, some had businesses and one was a millionaire's wife. Jen had a few years left before all eyes fell on her life choices. Maybe this was why carefree rebellion came so easy for her; after all she had the money and the family to fall back on when the time was right. And this is how I viewed Jen for most of our relationship. In truth, she never said much about her family or her life outside of us. She once alluded to the fact that they weren't the white collar type, but this was as far as it went. I guessed she liked the cloak of mystery adding to her mystic.

"I didn't get you anything, but you can have some of my weed," Jen said, removing her crinkly platinum blonde hair from her eyes. Like Becky, she liked Madonna too – from the lace and chains it was obvious.

"Thanks but I'm more of a drinker," I said, holding up my paper cup.

"That's cool, um, is it okay if I spark up here?" she asked, surveying the hall.

"How about upstairs, we'll open the window?" Becky quickly interjected, not giving me the chance to appear uncool. "Come on Lisa, you can have a fag," she said, leading the way. Our 'Say No To Drugs' pact, which went back to our squat-over with Dave, had recently altered to accommodate Becky's experiment with weed. Which 'coincidentally' coincided with meeting Jen.

The arrival of Jen brought drugs into our inner circle. And wild and vulnerable as I was, at this stage, for some unfathomable reason I had a blockage when it came to taking them. I had no real experience with drugs, so there was no rational reason why they should frighten the life out of me – but they did. I had all the characteristics, all the opportunity, and yet I remained illogically impermeable to their allure. And much as I too wanted to impress Jen, time after time I said no, and kept saying no. Even when I was drunk, which I was with greater frequency, something inexplicable pinned me to the wall, denying my participation. If there was ever a case for a guardian angel, I think this was it.

"So what do you think of Jen?" Becky asked giddily. Jen was her find, and she was proud of it.

"Yeah, she's cool. I'll be back in a sec," I said before squeezing myself into the living room to lower the music, at the behest of a burly London bobby who was now standing with arms folded on my doorstep.

"Great party Lisa!" a voice called from the crowd. It was Elizabeth, a girl from school who I'd been friends with for many years, but it was only since puberty that I had begun to notice just how beautiful she was – silky dark locks, almond green eyes and the most perfect lips. If there was ever a girl every schoolboy fantasised over, it was Elizabeth.

"I just have to turn it down!"

"What?"

"TURN IT DOWN," I mouthed, doing the actions.

I closed the door as the squad car pulled off down the street. I did a mental countdown: three, two, one and right on cue someone blasted the music up louder than before. It was the mid-eighties and there was defiance in the air. A divisional wind of "us and them" had swept across the country, whirling up dust devils in every underprivileged neighbourhood.

Squeezing myself through the bodies jamming the hall, I finally came up beside Elizabeth. "Hey, you all right?" I said, close enough to smell her sweet perfume.

"Oh yeah, I'm having a great time," she said, patting my arm lightly. As my skin excitedly registered the touch a tingling charge raced through my entire body. I had an almost uncontrollable urge to fling my arms around her and kiss her. Before Helen I hadn't fully realised that the pain I was feeling was caused by a lack of affection, but now my starvation was exposed I couldn't help the cravings. If there was one girl on the planet that could take the place of Helen, it was Elizabeth.

"You want a drink?" I asked sheepishly.

"I'm good," she said popping her plastic cup up. "What do you think, do you think I should go talk to Kevin?"

Kevin: jeans, biker jacket, good looking, tall, cocky, he had no problem getting a girl and he damn well knew it.

"He's hot, isn't he?" Elizabeth gushed.

No, he's a dick. He's totally wrong for you. He'll use and abuse you. That was what I wanted to say as I swept her into my arms.

"I'm going to talk to him, maybe tonight will be the night."

"Oh my God, she's telling me she's a virgin," I thought, feeling an immediate need to save her. But how? I was more than impotent – I was invisible.

As I watched Elizabeth wading towards her mark, my impotency slung a ball around my neck and flung me to the ground. I knew that come tomorrow Elizabeth would pull a friend aside and rejoice her passing into womanhood, and suddenly I hoped that the friend wouldn't be me. In an instant, Elizabeth had gone from a childhood friend to someone to be avoided. It seemed that my fear of telling the truth about my sexual identity had unleashed a virus that was set to taint every relationship I had.

I turned and fled into the living room. The music was still blasting, everyone was still smiling and all I wanted to do was to take down the Samurai sword from the fireplace and plunge it into my heart. A bit extreme, I know, but it didn't take much then days to send my mood plummeting, and the happy couple coming in, and the lights going down, and the music slowing, was as sure as anything to make me put my hands upon that sword.

As I watched their arms going around each other and their mouths seeking each other, something powerful rose in me – hatred. I hated Kevin, I hated him for everything he was and for everything I wasn't, I hated him with all the envy and spite I could muster, but much as I hated him, I hated myself more - much more. And with no perceivable way out of my wretchedness, I decided that it was once again time to get wasted. It wasn't the first time I had turned to drink in an attempt to float my way out of my choppy nightmare, and unfortunately it wouldn't be the last.

* * *

The months leading up to my June finals came and went in a blur of what might have been. Much as I wanted to do well, much as I might have been able to cram, I just couldn't do it. I couldn't get the day started, I couldn't set any intentions; all I really wanted was not wake up in the first place. And when I was awake, I sought to distract myself with Becky and Jen. The three of us had by now become quite the dysfunctional trio. Living with parents who were fully occupied with their own survival meant that it was child's play for us to go wayward. Despite the fact that we were still so young, even staying out for a night here and there was never a problem for any of us. It was less of a problem for me because my father had no problem bolting me out, if I came home later than him. At sixteen, it was an unnatural freedom to be given. One that allowed me to push my boundaries beyond the safety zone. Still, what thought did I give to that? I was young and I was growing more rebellious by the day. It quickly reached the point where we went to practically every party we heard of. It never mattered what day of the week it was, how far it was or how late; if it was a chance to escape our home lives, we'd be there.

Living the carefree life, no matter how illusionary, does not bode well for academic success. When my results came in August, I was actually surprised that I had passed - a bare pass but a pass nonetheless. Aced or failed, it didn't matter a jot to my father. When so many parents eagerly awaited the all-important results, my father never even asked.

It was hard to equate the shadowy father of my present to the hero of my early days. And I suppose it was hard too to equate the person I was becoming to the one I had been. I was moody and hopeless, and I was staying away from home more and more and drinking more and more and hurting my inner self more and more. The dismissals, disapprovals and judgements, the lack of empathy, the lack of love, had dug at my self-worth. I had turned inward and I had turned angry to hide my pain. Even though I told myself that I no longer needed approval from anyone else but myself, the truth was that my self-esteem was so damaged I was incapable of approving of any part of myself, let alone loving myself. The reality was that the wounds inflicted by the cold and threatening environment were still very much open and available for every sort of unethical manipulation my father choose to come up with. And though I couldn't see it, I was with all certainty heading down a dark road that was only going one place – a broken life and a broken soul.

* * *

Come September, my bare pass had managed to get me onto a year's training course as an introduction to becoming a chef. As good an idea as any, I thought with as much enthusiasm to fill a half a teaspoon. Still, I dug deep and found the motivation to at least turn up on the first day.

For the next three months I struggled to walk the path of someone who had a future. Outflanked on all sides, the development challenges faced by every teenager became an epic struggle to me. To begin with, I wasn't adjusting at all to the biological changes assaulting my body. And with no boundaries at all to establish safely or otherwise, my expanding social network had, by now, one overriding trait in common – dysfunctionality. So it was hardly surprising that my life-goals at this stage were less substantial than a mirage. The only task I was aceing in the Adolescent Development Department was the 'understanding of one's sexual orientation' task. In this I excelled: I now understood that I was heterosexual, no question about it. I was heterosexual, yes, and male, yes - oh, and in the wrong body.

CHAPTER 8

My plunge through the cracks of society came in three distinct stages. The first started almost immediately after dropping out of the training scheme. I'd lasted three months, which under the circumstances was a minor miracle. I remember waiting for my father to come home, so I could tell him the news. It would be bad news for most parents, but I didn't expect that in my case.

"Dad, I'm not going back to that course."

"Do what you want, just don't look for any money from me," he said, and that pretty much summed everything up for me. He left for the pub soon after, while I went upstairs and threw a few clothes into a rucksack for the weekend and headed off to find Becky.

"I've left. I'm not going back on Monday," I told Becky.

"You could get a qualification," was Becky's feeble attempt to talk me around.

"Is it okay to crash here tonight?" I said, feeling the iron bar that was growing daily on my back.

"We're family."

"Can I come with you to Islington tomorrow?"

"You want to go now?"

"Will your Mum let us crash?"

"If she doesn't we'll squat, we'll find Jen. Why don't we go and decide if we want to come back?"

"What about school?"

"You finished, and look at you."

"Yeah, all right, why not?" I had finally run out of excuses, and this time as far as I was concerned I had responsibility to anyone, least of all myself.

Sitting on the upstairs of the bus, looking out at life carrying on below, I was overcome with a huge sense of relief. As younger children, Becky and I had invested so much of our dreams in the grand adventure we would have when free of our home ties. All we really wanted back then was that half chance of a happy-ever-after. Although the dreams had faded considerably, their memory sufficed to quieten what fears I had of leaving home. Even Becky's dreams were tainted of late. There wasn't much talk of bright stages and glimmering entourages on our silent journey away from home that night.

Our security for our future amounted to some loose change and a couple of cans of beans and soup wedged into Becky's rucksack. We had no clue where we would stay this night or any subsequent night. We had no clue how we were going to feed ourselves after the soup and beans were gone. We had no clue what dangers came with the lifestyle that afforded someone with nothing. We had no clue, either, about the countless teenagers that had been forced to take the same silent bus ride only to wind up in prostitution, in prison or dead with a murderous syringe in the arm. And we had no clue what alone and unprotected really meant – but we would learn, like all the others, soon enough.

We found Jen later that evening having a fag and a coke in a local chippy. Her eyes were puffed from lack of sleep.

"We've done it, we're out of there, both of us," Becky exclaimed triumphantly, dropping down beside her.

"Cool. You got money for a single or we'll be chucked?" Jen replied, stubbing her fag out on the top of her can. "Any fags?" she asked, playing the pauper.

The truth was that when Jen wasn't out partying or playing the pauper with us, Becky had heard that she lived in a mansion with her parents. Why she chose to hang with friends out of her social set, I never knew. Whenever we asked about her parents, she just said they were very old and didn't get her. This we could relate to, so we never pushed, and eventually we stopped asking. As far as we were concerned, loaded or not, Jen was one of us.

As it happened, Becky had just enough cigarettes to go around and I had just enough money for a round of chips and coke.

"My mum has a boyfriend over, so can we crash with you Jen?" Becky asked, keen to see exactly where Jen came from.

"If you want to go to bed by ten you can," Jen replied. Old as her parents may have been, she could stay out when she liked and go home when she liked. That just didn't sound to me like the old fogeys Jen tried to portray.

"Anyway, I'm not heading home, some popheads I know are having a party in their squat. Come it'll be chilled."

"Chilled?" I asked, not exactly up on the squatting scene.

"Yeah chilled, no crackheads to fuck with you."

"Right," I said, not liking the sound of that at all.

"So Becky tells me you're a lesbian?" Jen said randomly.

"Um no, not really. I tried it once."

"Yeah me too, when I was off my face, maybe twice, can't fucking remember. You got any money for the bus?"

"No, nothing," I said, pleading with myself not to turn scarlet.

"We'll hitch, no biggy."

"You think she could get a job here?" Becky asked, as if suddenly realising our grand adventure might require funding.

"Only if you move over there quickly."

"Why?" I asked, not getting it.

"Because the prick who owns the dump has it in for me."

"Why?" Becky asked, hushing her voice.

"Because he wants to fuck me out, but he can't."

"Why?" Becky and I asked in unison.

"Because I told him if he did I'd tell his misses we did the dirty deed."

"Did you?" again in unison.

"No, but he would and his wife knows it."

"Is that him?" Becky asked, spotting a heavy-set man come out from the back.

"Yeah that's the scumbag."

"Wow!" Becky said in admiration. Jen was increasingly becoming an icon to her. Most, I suppose, would have assumed that Jen was the oldest amongst us, but in reality, she was only fourteen at this time. Though it would be a couple more years before I found out that truth.

"Maybe he'd be desperate though, no one stays long in this kip."

I don't know if Jen's story was a tall tale or not. Maybe there was something between her and the owner and maybe there was not. Either way, by the time I'd finished my last chip my determination not to take the last bus home, ever, was enough to lift me from my seat.

"Hi I'm Lisa and..." off I went telling Tony, the owner, everything about the course I'd been on – everything apart from the fact that I didn't finish and I wasn't qualified. That being said, the way I saw it, this was a chip shop so I really couldn't see how such technicalities mattered.

Tony was middle fifties, overweight, overbearing and from the flavour of his Cockney accent, probably of Italian extract. Slumped over the counter, he listened to me like a suspicious police officer, not buying a word of it. When he finally straightened to speak, I fully expected to be turfed out on my ear. Instead, he turned his back on me to fetch an apron. Leaving me standing, I was about to turn on my heels, when his index finger beckoned me closer.

"You rob from me, I'll have you nicked. Part-time, you get coffee, no food and no freebies. You give me shit, you're out. They give me shit," he continued throwing his head at the table, you're out of here. And just so we're clear, I don't give a toss about your fancy pants qualifications. In the kitchen, waist-high to your mother's table is where you learn to cook."

I went back to my seat happy that Tony and I were on the same wave length, at least regarding my qualifications.

"Well?" Becky asked eagerly.

"I can work a few hours at the weekend."

So this, and other such precarious working arrangements is pretty much how we figured we would feed ourselves. As for accommodation, our first night was spent, as Jen had suggested, squatting in a ground floor flat in a worn-out council estate in a place called Stoke Newington, which was about two miles from Islington. Not having the bus fare, we ended up hitching. Eventually we bummed a lift from a middle-aged van driver. "I don't usually pick up hitchers, but I've daughters meself," he said, letting us squeeze into the two seats beside him.

"I'll let you out here," he said, pulling up on the outskirts of the estate. "No offence like, to anyone, but me van's me job," Which I thought spoke volumes about the neighbourhood we were visiting. The fact that a fully-grown man with muscles and a machine to protect him wouldn't cross the threshold of the estate made me wonder just what we were getting ourselves into. Both my stomach and my feet became heavier as wonder turned quickly to worry.

"That's it there," Jen said, pointing to a boarded-up dwelling. From the outside the small building looked like it might well have been gutted. There wasn't a pane of glass left in the rain-streaked structure, which could have done with a repainting a decade or so ago. If rain and boarding was the problem on the outside, a lack of furniture, fittings and utilities was a definite drawback on the inside.

Having been left standing at the front-door for a moment, we took ourselves around the back to where one of the boards was loose.

"You sure this is okay?" I asked, feeling like we were breaking and entering or, if not that, maybe we were just being rude.

"It's a squat," Jen said almost accusingly from the inside.

"Come on Lisa, it'll be fine," Becky said, following Jen's lead.

Inside, we found a boy a little older than us sitting in an armchair listening to a Walkman. Seeing us enter, he pulled off the headphones. "Got any food?"

"Beans and soup," Becky said, digging in her bag.

"That'll do," he said, setting his Walkman aside. "Here give us the beans, I have a knife."

"Don't you have a cooker?" I asked after watching him hack open the can and start eating.

"It's a squat love. What, you out on your holidays?"

"No, we've left home," Becky said, feeling the need to explain herself.

"Well if you can find a place later you're welcome to it," he said, putting his headphones back on.

Later, bodies seemed to come out of the rotting woodwork, as did the thick smog that descended from the rafters. If the carpet had anything that resembled threading it must have been hidden under the objects that stood in for armchairs and couches. Any notion of glamour that had survived Dave's squat was quickly vanquished the moment I set eyes on an assortment of unwashed mugs which would have delighted any microbiology student intrigued by living detritus.

I don't know if my question about the cooker had anything to do with it, but later, our friend from the armchair, along with some of the least sober of the bunch, decided to hack the electricity box. However, this plan was quickly abandoned after a couple of life-threatening sparks shot out at them.

"Fuck it, let just get a bunch of candles," someone suggested. I did wonder just how long they had survived without this notion ever arising. I also wondered, in all innocence, where they were going to buy them. It was a strange night, to be sitting there amongst strangers sharing cold beans and soup by candlelight. And I guess, this is where the illusion of rebellious nobility might swoon in. Far from palatial, the squat was cold, damp and stale. Still, on the positive side, our fellow squatters were as Jen had said, "weedheads" who only wanted to listen to reggae music and get stoned.

Our popularity soared the second day, when it was discovered that my couple of hours working was enough to bring back a bag of shopping. It didn't go far, barely making it through the door. As soon as the weed wore off the "munchies" kicked in, and I guess my small bag of groceries was worth its weight in gold – at least that's how they treated it. I suspect we would have stayed a lot longer than four days had the police not arrived on the fifth morning, early, to move us on.

"Go on, get on with you and don't come back," the officer said, warning us off.

How strange that he didn't bother to ask where we were heading to. After all, we were a bunch of kids being left to our own devices, and these devices amounted to walking roads and estates looking for another place to squat. Sometimes we'd get lucky and we'd have a toilet which came with the optional risk of catching typhus or some other Third World disease, but mostly running water and sanitation were a luxury. Mostly the best thing on offer was the supermarket toilet – there at least there was hot water.

About three weeks into the grand adventure, I was tracked down by my brother Gavin. "Dad's looking for you," he said, coming into the chipper.

"Yeah" I said, not knowing what else to say.

"So you coming?" he asked, taking a seat.

"You want a single?"

"Yeah, but I've only bus fare."

Becky and I decided that maybe we could go home and see how our absence might have changed things. It was much harder than we'd imagined roughing it. So home we went, a couple of cans lighter.

Waiting for my father's return mixed my emotions up like clothes in a tumble dryer. I just didn't know how to separate everything I was feeling. I was in many ways glad to be home, especially glad to have running water and the like, but there was also the mounting apprehension of seeing my father.

"Hi Dad," I said, walking in on him in the early morning. I had decided to try and keep my job at the chippy for the time being anyway. It was manual and it was minimal but it gave me some independence – even if it was only a couple of quid, less now with the bus fare.

"What, you want a fanfare, a marching band, yeah?"

"No, I was just..."

"Go on get out, will ya."

Becky didn't get the marching band either. I felt like a fish that had leapt onto the fishmonger's table and got gutted for his troubles. Realising, like the fish, that if I hung around I would either end up rotting or beheaded, I looked for my only escape beneath the surface in the gutters. Desperate for sanctuary, I cast myself into the murky undercurrent, not knowing what lay ahead.

* * *

As the weeks turned to months, my ability to keep swimming in the darkness was greatly curtailed. I was exhausted with the greyness of my existence. Working while others partied was a bigger drain on me than hunger. Becky got work where she could. Both of us realised that the only upshot of having a few quid was that it enabled us to feed not only our stomachs but our developing addictions – mine for drink and Becky's for drugs.

While my addiction worked on me at a slower rate, Becky's quickly kicked her from weed up to amphetamines. Speed, the amphetamine of choice, was popular amongst teenagers for the simple reasons that it was relatively cheap and readily available. And where other more expensive drugs exalted you higher momentarily, speed allowed children such as Becky to remain "buzzed" for hours at a pop. The downside, and there was always a downside, was that when it wore off the low burrowed deep, ensuring a repeat market of eager users. Caught up in this very effective loop, children from both ends of the social spectrum went easily from dabblers to full-on drug users – children like Becky and Jen. It wasn't long before I was the only one capable of going out to work, and that was saying something. Not sleeping, not eating, not functioning, it became increasingly hard for me to hold down a job for more than a couple of days. Which meant there were times when we had the option of starving or going home.

Sometimes upon my return, I would run into Karen and Gavin and sometimes I would not. I'm sure there were months on end when we didn't see each other. Not that it really mattered, as we were by now troubled planets orbiting around our own dying suns. Gavin especially was having a hard time of it. He exhibited all the hallmarks of heading down the same road as me. I did what I could to discourage him, but it was like a feasting lion telling a starving cub not to eat. He neither listened nor heeded my warnings. As for Karen still dating Craig, she was far beyond listening. Sometime into my second year of squatting she got pregnant – at fifteen.

Like a thief in the night, I continued to appear now and again without warning. During these visits home, I would keep my head down as much as I could, but it never took long, usually no more than a day or two, before my father gave me good reason to pick up my rucksack and disappear again. It was this situation, repeated in dysfunctional homes up and down the country, that generated the teenage squatting phenomenon of the 80s. Mirroring Becky and me, nearly all of the teenagers in the various squats we moved between came from troubled homes. Living in abject poverty, as we lived, wasn't easy on any of us. Although I'm sure, in the right circumstances every heart had the potential to glitter like any saint, living as we did caused every heart to dim as our precarious existence honed the "survival of the fittest" instinct into every one of us.

Soon every line of the handbook was etched in our minds; If you had money, you hid it; If you had drugs or drink, you hid it; If you had food, you ate it; and if you had none of the above, you acquired it. Maybe there are people who would starve themselves for their morals, but I didn't come across any squatting in London. Wrong as stealing is, hunger is worse, and that's how we saw it. None of us wanted to be on the streets, none of us asked for it and none of us intended to die because of it – though many did.

I remember one day in particular when we hadn't eaten for two days and we were all starting to look at each other weirdly, so someone suggested, I can't remember who, going down to the local fish-shop, ordering the food and legging it as soon as it was handed over. It seemed a clever alternative to starvation or worse.

"Right, who can run and hasn't been nicked?" This was the best method of selection we could think of. In the end, a guy and a girl, both relatively new to squatting, were selected for the job. The boy had started a fling with Becky and her staying put pretty much guaranteed everyone would get their fair share. As it happened, Becky as security held up, and ten of us sat around happily sharing the spoils. Moments like these, rare in their serenity, threw out some light into the grey. Ten eating by candlelight, but how many would end up dead with the label of 'junkie' or 'prostitute' pinned to their unclaimed corpses? How many would end up in prison or crippled from the drugs? And how many would come out intact by the end of this grand adventure? None, as it happened, this answer I can be sure of.

Living such a precarious existence, your old life, your old ways and your old self are quietly forgotten. Little by little you sink a notch lower. When only survival is on your mind, you readily place yourself in the firing line of bad choices. And like attracting like, it isn't long before negativity surrounds you, darkening every waking day.

From the start I never really imagined myself living in some teenage utopia free from parents. In fact, my perception of the world was that it was big and it was bad and it was scary. Ironically, this perception had largely been formed by my father. Night after night we would sit watching the evening news, and night after night my father would drum the dangers into me. "The world is filled with people out to take what they can get from you," he'd say.

When I left home I was innocent, emotionally unstable and extremely vulnerable, and yet ironically, this was the very father who had pushed me head first out into the same savage world. No, despite the chips and the candle lights, I didn't enjoy my freedom because as my father had warned, a world without boundaries can be an extremely dangerous place – and that was before the epidemics of heroin and Aids.

* * *

During the three-year period from 1984 to 1986, I had no meaningful relationship to speak of. I had one or two drunken tangles with girls at squat parties which amounted to nothing more than hazy memories. My secret remained tightly locked, and I passed mostly as a sexually inactive lesbian. Which was as good as it gets, I supposed, on the sexual front at least. By my eighteenth birthday, nothing had really changed, nothing for the better anyhow. My situation still sucked. My mental health was wobbling. My drinking had gone from entertainment to medicinal, and my denial - well that was stellar, so stellar in fact that I had become known as the frigid lesbian who had the unfortunate habit of being attracted to "straight" women. 1986 turned out to be a pretty uneventful year. Granted, it had started off badly enough with a spell of sub-zero temperatures making life in a fridge preferable to the squat. Spring came promising newness, but it lied, and then there was the catastrophe of late summer.

By late summer, Karen, now 16, was having issues with her boyfriend, Craig. In all honesty, I never liked this bloke. I know he was the father of Karen's child. I know she had a home with him. I know she said she was in love with him. But all this knowledge couldn't alter the facts of our first meeting. I had come home from school, gone to my bedroom and found this butt-naked guy humping my thirteen-year-old sister. Before a word could drop from my mouth, my father walked by and looked in. I don't know which shocked me the most, whether it was my father walking on or this naked bloke continuing on. Either one, my impression of Craig from that moment on was forever tainted. The guy was a creep.

And so with my father walking on as he liked, I turned and lunged at Craig. I didn't want to be within a thousand miles of his naked flesh, but I had to get him off Karen. He was nineteen, I was fifteen, but I didn't care. We tussled on the floor for a moment before he gave up trying to get the better of me. I may have been inside a woman's body, but all my instincts were red-blooded male. I was just like any boy trying to protect his little sister.

"What the fuck is wrong with her?" he shouted, grabbing his trousers.

"Lisa, for fuck sake! Dad knows, I told him, me and Craig are steady now."

"Karen you're thirteen!"

"It's none of your business!"

"Fuck this, I'm going," he said pulling on his T-shirt.

"No, stay!"

"Nah you can shut up, its gone," he said, moving to the end of the bed. "What, you want to watch me put me fucking socks on?" he spat.

Pulling back from the door, I turned away to shouts of, "Stupid slapper."

"It" might have gone, but unfortunately he remained. And with all of my subsequent protests falling on deaf ears the only way I could maintain the semblance of a relationship with Karen was to stay well out of their way.

Three years on and I was still trying to stay out of their way. I only went on the very rare occasion to visit, mainly to check if Karen was okay and to see the baby. It was November; the day is etched in my mind. The weather was giving no surprises, it was cold and damp and typically British miserable. It was the middle of the afternoon. I presumed that Craig would be out, but he wasn't and his presence ensured the visit would be very short and very awkward.

"Get us a cup of tea," Craig said, ignoring the fact that the baby was hungry on her lap.

"I have to feed the baby first."

"I said get me a cup of tea," he repeated this time

punching her in the arm.

"I'll get it, I'll get it!" I said, mainly out of shock.

"I said she'll get it."

"Here, give me the baby Karen," I said, standing and taking the baby from her.

"You think you're big hitting on her like that?" I asked when Karen had left the room.

"And what the fuck is it to you bitch, what you feelin' left out or something?"

Having the baby in my arms, what option did I have but to leave the room? Finding Karen in the kitchen, I asked if she was okay.

"Yeah I'm okay."

"What you two fucking yapping about?" Craig said, appearing at the door. "Time she slung her hook," he added throwing his head in my direction.

"Don't worry I'm going, but if you touch my sister again..."

"What? Get your fat face outta here before I do somethin," he said, coming for me.

"No Craig!" Karen screamed, fearing I'd get a taste of what he was really like.

Craig was the type of man who liked women to be seen and not heard. And viewing me as a woman, he didn't take kindly to my interference. Shaking badly, I fled the flat, feeling the pangs of having to leave Karen and the baby behind. I wanted to get her away from him, her and the baby, but where would I take her? Would she even come? Not likely.

Knowing that Becky was around at her mum's flat, I went to find her. Like mother like daughter, I guess, because Becky's mum Cindy had a drugs problem. She also had man problems, more often than not. I suppose, unlike her daughter, being on the wrong side of thirty made her more lenient with the men in her life. Most were on drugs, most were bad news, but still dependence of any kind is a frightful taskmaster.

Cindy's latest "fella", as she called him, was Jeremy, a tough Cockney geezer who unsurprisingly liked beer, football and greyhound racing. He also liked cocaine and the art of extortion – this I wasn't to find out until later, after I went and spilled my guts out to Becky and her mum, and after I agreed to let Jeremy and his friends go around to Craig's to have a little "word in his ear".

The fact that Jeremy's Ford Cortina was so stuffed with friends that Becky and her mum had to stay at home should have said something to me, but it didn't. We, all five of us, arrived at Craig's flat.

"Wait with the car," I was told as the others piled out.

From the pavement I watched as the door opened and the four piled in. They do say hell is paved with good intentions, and I might also add, bad choices. And as far as bad choices went, this one was outstanding.

"What the hell did they do?" I screamed at Becky after she told me that Jeremy's little word to Craig had included stealing all his cash and jewellery.

"Where is it? I want it back!"

"It's gone. I'm so sorry Lisa."

"Get it back! I don't care, it goes back or I mean it!" I said almost hysterically.

"Shut the fuck up Lisa and listen. You can't do anything, do you hear me?" said Jen. I looked at her; her eyes were fixed and her voice was cold. "These guys aren't the sort you can mess with. You'll have to keep your mouth shut."

"But you don't know him, he'll call the police."

"Well if that happens, you keep your mouth shut, you

can't grass on them, you understand what I'm saying?"

"He won't call the police, he'll be too afraid."

"Well if he does, you take the rap if you have to."

"What? I could go to prison."

"Don't be ridiculous, it's a first offence, isn't it Jen?" Becky said, trying to remain calm.

"Yeah, you'll probably get probation."

Prison? Probation? The situation had got way out of hand. How stupid could I have been? Had I not learnt anything from my time on the street? It appears my trust in the world hadn't faded as much as I thought, though in the circumstances I now found myself discovering I still had some virtue was absolutely no comfort to me.

"I can't go to prison," I said weakly.

"If you grass them up and get sent down too, you won't last a minute inside."

"But if she tells what happened, she'll get off," Becky reasoned in all innocence.

"Are you stupid or something?" Jen snapped at Becky. "If they go down, they'll send someone for her. I'm not fucking around. I know this world. You get caught, you do the time, then you forget about it."

I suddenly understood that Jen's intimations about her family's ties to the criminal world were anything but glib remarks. And this scared me.

"What will I do?" I said, crumbling.

"I don't fucking believe you two! I leave you for a second. Becky, what the fuck were you thinking?" Jen said, angry that colours of her other life had been dragged into this one.

"I was trying to help. It wasn't my fault!" Becky replied, close to tears.

"What should I do Jen?" I asked, desperation swamping in.

"You'll have to get out of here until things cool off. Go on get your stuff," Jen ordered.

"Wait! Hold a minute!" Becky said, holding her head.

"You shut up! Go on get your stuff."

The absurdity of the situation suddenly hit me. "I think I'm going to be sick," I said, doubling up.

"He mightn't call the cops. Wait!" Becky shouted, almost as frantic as I was. "He mightn't!"

"Becky, you're not helping. Christ, remind me not to do a fucking robbery with you two," Jen said, walking towards the door.

I looked at Becky for guidance. All she could give was, "Maybe he won't." But maybe wasn't enough, because deep in the pit of my stomach I knew he would.

"I can't go to prison Becky," I said, feeling the tears welling.

"I know, look it'll be all right I promise," she said, putting her arms around me.

The thought of prison churned my stomach. Earlier in the year prison riots had erupted all across the country. Images of convicts on roofs burning bedsheets flashed across the media. How could it be that I might very soon be amongst them? It was surreal and it was terrifying.

In spite of the life I had lived, I had done my level best to stay out of trouble. I had continued to stay off drugs, even as temptation grew, and I only stole food when I was literally starving. But this wasn't shoplifting a can of beans, this was something far worse. I now had to consider how much trouble robbery, assault and battery would pile upon me.

* * *

Later that evening I found myself a fugitive in a squat about twelve miles away. For three unending days I cowered inside, feeling the world closing in on me. I couldn't eat and I couldn't sleep and I couldn't think of anything worse than getting carted off to prison. When on the fourth day, a loud bang came on the door everyone else immediately suspected another morning raid, but I knew different. There wasn't the scene of a body being grabbed half way out the window and then flung to the floor for handcuffing. No, my arrest and handcuffing was far less dramatic, but nonetheless terrifying.

I was hauled off to the local police station, pushed into a holding cell and left for a couple of hours before being taken out into a windowless room for questioning.

"We know you didn't do it on your own, so you might as well give us the names," a detective said, turning on the tape recorder.

"No, I can't…" I said, breaking down mid-sentence. I had no idea what was going to happen to me. No one knew where I was, so no one was coming to help me. I was too naive to know that I should have had a solicitor present. And if Jen hadn't enlightened me, I would have also been too naïve to understand that giving up a member of the criminal underworld was as good as signing your death warrant.

"You want to go to prison do you? Know what happens to nice girls like you? Come on Lisa, we know those scumbags have nothing to do with you."

"I can't remember, I was drunk, no, there was only me."

"Maybe some more time in the cell will help you remember," he said, rising and banging on the door. "You know I've seen all sorts come and go and I can tell you. You'll never survive prison sweetheart, trust me, I'm never wrong."

This detective, cold and mechanical, knew very well that

there were others involved in the attack on Craig. He also knew that my unwillingness to grass them up meant that they were a collar worth going after. He held me over for three days, doing his level best to grind the names out of me. I guess playing all his hands and coming up empty persuaded him to settle for what he had – me.

After three days in custody I was finally charged. I had to spend another night in the cell before being brought, in the morning, to appear before Wood Green Crown Court. Having not washed for four days, I can only image what impression I presented. Whatever that picture, it wasn't one of unquestionable innocence. I guess the judge was just going through the motions, following procedure, and that procedure meant that I was released on bail, freed to contemplate an impending trial by jury.

After leaving the court I went looking for Becky. I found her staying over at a friend's house, and that was the way of it, squatting or staying on somebody's couch. It was about a month after this, mid-December, when I got word through Becky's father that my parents wanted to see me. It had been four years since I had seen them together – not exactly the reunion I had imagined.

The Christmas season had arrived on the street where my father and I met. He pulled up in his Ford Escort, and I was surprised to see my mother sitting beside him. I climbed in and he pulled off without saying a word.

"Hello Mum."

"Hello Lisa, how are you love?" My mother said, turning her head to look at me.

"How the hell is she?" my father sneered.

And this was all it took. The plan was to go to some nearby pub to sit down and discuss the seriousness of my situation. But as it happened, this was far too much to hope for. Each blaming the other, the journey quickly came to an abrupt halt. My mother got out, I followed soon after and that was that. The next time I saw my parents, they were sitting away from each other at my trial.

It took over six months for my case to go to trial. It was by now the summer of 1987, and I had just turned nineteen. The trial lasted for three days. A jury of my peers sat in judgement. I pleaded not guilty to all charges. My state solicitor assured me that no imprisonment would be forthcoming. He pointed strongly to the fact that Craig's claims of battery were unfounded and unsupported by any physical evidence. I had found out from Becky that in fact Craig had been shoved against the wall, held by the neck and had his wallet and jewellery taken. Nevertheless, a crime had been committed, and I was the only one in the dock. I suppose, to be fair, the real charge I should have been up for was perverting the course of justice. I would have readily accepted this. I was perverting the course of justice, but as I saw it, what choice did I have?

The jury listened to the evidence from both sides, and after a brief recess they returned to deliver their verdict. "Guilty!" I could hardly stand as the sentence was handed down. "Eighteen months' imprisonment." I could feel my head spin as my solicitor quickly turned to assure me that the sentence would be reduced because it was my first offence. I heard these words, but they mattered little, the fact was, ten days or ten years, I was going to prison.

In the four years since I had left home there was hardly a day went by when I didn't have to consider where I'd be sleeping next. Now, for the next six months I knew exactly where I'd be sleeping, and the prospect scared the life out of me. Hearing the keys turn for the first time in my cell door in London's Holloway Prison, was by far the worst sound I had ever heard. If the largest female prison in Europe was built back in 1852 to terrify, it certainly didn't disappoint.

I had felt loneliness before in my life, but this was something far worse than any of my nightmares. Lonely and claustrophobic as my little cell was, I knew that in the morning I would have to step out into the general population. I knew I'd be singled out. I knew I'd be tested and taunted, and I knew if I showed any weakness, I would be devoured.

Knowing all this too, the guards kept a close eye on me throughout my first full day in prison. I kept my head permanently and only spoke to the other inmates when I was engaged. As it turned out, my stay in the infamous Holloway was only to last two weeks. After that, I was shipped out to spend the remainder of my sentence in an open prison in the West Midlands.

Cookham Wood Prison, located amongst the hills and fields of Staffordshire, was for the category of prisoners who weren't considered a flight risk. The truth was that my first week in my new surroundings was a living hell. Nothing to do with the regime per se, but everything to do with the bullying and intimidation I received as a welcoming present from some of my fellow inmates. Being new, I was immediately targeted by the resident bullies, and just like the playground, these bullies systematically tested me for weaknesses. It seemed violence and theft were an accepted way of life within the walls, a pastime even for some, a novelty that newcomers like me were duty bound to provide.

To begin with, I took the intimidation and abuse like a punch bag. I'd take what was flung at me, praying for it to be over, praying to hear the noise that would send me back to my room. Inside, behind the locked door I'd wait for the light to disappear so I could slip away with the darkness. I considered it a blessing when sleep came quickly. The nights when it didn't were the worst.

About a week or so into my sentence, the morning routine found me sitting alone. My appetite was poor, but I knew I had to eat, so I tried to force some toast into me. All the while, sitting there, I had my eyes to the table and my shoulders tight, trying to make myself as small as possible. I slowed my chewing as a dark-haired woman sat beside me. I didn't really get a good look at her to determine her age before her hand hit my cheek with such force that my whole head moved to the side.

"Bitch!" I screamed impulsively, as years of oppression flowed out of me like a swollen river running riot. Without thinking I grabbed her by the back of the head and dragged her down onto the table.

Before either of us could react we were both hoisted into the air and flung onto the ground. It didn't matter who did what, fighting was fighting and it got you three days' solitary confinement, for the first offence. It wasn't so much being confined in such close quarters that bothered me, it was the circular thoughts of what lay ahead that tortured me. No matter how I tried, I just couldn't erase the taunting words of the officer who had interrogated me. He had prophesied my doom, he had spelled it out for me in no uncertain terms and now, to my horror, his visions were starting to come true. I seriously doubted if I had the mental strength to take me through another day, let alone months. Since leaving home, thinking was something I had tried to avoid at all costs, and now, confined with only my thoughts, four years' worth were starting to get the better of me.

When my confinement finally came to an end I was so much the worst for it. My mind was starting to panic and my stomach was weakening to every dark thought that jabbed at it. Let out once more amongst the general population, I was sent back into the same canteen, where only trouble awaited. Walking slowly to my table, I clenched my stomach waiting for the attack that would inevitably come. When it came I would defend myself as best I could. It would land me back in solitary, but what else was there to do?

Sitting at a table well away from the serving area, I put my back to the wall, lowered my head and said a silent prayer. I had not thought of God or angels since I was small. But seeing no way out of the hell I was in, somehow it just seemed appropriate. In reality, I don't even know if you could call what I said a prayer or not - it was, I guess, an internal vocalisation of desperation. Mostly, I prayed for invisibility, a tall order I know, but that was the only thing I really wanted – invisibility, or the ability to walk through walls.

Gathering my nerve somewhat, I began to wade through the scrambled egg on my plate. But before I could put a morsel in my mouth I was frozen by the appearance of a presence. A woman in her forties, slender, well groomed, short blonde hair, plopped down opposite me and immediately started eating. I could hear the bread roll breaking, the butter spreading. Within seconds she had attracted a group about her. Each was of a similar age and each one was equally well-kept.

As the chatter rose I felt like a little mouse between the paws of a well-fed cat. The woman finished eating and still I kept my head down. The conversation seemed to be orchestrated largely by the first woman, whom I presumed was the kingpin of the group. Her name was Beth, a fellow Londoner, who had queen-like status in the prison because of her husband.

"You like solitary?"

A full ten minutes it had taken for these words to finally come. Anticipating the very worst, I tightened, wondering from which direction the first blow would come.

"Solitary, you like it?" Beth repeated.

"It was okay," I said looking up for the first time.

"Okay she says, so you'd like to go back?" Beth jested, causing the table to erupt in laughter.

"No" I said, open and honest.

"Your first time inside, yeah?"

"Yes."

"We know it is, don't we ladies. You did well to survive Holloway, first time and all."

Apparently Beth and I had been transferred from Holloway at the same time. I hadn't noticed her, but she had well and truly sized me up from the get-go. Now, there was only one question, which would be the difference between sanctuary and no sanctuary.

"What you in for?"

I told them. The real clincher for me was not whether I was innocent or not; it was the fact that I had acted to save my sister. This was all Beth and her mates, as she like to called them, needed to hear. They were all mothers, so they totally related to the sincerity of my actions.

"What have you signed down for?" Beth asked, referring to the number of daytime activities offered by the regime.

"Nothing so far," I said, still as timid as I had begun.

"When it's raining, you go for the gym, and when it isn't you go for the garden. And when you're in here you sit with us. You got that, right?"

"Right." And there it was, my protection, my sanctuary, my saving grace.

Being under Beth's protection meant that the rest of my

time went by without any major incident. Oh, I still had to endure the occasional taunt, the occasional dig in the ribs, but by and large life inside became bearable - pleasant even, on occasion. With three months of good behaviours under my belt I received the news that my sentence was being reduced by a full two months and my probation thereafter to eight.

"So keep your head down for the next four weeks and you'll be out of here," the officer told me, closing my file. "One more thing," he said, seeing I was about to rise. "We've received a visitation request from your mother and brother, they want to come see you next week."

I looked on blankly for a moment. I really didn't know at this stage whether this was a good thing or not.

"You don't have to see them," the guard continued, reading me.

"No that's okay, please tell them they can come."

A week later, as advised, I sat in the family area waiting for my visitors to arrive. The room was bright and full of chatter. The excitement of family coming together was infectious, and by the time I saw Mum and Gavin come through the doors I was genuinely happy to see them. Spotting me, Mum gave me a big wave. I waved back, pretending we had been magically transported back to happy times. Knowing my capabilities for day-dreaming had been removed long ago, I knew the act could never last. Still, I still had enough heart not to want to hurt anyone.

Mum sat down and pulled me out a yellow T-shirt with Cheers emblazoned across it, celebrating the popular American sitcom, which was basically, as far as I saw it, about a bunch of lonely souls bemoaning their sorrows on the way to drowning them. I guess she thought it would cheer me up, make me laugh or something. Ironically, she had given me this present in all goodness, not knowing how close to the bone the symbolism actually was. It showed, in many ways, just how far apart we had all become. I so wished it was all that simple, a simple gift and everything was erased, but that was impossible, far too much water under the bridge I guess.

Lacking the appetite for exuberance, I gave my mum a gentle smile, it was all I had. After the T-shirt came a box of chocolates and some pleasant enough chit-chat. After that, in came Mum's new boyfriend John, which really didn't improve matters. After that, came the endless remonstration about Dad, which really, really didn't improve matters. And after that, they left – no discussion of what I would do or where I would go three weeks from here. Gone. Gone. Gone.

* * *

When my release date finally arrived, I walked out a free person with just enough money in my pocket to take the train back to London. The weather was wet and wild, a violent storm had struck overnight and was still in full force, battering all parts of the country. Making my way to the train station, I looked at the many branches savagely ripped from trunks and wondered if I would make it back to London at all.

At the station, there were long delays. My summer attire made the wait all the more miserable. I told myself I should be happy to be free, but I just wasn't so sure about that.

Two hours late, the train pulled into the station. Finding a seat, I sat looking out the window waiting for the inevitable moment when I would have to contemplate my future. Putting off the inevitable, I picked up a discarded paper from the floor and began scanning it. Finally, I rested on a story bemoaning the spectacular failure of the £1 million operation Deepscan, to locate the legendary Loch Ness monster Nessie. How strange, I thought, that someone would pay so much money to search for monsters. It didn't seem fair in this world. Feeling my thoughts swim towards the desolate shore that was my future, I suddenly wished I had chosen a different story.

When I finally stepped off the train in London I was shocked to find Becky and Jen waiting for me.

"I would have hitch-hiked, but 150 miles…" Becky began to say apologetically.

"Is a bit much," I interjected, making it easy for her.

"And Jen was away for the summer, weren't you Jen?" Becky continued.

"Where?" I asked, as Jen lit up a smoke.

"America," she said after exhaling. "Here, you want one?" She offered this as a gesture to represent everything she would never say.

"So what was it like inside?" Becky asked innocently.

"Fuck sake, how do you think it was?" Jen snapped, shutting down the conversation.

I really was glad to see them both, maybe not as much as I should have been, but glad just the same. They couldn't have known this, but behind the smiles and frivolity something had changed. Nothing to place your hand upon, but I could feel a cooling breeze blowing tiny cracks in our relationship.

CHAPTER 9

—✦—

As part of my release conditions, I was required to sign with a parole officer every week in Tottenham, eight miles by bus out of Islington.

"Here," the female parole officer said, placing a form in front of me, "fill that out to apply for housing support."

"Will I get something tonight?"

"There's a waiting list."

"How long a waiting list."

"A long one. I can't tell you exactly, maybe weeks, maybe months."

"So what do I do now?"

"Don't you have family, friends? Or I could give you a list of shelters if all else fails."

It was October now, so that ruled out the option of sleeping on a park bench. I wondered if it had been the summer if this would have been added to the list. Not liking too much the sound of "if all else fails", what option was there other than to seek out squats and couches again?

The whole dire experience of going to prison had a lasting impact on my mental wellbeing. "He who lives without hope is truly lost", I remembered reading once, and as far as close to the bone gets, this was as close as any. Whatever picture I held for myself during those brighter days was now obscured from layered darkness. If by some miracle I had awoken one morning to find myself placed in the right body, my new body and I would have immediately had to set out in search of my authentic self. Whoever and whatever that was, it was lost. In all honesty, at this point in my life, I had absolutely no clue who I was, other than someone whose constant need for food, shelter and forgetfulness occupied every waking hour. Even with a new body, a greater miracle would be required to reunite me with myself.

Now at this point, I had got into the habit of saying the occasional prayer here and there. After all, I had survived prison, so I never saw the harm. Not being especially well acquainted with God, I never saw the logic in blaming him for any of my problems. I mean, why would I? I knew all too well that all my problems were without a shadow of a doubt man-man. And so I figured, if man had failed me, why not seek out some higher power? I was so low at this point that it was logical that only that would suffice.

And then, lo and behold, a couple of weeks later to my absolute amazement the most bizarre offer came my way. Florida.

"Why don't we all go?" Jen asked Becky and me, waving a letter in our faces.

"Florida! Are you serious?" I said. "Are you high? is what I could have said.

"No, I'm just fucking with you. Yeah, Florida, next

September," Jen said in her typical banal fashion.

"For how long?" Becky asked, less than enthused.

"Three months."

"Months?"

"Oh shut up, we all know you won't go," Jen said, frustrated. She knew only too well that the fact that Becky had a new boyfriend ruled her out automatically. Whether her relationship would last until next September was another matter, but in Becky's world this, like all of the others, was the one – the one who would stay with her forever.

"What of it, Lisa? Your probation will be up by then, right?"

"Yeah, but Jen, I can hardly afford fags."

"I wouldn't be into it, boyfriend or not," Becky said, as a retort to Jen. "I've got better things to be doing with my money."

"Yeah, like buy drugs," Jen quipped.

"Says the one!"

I don't know if you could rightly call either of them addicts at this point, but they certainly weren't far off. What was most worrying from my perspective was to witness their occasional dalliance with crack cocaine. Pot was one thing, cocaine was another. They may have fought like cats and dogs, but one thing they definitely had in common was their belligerence when it came to any warnings about drugs. Given the circumstances, given the company, it was a miracle that I continued to live drug-free.

While the grace of remaining drug-free wasn't recognised by me at this time, the miracle of being invited to Florida certainly was. While I was in prison, Jen had spent the summer there and had sparked up a friendship with a girl called Leah. It seemed Leah was dead keen to have Jen stay with her next September. It was December now, and with no warmth other than cold damp clinging to your bones, who wouldn't salivate at the thought of blazing orange heat?

"But she's never met me, why would she want me over too?" I said, not at all understanding why the offer was being extended to me.

"I checked and it's cool. Why would I be asking you?"

"Jen, I've five pence, if that," I said, tapping my pockets.

"We go September, so that gives us nine months. We'll make it, come on it'll be wild."

"Are you forgetting, I've a prison record! How the hell am I going to get a job?"

"Her parents won't pay for her ticket," Becky interjected.

"Neither will mine, so it's either get a job or go nicking."

"Are you serious? No way, I'm not going back to prison." This was probably the first time I had snapped at Jen. But I was adamant.

"Right well, we'll both get jobs and pool the money. I know a guy who owns a club, we can do waitressing, the tips are good and he owes me a favour."

"What favour?" Becky asked suspiciously.

"He fancies me, as it happens, so he's gonna owe me one isn't he? Leave it at that and I'll sort it."

"Jobs, just like that?"

"You're not coming, so what's it to you?"

"Just saying."

"Right," Jen said, focusing on me entirely, "that's settled then, you and me are going to Florida next September. I'm gonna ring Leah later. Yeah?"

"Yeah," I heard myself saying. What was wrong with me? There I was at it again, setting myself up for another kick in the teeth.

Although I expected the plan to come to nothing, by the

New Year there I was, just as Jen had said – well, not exactly how she had said it, but nevertheless, there I was slogging my heart out waitressing and there she was, well, getting the money elsewhere! Still, little by little the money mounted and little by little a small flickering light called 'hope' re-entered my world.

Nine months of hard slog and ass-slaps, nine months of precarious living, nine months of recovery from the ordeal of prison, but by September 1988, aged 20, I had done it – I was on my way to the land of hope, to the land of the free.

My wait for Jen in the terminal, with a golden ticket clenched in my hand, was a test of self-control on my part. I could hardly contain myself. Expelling some of my charge, I chatted to whoever was willing to have their ear reddened for a spell. By the time the plane pulled off the runway, like the plane my excitement was rising – moment by moment it scaled new heights. This time last year, I was pulling up weeds in the prison garden, and now I was sipping a coke and vodka on my way to Florida, no less. How was this even possible?

Now had this not been back in the day when no visa was required, the reception I got from the friendly customs officer might have been a whole lot different. The only question the officer with the gun ask me was who I was visiting. And getting a reasonable enough answer, he rubber-stamped my papers for three months and welcomed me to the USA. As I walked away from the counter, every American movie, every drama I had ever seen fought for a place in my head. While watching and absorbing the American culture as a child, never once had I imagined that one day I, of all people, would be standing in the land of Dirty Harry, Starsky & Hutch and Kojak. America was the dream. And I had arrived in the land of better everything;

movie stars, cars, houses, clothes, food, jobs, opportunities, you name it America had it – only better.

Even flying straight into Hurricane Gilbert couldn't dampen my enthusiasm, nor re-routing to JFK, and even the 36-hour bus journey down the east coast of America couldn't kill my grin. What did make it fail momentarily was my walk through New York's Penn Station, where I saw two worlds shadow each other silently. Once I had noticed the first of Penn's homeless I couldn't help seeing these poor lost souls everywhere – under benches, in corners, along the skirtings of walls, wherever dust settled, there they were. Even outside, box after box accompanied us down the street. My life had been hard, squatting had been hard, prison had been hard, but this was something different. This was desperation en masse where it just shouldn't have been.

Halfway down the street, these sights got to me. I couldn't help the feeling that was slowing me – it was pity. I stopped to drop three dollars into a lap. I'm not sure who was hiding under the hood, but whoever it was nodded, acknowledging my gesture. His connection to fellow humanity was so fragile that he couldn't bring himself to look into another's eyes. If it had been London, I doubt I would have been so shocked, but this was America, the last bastion of hope for the rest of the world. Suddenly the darkness of the picture gripped me with such fear for my own preservation that it was all I could do to get away from it, to forget it. I now understood how the two worlds could co-exist in such close quarters; it wasn't because of cold-heartedness or greed, it was out of fear.

"Do you think you can get me my job back at the club?" I asked later on the bus.

"Why would you want to?" Jen asked, turning over to go to sleep.

"Because I don't want to end up in a box."

Jen turned back and looked at me for a moment. "You know what I say, fuck the future."

"But don't you ever worry about it?"

"I worry that my arse might collapse."

In the four years I had known Jen she had never changed. At eighteen, she was as fresh as ever. She had her look and she had her undeniable charms. She had her men, but not in the same way Becky had; Jen would never let anyone have a hold over her. I never understood what stirred such rebellion in Jen. Whatever it was, it ran dark and it ran deep and it wasn't something she was ever willing to talk about. I guess she had her demons, just like me. And I guess she figured that somehow the world owed her. Maybe that went some way to explaining just how Jen had the neck to land both of us on the doorstep of this lovely picture-perfect bungalow and expect free board for three months.

Standard beside Jen with our rucksacks on our backs I felt my nervousness knot inside of me. I hoped with all my might that this time promise wouldn't disappoint. It was Leah, tall and tanned, same age as Jen, who flung the door open and ushered us in like old friends over for dinner. Inside, there was no time to take in the surroundings before Diane, Jen's mother, came through from the kitchen wearing a smile, jeans and flip-flops.

"Welcome! Welcome! Jen, still pretty as a postcard, and you must be Lisa. You hungry sweetheart? Of course you are, come on get yourselves over to the table. I've everything waiting for you. You poor things, all that way by bus."

"You've a lovely home," I said, trying my best to make a good impression. "Beautiful smell too."

"It's Mum's new rose incense," Leah said cheerfully.

"Leah's favourite so far," Diane said lovingly.

As I watched Diane drape a motherly arm over Leah's shoulders, listening to the tale of our journey I left a lightness shine through the air. Suddenly, I wanted to be visible, I wanted Diane and Leah's attention. I wanted the warmth that radiated from them. And for the first time, for what seemed like an eternity, I wanted love. In the midst of such stirrings it didn't take long for my knot to untwist, for my drudgery to lighten. Yes, promise had delivered, and then some.

I immediately took to Diane, which was a major departure for me. As a result of my recent past, guardedness had overshadowed my natural inclination for friendliness. But, here in the bright warmth of Diane and Leah, I felt my arsenal being disarmed.

"Thirty-six hours on a greyhound bus, here let me give you a hug," Diane said playfully as she walked over and gave Jen and me just that. As her arms fell away from me I hoped she couldn't detect my awkwardness. It had been so long since genuine affection had come my way, I hardly knew what to do with it.

After getting us settled at the dining table, Diane disappeared into the kitchen. I took this opportunity to have my first glance around the room. It was so different from the rooms I had occupied in London. The air was fresh, and the woods that dominated the room, floors, table and sideboards provided a natural palette for the many ornaments and trinkets that intrigued my vision. Large rubber plants, some on floors, some on sideboards, put an exotic gloss over everything, in the same way as the flickering candles added an extra touch of magic. Feasting on all the brightness, on all the colour, I suddenly felt like a child again, wanting to get up and touch everything.

"You have so many beautiful ornaments, Leah," I said, turning in my seat to admire the ones on the sideboard behind me.

"Mum runs a New Age shop, so she sources it all herself."

"What's a New Age shop?" I said, in total ignorance.

"She sells things that help people connect with their spirituality."

"Like to God?"

"To God, to Nature, to Spirit, to the angels," Diane said, laying a large baking dish beside me. "If you like, I'll do an angel reading for you sometime?"

"What's that?"

"It's a way to talk with your angels."

"Wow, yeah that sounds fun," I said, wanting to please her.

"How about you Jen?"

"No offence, but I don't believe in any of that."

"That's okay, no one has to do anything they don't want in this house," Diane said, carefully taking off the dish-cover. "Now, who wants meat loaf?"

"What is it?" Jen asked bluntly.

"Haven't you had meat loaf?" Diane asked cheerfully. "Oh you're in for a real treat," she promised, after we had both shaken our heads.

Savouring my first mouthful, I wanted to cry. It wasn't so much the delicious flavours, which I really appreciated, it was the lovingness that swirled around the table that moistened my eyes. This simple slice of family life was so intoxicating, I would have happily sat around their table spooning meat loaf and salad into my mouth for the rest of my life.

"You know, don't let the cardigan fool you, during the sixties mum was a hippy, and I'm talking flower power and Woodstock."

"What's Woodstock?" I asked.

"A really famous music festival."

"Lots of music, lots of flowers," Diane explained laughing, "and lots of love. We were young, like you girls."

"Did you take LSD?" Jen asked, suddenly intrigued.

"Oh, just a little pot, you know, to try it. But it never had much of an effect on me, so I never really bothered. You know, it's such a lovely evening, why don't you girls go out to the jacuzzi while I clean up?"

Homecooked meals, jacuzzi, are you serious? Seems I had died and gone to Orlando, Florida.

"The stars will be out soon, it's pretty cool," added Leah.

"Sounds amazing," I said, grinning widely.

"How does that sound Jen?" Leah asked politely.

"Why not?" Jen said, looking at the kitchen door. "Do you have any weed?" she asked quietly.

"No, but we've beers."

"Beers are great!" I said enthusiastically.

Leah smiled than turned to Jen. "We can get some weed in the forest tomorrow, if you like?"

"What about now?" Jen pushed.

"We can't go now Jen, it's not safe."

"Serious Leah, beers are great, stop worrying," I said, pushing back.

"Tomorrow, first thing, right?" Jen said, making a point of it.

"Oh sure. You see, we usually don't bother until the weekend."

I might have stayed annoyed at Jen for being so pushy, but Jen was Jen, and I knew her drug habit was not so much under her thumb as she liked to make out. I only wished she could have been contented with just the beers, drugs, squatting. All that was London, and I, for one, needed to leave London as far behind as possible.

As if in answer to my prayer, as soon as we stepped out the back the stars seemed to switch on and the warm southern breeze came and blanketed us all the way to the jacuzzi. As I slipped under the warm gurgling bubbles my body twitched as all the grime of London feel away. I closed my eyes and smiled, allowing an ancient memory to come to mind – this was good, this was real good, this was living.

I awoke to what I can only describe as the official dawn chorus. Diane's home, in what they called a suburb, was bang smack in the middle of nature as far as I was concerned. I mean, with a forest literally on your back door you couldn't get much closer if you pitched a tent in Sherwood Forest. After soaking in a couple of bars of music, I strolled into the kitchen to find Leah had breakfast waiting for me.

"You ever get alligators here?" I asked, thinking of all those swamp movies I had seen.

"No, there's no water close. We get mostly raccoons, sometimes rabbits and squirrels. We leave food out for them, it's pretty cool."

"You been here long?"

"A couple of years, but there's a shop Mum's thinking of buying, so we might be moving."

"Oh," I said, hoping it wasn't any time soon.

I was on my second waffle when Diane strolled in, brushing her blonde shoulder-length hair. "I'm off now girls, there's money on the counter and food in the fridge. I'll see you later."

"Normal time?"

"Normal time, if I don't have a reading, I'll phone you if

plans change. I haven't forgotten about you, Lisa."

"Great, look forward to it."

"Okay, make sure you girls have a super day. And if you get bored drop in."

"We won't," Leah said laughing.

"I know," Diane replied tugging playfully gentle at the ends of her daughter's blonde hair.

After Diane had gone, I sat wondering just how someone could be so nice. Her hospitality, her kindness to veritable strangers was unfathomable to me. I had to admit to myself that I found it somewhat peculiar at first, I guess mainly because I had just grown so used to cool distance between myself and others. Even with friends, even with Becky and Jen, there were just too many layers, too many barriers, too much hurt to make it any other way. With my faith in human goodwill devoured by abandonment and prison, I couldn't help the little light going on to wonder if the heart that Diane and Leah displayed so openly was just another facade set to fade.

After Diane left, Leah and I sat in the garden waiting for Jen to stir. After an hour of sun soaking, she finally sauntered out in shorts and a belly-top.

"Is that the woods?" Jen said, pointing to the tree line at the end of Leah's garden.

"Well, we have to trek for a bit."

"Okay, can we go now?"

"Don't you want breakfast?"

"You have a Coke?"

"Sure!"

"That'll do, I'll have it on the way."

I had in all honestly never seen Jen so eager to do anything. As we started out, I quickly gathered that she must have known about this enterprising cottage industry that Leah and her friends had going. In the four years I'd known Jen, the closest she'd got to a wood was striking a match. There had to be drugs involved. I did also wonder whether the attraction in the woods was the primary reason Jen was in Florida in the first place.

"Is it okay if I bag enough for a couple of days?"

"Oh sure, help yourself, as you can see there's plenty."

"You want some?" Jen asked Leah, probably making sure she didn't have to share.

"No I'll get some on Saturday. What about you Lisa, do you want some?"

"No, I'm not into that."

"I'm not big into it either, a puff or two at the weekend does me."

Being around Leah with her laid-back ways was pure tonic for me. Even my drinking moderated and changed function. Whilst before it was poured into me for the purpose of rendering me unconscious as quickly as possible, now, around Leah and her friends, I was drinking and laughing like I was one of them. And in this sense of belonging, I felt my healing begin.

Leah in her kindness was every bit her mother. She introduced us to all her friends and made sure we were the centre of everything. On a trip to Tampa Bay, she took us to a beach party to watch the sunset. As the last of the rays dipped into the still ocean I thought to myself, this is how life is supposed to be lived. After leaving prison the minor connection I had taken up with God above had not been maintained, on my side at least.

In truth, I had never turned a single brain cell over to consider my place in the grand scheme of things. I wasn't religious and I wasn't holy. I had no faith, if faith meant conviction. But nevertheless, standing on the edge of the shoreline bathed on all sides in flickering golden light, I thought if there was ever a case for the existence of an Almighty Creator, then the celebration in my heart at that very moment was surely it.

When joy comes hope quickly follows, or so it was in my case. A couple of weekends of campfires and roasted marshmallows and my life in London was soon forgotten. Being in Florida was in many ways like being out of time. Where there is time there is pressure, and where there is pressure there is stress. Having no time allowed me to rise above all the binds that fastened my problems and issues to me. I never spoke of my past and I never thought of my future. Living in the no time, or at least the now time, rested my mind in such a way that it stuck exactly where I wanted it to, and never once wandered. I had decided not to allow my complex sexual issues to board the plane with me, and leaving them at home in London gave me great solace. There were no pressures for me to become romantically involved with anyone. It was cool either way. Jen had her flings and Lisa had none, and no one saw anything unusual about this – even me.

As if to celebrate the return of joy and hope to my life, Leah took us to Walt Disney's inspirational Epcot Center, where a plaque at the entrance read: To all who come to this place of Joy, Hope and Friendship, Welcome. By now I was rising high. The Starship Enterprise could have floated over town and beamed me up to have a beer with Captain Kirk and I wouldn't have blinked an eyelid – London was a universe away.

It was on the occasion of our return from the Epcot Center that Diane pulled me aside. "I promised you an angel reading, didn't I. how about now?" She sat me at her kitchen table, went to a drawer, then returned with a small box. I'd expected her to light a few candles, put on some appropriate music, maybe some chanting, but she just sat beside me and smiled.

"You're not nervous are you?" she said, as if picking up on the cartwheels churning in my stomach. Suddenly, I was nervous. Suddenly, I was afraid my two big secrets would be uncovered – my gender identity and my prison record. Strange now, to lumber both together in the same basket, but to me at this point in time, they were one and the same.

"So, let's see what the angels have for you, okay?" she said, shuffling the deck. Looking at Diane, dressed in her pink cotton trousers and matching T-shirt, she really was the farthest from crystal balls and dangling earrings you could get.

"Okay, it seems you're here to help. Like me you're going to help people," she said smiling. "Okay, another," she said, taking a second card, "This is a communications card, you'll be somehow involved with communications to many people, most likely you'll be involved with the media."

"What, like the papers?"

"Something like that."

Diane went on to pull some others, I can't remember the specifics, but in summation I remember her telling me that one day I would be put on a spiritual path. I nodded gratefully.

After my reading, I thanked Diane and went out to find Jen and Leah. I had a giggle with Jen about the fact that I was going to be in the papers and left it at that. But to be perfectly honest the information went in one ear and came out the other. The insight she was giving me, although in hindsight I now see as being profound, at the time just didn't resonate with me. Even that day with Candy in the car park, I didn't tie in my experience with Diane. It wasn't until later that the pieces of my life started to fit together. I guess in the great scheme of things our spiritual journey is mapped out by the divine – divine timing, as they say. Diane's wisdom may have appeared to fall on deaf ears, but I do believe that somehow her words nourished the spiritual seeds that were already germinating deep inside me.

From here, Diane allowed our days to proceed with ease through her continual provision of meals and spending money. This act of generosity and kindness, performed every day, for three months, was pretty amazing by any standards, even more so when you consider that the only source of income she had was the modest income she made from her small shop. She never spoke much about her spirituality, however in hindsight I see it must have run deep within her.

Moving home in anyone's language is a biggy, and Diane orchestrated a move from Orlando to Key West, some 400 miles, with all of us in tow, without missing a beat. She was amazing and she was an angel and I have never forgotten what she did for me.

Like every dream, there comes a time when it must become reality or fade. Even if life wouldn't be the same back in London, I hoped that I could hold onto some semblance of the happiness I was now accustomed to. I liked being happy. It wouldn't be Florida happy, but I was determined to find a way to create a new London happy, in whatever form that would take. Firstly, there was stability, I would have to find a job that would enable me to put down roots, even if it was only within a bedsit. Secondly, there was peace of mind; I wanted to resolve my relationship with my father. I knew this would mean building a bridge over stormy waters, but I had hope now that one day things would settle down and once again we could meet on solid ground.

Saying goodbye to Diane and Leah was hard. I had grown very attached to both of them. They had filled the many holes in my heart with kindness, and it was hard to wave goodbye to that. We kissed and we hugged and we promised to write and we promised to return, and then we were on our way home.

As the wheels hit the runway and I looked out upon the grey British morning, the strange thing was I actually found myself excited to be home.

Lee as a child called Lisa

Lisa with pigtails

Graduating from the University of Hertfordshire

Visiting a Mayan temple

Lee today

CHAPTER 10

We arrived back in London in the midst of the Christmas run up. Instead of adding to my misery, that year the crimson cheer actually reached me. I walked tall amongst the shoppers with a smile on my face and the smell of Florida still fresh on my clothes. Florida had strengthened my back and taught me to hold my head up to the sun. It had taught me that there were good people in the world, and that no problem, no matter how great, has to be permanent.

In addition to security and peace of mind, the third thing I was determined to face was my sexuality. I had not spoken to Diane about it, though I wished I had. The way I spun it for myself, the dream was just too good to spoil. If there was ever a person who could have helped me, it was her. Under the glow of the Florida sun, I might well have believed that the fear within had been bleached out. In reality, fear was hiding deep within me, still able to reach its tentacles out to fool me. I came home with the delusion that I could perhaps find everlasting love, even under the guise of a lesbian relationship. I guess it is a toss-up as to which is worse, false hope or no hope.

I was more open about my desire to build bridges with my father. Jen and I had gone our separate ways, so my course was straight home to find my father. I didn't expect hugs and kisses, I didn't even expect courtesy. I knew I would need a flak jacket and a helmet, but I was ready to put up with all that.

I shuffled my luggage between my hands as I walked the small path that led to my old front-door. I felt a twinge that required some deep breathing before I could ring the bell. I set my feet firmly on the step, yet every other part of me was telling me to turn the other way. I waited for a moment. The weather was cold and I really wanted to get in and scrounge a jumper from Gavin. I waited another moment and still no answer. I put my bags down, having decided to look in the window; maybe my Dad was having an extra day off and was ignoring everything. From the gap in the curtains I couldn't really see much of anything.

I left the front and went round to the back window. The kitchen was empty. Even the table was gone. Maybe he was remodelling the house, which was a good thing, I thought to myself coming back to the front. Before the breakup my father was pretty handy when it came to decorating. If he was remodelling as I suspected, then that was a really good sign.

I rang the doorbell again, just in case.

"Is that you Lisa?" A soft Irish lilt came from behind. I turned to find Mrs Burke coming towards me. "Lisa sweetheart, the colour of you, look at you, don't you look grand!"

"Hi Mrs Burke, yeah I've been in Florida, so I have."

"Florida! Good for you girl."

"Do you know where Dad or Gavin are?"

"They're not there Lisa, haven't you heard?"

"Heard what?"

"Why don't you come on over, I've a pot under the cosy."

"But where are they?" I said, staying put.

"I don't know sweetheart, God's honest truth. All I know is that the house has been sold."

"Sold? But I came back before Florida, he said nothing, how can it be sold?"

"I'm sorry sweetheart, look no point standing there, come on over to ours," she said, turning back down the path.

I sat shell-shocked in Mrs Burke's, clasping a mug. Mrs Burke had always sworn that a cup of tea solves everything. However, on this occasion, even she would concede that the tea failed badly.

"Look Lisa, the one thing you know is that I'm not a gossip," Mrs Burke said, sitting down opposite me. This was true, and this made my expectations for a happy conclusion nose-dive. "You're old enough, so I think you should know what everyone else is saying." She offered me a biscuit, as if to sweeten the poison coming.

"Okay, thanks," I said steeling myself for the very worst.

"As far as I know, your Dad has got himself messed up with a scarlet woman and he's sold the house to go off with her."

"A scarlet woman? You mean a prostitute?"

"I'm sorry Lisa, my Paddy swears it's the truth, and you know him."

"What about Gavin?"

"Poor thing was spending the weekend at a friend's and came home, like you, to find the house in the state it is, even the electricity was off. He went looking for your Dad, and when he came back an estate agent was at the door letting himself in. Gavin wanted to go for him, but luckily my Paddy was there to drag him off. I'm so sorry to be tellin' you all this."

"It's okay, go on."

"Well, we took him in for a couple of nights, then he said he was going to your mum's."

"Is she with her boyfriend still?"

"Sweet Mary and Joseph, but you know your mother got married?"

"No, no I didn't."

"Honestly, I'm sorry now I came out."

"It's okay, so they're all living together?"

"No, you see, I was worried about young Gavin, so I made it me business to see if anyone had heard anything, and well from what my Paddy found, Gavin and your mum are back with her dad."

"Right."

"You don't mind me sayin' all this, do ya?"

"No."

"Well, by all accounts her fella wasn't up to that much and he didn't want Gavin with them. So I heard your mum just packed up and told him to go sling his hook."

"Right."

"So, you going to go around?"

"No, the house is tiny as it is."

"It is, so where will you go?"

"Back."

I don't know if I had more anger for my father or for myself. Yet again I had hoped and I had been piked. And back is precisely where I landed, instantaneously, straight back to my cold-hearted hopelessness – but this time with a vengeance.

I just couldn't fathom how my life had gone down the toilet so fast and so efficiently, and to be perfectly honest, at this stage I really didn't care. I was done analysing. I was done reaching into the past. And I was done attaching hope to my future. All I wanted now was peaceful oblivion, even if I had to drink copious amounts to get it.

"But preferably not with the added option of a cardboard box," I told myself as I descended into the Underground. Low as I felt, I still wasn't ready for that. Although I certainly wouldn't have been the one to go looking for it, I guess, somewhere, slugging it out to the death with my rising fear was hope. I wouldn't have gone looking for it, because I sensed with each step I took that hope was being pulled asunder.

I suppose I could have dug in the bottom of my case and pulled out the yellow T-shirt my mother had given me. I could have put it on and knocked on her door. Maybe I could have done this, if it wasn't for the niggling feeling of anger I had towards her. She had in the end done the right thing by Gavin, this was good, but I couldn't suppress the voice that shouted, "Yeah, but what about me?" Nor could I silence the other voice that screamed equally loud that she was partly to blame, along with my father, for me winding up in prison. With all these voices screaming in my ear I could still hear the small voice that whispered, "put on the T-shirt and go." I couldn't hear anything above the anger, so I kept on, lower and lower until I finally reached the bottom.

My first few nights back in London were spent on a friend of a friend's couch. It didn't last long, it never did, so in desperation I had the bright idea of paying a visit to Sally, my ex-probation officer. My name had been a year on the housing list, so I figured it was worth a trip. Either that or sleep rough in December, sure it was worth a trip.

"You're in luck, there's a place for you in shared housing,' she said. 'It'll take a fortnight."

"But what am I meant to do until then?"

"Friends, family?" Sally said, looking at me over her glasses.

"I have no one. If you don't sort me out I'll be on the streets."

"Okay, give me a sec, I'll see if I can get you into a hostel."

"In Islington?"

"No, here in Tottenham."

"What about food, is there an allowance or something?"

"You can apply, but without a permanent address it will be difficult. Here, take this," she said, scribbling on another scrap of paper. "That's the address of a charity that will give you some food."

If it wasn't for the charity of others, I would have been forced onto the street to steal or starve. I was walking a fine line, and I knew it.

As far as the accommodation went, of course I would have preferred to have been housed in Islington close to Becky and Jen, but it wasn't too far, and anyway I really didn't have too many options floating around. And I would have preferred to have gone straight to the shared housing. "But how bad can a hostel be?" I thought, walking out and looking at the scrap of paper with the address neatly inscribed upon it.

It didn't take me very long to find my destination, and on the outside at least the building looked pretty harmless. It was old and in desperate need of a new paint job, but from the entrance onwards that's where things started to deteriorate. Take it from me, when you find yourself in a bind, never ask yourself, how bad can something be.

With the rise of property prices in London the strain on social housing had never been greater. With houses becoming such an asset, every squatter knew their time was rapidly coming to an end. 1988, the year I became homeless and rootless, was the zenith of the homelessness crisis in London. It would be a further two years until the social consciousness of the wider population would grind some cogs into action. But for now, what constituted as the social housing network was about to collapse, any minute now, under the strain of the sheer numbers being forced onto the street – people just like me.

The hostel I had entered was run by a charitable organisation. The heady smell of mildew and mould accosted you when you entered the hallway, and I'm sure it was a deliberate way of making all but the most desperate turn on their heels and run straight out the door. Hostels in London at this time were getting the most horrendous press, and, standing in this field laboratory, I could see why.

But sadly, the general health hazards were the least of the problems. A series of tragic fires had demonstrated, all too well, the appalling way the homelessness issue was being ignored. Greed had created the problem, but greed wanted nothing to do with the fallout. In one fire, in North London, eight women lost their lives. Not only were these buildings lacking basic fire regulations, they were hopelessly overcrowded with the most vulnerable in society, many of whom suffered serious mental health issues.

If I could have run away from this place, I most certainly would have. It was in every way demeaning to the spirit and a place of danger to the physical. Fires weren't the only thing you had to worry about, as there was also the very real threat of serious violence. Bringing together such hopelessness, such vulnerability, such mental instability and such volatility into a melting-pot with no security or provision for the specific needs of such residents had created a volcano ready to erupt.

No sooner had my room been pointed out and I stepped inside a fellow resident came to call. "Give us your fuckin' bag or I'll have ya," he said, ripping the plastic bag from my hand. Before I could think to scream he had disappeared into the low light of the narrow corridor. Afraid to follow, I quickly ran to the door and fumbled the bolt across. I looked at the door, wondering how on earth I was going to survive two weeks of this. I really didn't want to be hiding like this, I didn't want to be there at all, but what choice did I have?

Too afraid to venture out, I stayed in my room until morning. And when the morning finally came I was drained by the lack of sleep and the constant worry that someone would force their way through the door.

A couple of days into my stay and I could have written the A-Z of hostel survival. Among the highlights there would be: lock your door immediately and keep it locked; Whilst in transit from room to street, keep head down at all times and talk to nobody; where possible sprinting is preferable to walking; where possible a park bench is preferable to a hostel. In summary, the absolute necessity to avoid hostels at all costs can't be understated. And this is why so many homeless people, weather permitting, choose to bypass the so-called "buffer" that hostiles are supposed to provide and instead head straight for a box in the street. However, in the middle of winter, going onto the streets would have done nothing for me other than quicken my end.

The plunge of going from the sunshine of Florida to the homeless shelter was so startling that it landed me in a deep crevice of depression. Listening to the shrill cries of my fellow residents nearly sent me demented. Every time I heard someone banging on my door I thought this was the time someone was getting in. After a week it had become all too much. Sitting on the bed listening to the darkness, I said to myself, "You can go on listening to this and before long you'll be joining them, or you can drink."

The next morning, I took a tape recorder and some tapes out from under the bed and went down to the local market to flog them. The tapes were expensive in those days and combined with the tape recorder they bought me a couple of nights' peace.

With only three nights to go, I went walking down the market and bumped into a girl I recognised from a squat in Islington. Her name was Mary, and she was nineteen or twenty, around the same age as me.

"Where you staying yourself?" she asked, running a hanky across her nose. She looked poorly and her face had a greyness too it, which I knew had more to do with drugs than a seasonal cold. "I'm at a squat in Kentish town, why don't you come back, we can listen to some music."

I knew the squat wouldn't be up to much, but anything was better than the shelter. Actually, being around a friendly face again was comforting. I hadn't seen Becky since arriving home, which meant she was off with a bloke, nor had I seen Jen since leaving her at the Tube, nearly a fortnight ago. I bought a couple of tins of beer with the money I got from selling the last of my tapes, and Mary and I headed back to the squat.

Inside, we settled down. Mary pushed some rubbish off a mattress and we settled down on it. I opened my bag and handed her a tin. She put on some music and we started to chat.

It didn't take long for the room to fill with people Mary knew. One of them, a bloke a little older than us, sat down beside Mary and handed her what looked like a small piece of tinfoil. She dug under the mattress and pulled out a needle.

"What's that Mary?" I asked quietly.

"Heroin."

"Come on, why don't we just stick on the beers, we've enough."

"It's cool. I just need a little to take the edge off."

"Mary, it's bad news."

"It's only a little."

"I've some stuff we could sell, we could go to a club."

"Nah, I'm settled now," she said, lighting up her spoon.

Mary was petite as it was, so being underweight made her almost childlike. Like me, she had left home because of an abusive father, but in her case it was sexual abuse that had put her out on the street. As she rolled up her sleeve, I had to stop myself from putting my hand over my mouth. Her tiny arm was so pock-marked she looked like an eight-year-old with chicken pox. I looked down, as I knew the needle would soon pierce her skin. I couldn't watch. The horror of it all made me physically sick.

It only took a second for the chemicals to reach Mary's brain. I had seen it all before, the limpness, the "rush". Mary closed her eyes and leaned back against the wall. I knew she could be out of it for hours. Feeling the desperation of it all reach out and grab me, I did the only thing I could. I reached into my bag and pulled out my cans, one after the other, until I fell off to sleep.

The chill of the morning brought me around. The morning after is never a nice place to be, but it helps if you're not in a freezing room that even cockroaches would have a problem with. I opened my eyes slowly, feeling the carpet in my mouth, and looked over at Mary. It took a moment for the full horror of the scene to register, but when it did it reached into my stomach and pulled every ounce of me out.

Mary was dead. Her lifeless body was slumped against the wall. Her eyes were open, but I knew she couldn't see. Her lips were blue and her face was grey, and I knew the red would never be seen again in her cheeks. Mary was gone and not coming back, another statistic. Heroin was the method, but abuse was the cause.

Mary was not a junkie, not a statistic. She was a person, a beautiful soul. No one wakes up one morning and decides to become a heroin addict. If there's one characteristic of a drug addict, based on the poor souls I knew, I'd say they're all individuals who have been badly let down, one way or another. Why so many can't see the battered child or the rape victim behind the statistic, I may never know; perhaps it's the fear of acknowledging that something so awful could happen in a society which they need so desperately to believe is civilised.

After Mary's death I stayed in the shelter, locked in my room until I got word, three days later, about the shared housing. Despite my vigilance, by the time I left I'd been roughed up, spat on, verbally abused and burgled, on more than one occasion. I swore to myself that I would freeze in a ditch before entering a hostel again.

My experience in the hostel and Mary's death had taken their toll. How much more would I be able to stand? I didn't know. It was with considerable relief that I stood upon the carpeted lobby of the shared accommodation and took in the smell of cleanliness.

What was to be my home for the foreseeable future

housed a total of 12 women who had their own bedroom and shared, as the name suggests, communal areas such as kitchen and recreational rooms. All were ex-criminals, and all, it was hoped, would make their way out of their darkness with the stability that the house provided. From first look, I could see that some were genuinely getting on board with this ethos, whilst others were still actively using crack cocaine on the premises. In reality the charity running the home was under-funded and under-staffed, so it wasn't quite the ladder up from the gutter that they, or I, had hoped.

After being shown to my room, I immediately locked the door (old habits die hard), and got up on the bed. I knew I would eventually have to venture into one of the communal areas and meet some of the other residents, but with my hostel experience still in my mind, I wasn't about to rush.

As my eyes wandered about the small, functional room, I couldn't help crying. It had been only a matter of weeks since I had waved goodbye to Diane and Leah, my suntan had started to fade and all the good the trip had done for me was long gone. In the Florida sunlight I had fooled myself into thinking that everything in my life had been wiped clean by the fresh, wholesome air. For all to see, even me, I had the sparkle of a well put-together person with a solid emotional and mental state. But for all my three months away had done, it was only gloss. I hadn't been honest with anyone, least of all myself. I had allowed all my demons to fester in the gleam, waiting for their opportunity to bounce back with a vengeance, and that's exactly what they did from the moment I found out about my father's latest betrayal.

Sitting on the bed, in another strange room, and taking stock of my situation was no easy task. Coming off the heights of Florida I now had to find a way to deal with the fact that I was now lower than I had ever been. Although I couldn't have called it, what I was experiencing was the flashing warning signs of serious depression.

I spent my night curled up on my bed not wanting to move. I had exhausted myself by regurgitating the many scares of my past, and all I wanted to do now was to empty myself fully of all thinking and feeling. If I could have stayed curled up in a ball forever, I would have, the only problem was, I hadn't eaten or drunk in hours and the pangs in my stomach were getting in the way of me falling off to sleep. If I had had a bottle to hand, that would have done nicely, but I hadn't. And so, I decided, checking my watch, to go and try to put down a glass of milk or something. "2.30 am, it should be safe, there shouldn't be anyone up," I thought, pulling myself up from the bed.

Heading toward the kitchen through the low-lit corridor, I was happy to find the house sleeping. I was happy to find the kitchen in darkness. I fumbled on both sides of the door and finally found the switch. As the tungsten lighting flickered on, I was shocked to see it flash across the hunched back of a girl called Anita.

"All right?" I said, without thinking. Not getting any answer, I walked around the table to the fridge.

"Is it okay if I take some milk?"

She shrugged. Whilst pouring the milk I took a look at her, and the more I looked the more I was sure I recognised her.

"I know, you don't I?" I said, putting the carton back.

"I don't think so," she replied curtly.

"No, you know my friend Jen from Islington, bleach blonde bob."

"Yeah, I know Jen, from the clubs," she said, stopping to

sniff into a ball of tissue. "yeah I know her."

"You got a cold?"

Anita shook her head and sniffed again. I took up my glass, "You mind if I sit down?"

"No."

To me Anita looked like a small child who was going to burst into tears at any moment. I sat down opposite her and smiled whenever she looked my way. At this stage, I guess my depression wasn't so deep that I couldn't recognise the terrible suffering of the person sitting in front of me. In truth, what was left of my heart went straight out to Anita. She was mild and meek, and I had never seen someone so close to crumbling.

"You've been here long?" was my feeble attempt to break the silence.

"No, a week or so. I was in prison, that's how I got this place."

"You just out?"

"No, I was somewhere else."

"You from Scotland?" given Anita's accent, the question was unnecessary.

"Edinburgh, but I've lived in London since I was fifteen."

"How old are you now?"

"Twenty, but I look older don't I?" Anita said, starting to chew her knuckles.

"No."

"I do," Anita said, both of us knowing I was lying.

The fact was, I knew straight away that Anita had done drugs, a lot of drugs. It doesn't take a genius, once you've been around users for any period of time - like sirens, the signs scream at you. In Anita's case, I surmised that her poor physical and mental state were a result of a long-term habit.

"You like biscuits?" Anita asked, glancing at the door guardedly.

"Yeah, I like biscuits," I said, wiping the milk from my lip.

"There's some hidden under the sink. Quick, get them before anyone sees. I swear I'll go for them with that kettle if anyone tries steal from me."

I got up and found a half a packet of chocolate biscuits hidden behind the detergents. Anita was playing tough, but I knew she suffered with a gentle soul.

"I don't want one, you take what you want, but if anyone comes in, you say they're yours, okay?" Anita said anxiously.

"Okay," I said taking one and sitting back down. "Sure you don't want one?"

"No, but hand them over here, I'll hide them in my pocket."

As she placed the packet in her pocket, the cardigan she was wearing fell down on one side to reveal an angry two-inch scare.

"What's that?" I asked openly.

"I got stabbed," she said, covering it up quickly.

"In prison?"

"Before."

"Listen, thanks for the biscuit," I said as she stood to leave. "Oh, and Happy Christmas."

"Happy Christmas," Anita whispered, as she went through the door.

After that first encounter, Anita and I chatted every day. Little by little, we opened up to each other, and little by little we came to rely upon each other. Having so much in common, it really wasn't difficult for our friendship to blossom – both of us had come from broken homes, both had been to prison, both had few prospects and both had little hope. What we did have, for the time being at least, was each other.

Ten weeks had past, and I had not seen sight nor sound of Jen or Becky. Then out of the blue one afternoon, Jen appeared to check out where I was living, and then as suddenly as she arrived she disappeared. That was Jen, never one you could get your head around. In the absence of any solid friendship, seeing Anita had become the brightest part of my day, so I had got into the habit of popping in on her whenever I felt any of my wayward emotions rearing up.

It was on one such visit that I walked into her room and found her with a visitor. This caught me by surprise, because I had never seen her with anyone before.

"Not now, can you come back later," she said answering her door as if she barely knew me. I was about to turn around and leave when a good-looking woman came behind her and pulled the door open.

"Wait! No, it's okay, come on in," she said, smiling widely.

I looked at Anita, but she just turned and sat on her bed.

"Nah, that's okay," I said, finding it all a little strange.

"No, now don't be like that, you came to visit so come on in," the woman insisted. She was beautiful and confident and she had a definite authority about her that made you want to do exactly what she said.

"Hi, my name is Tina," she said, putting out a beautifully-manicured hand to greet me. She was, I guessed, in her early thirties. She had sleek black hair which fell to her shoulders, dark eyes, flawless makeup and gorgeous clothes. My initial suspicion was that she was from the charity, checking up on things. As it turned out, and not for the first time, I was way off base. Tina wasn't a charity worker at all, but said she was an old friend of Anita's. I was instantly happy to find that Anita had such a nice friend.

Her life mustn't be all that bad, I found myself thinking as I extended my own hand.

"So what line of work are you into?" I asked curiously, after we had dispensed with the usual chit-chat.

"I'm an ex-model and dancer, and I still do some work from time to time. I have my own studio now."

"Wow, have you met anyone famous?" I asked, instantly impressed.

"Oh lots, actors, musicians, you know yourself."

"So you run a studio just like Pineapple?"

"I do more private, one-to-ones."

"So you've a studio in your home, it must be big."

"It does me. I've a gym and a sunbed, you must come over sometime."

"Wow, sounds great, I'd love to. Maybe Anita and I could come over."

"Exactly, you and Anita."

To this Anita remained quiet. In fact, she remained quiet throughout, though I was too enthralled with Tina to notice.

"I really would love to see your house, we'll definitely arrange something, yeah?" were my parting words as I left Anita's room after that short conversation.

"Don't worry Lisa, we'll arrange something. Maybe go for drinks too."

"Okay," I said, feeling better than I had in a long time.

Later that night, I bumped into Anita coming out of the Kitchen. "Your friend's really nice," I told her in all sincerity. "You're lucky to have someone who cares."

"No one loves me," she said, putting her head down and walking on.

"Anita, you're so lucky," I said, catching up.

"Is that so?" she said coldly.

I hung back, knowing there would be no getting through

to her tonight. She was obviously having a bad day. We all had them. And we all knew it was just best to stay away and wait for it to pass.

What I intended to tell Anita, when she was in a better mood, was that she was lucky to have a friend who cared, and especially lucky to have a friend who was stable. Tina reminded me again, just as Diane and Leah had done, that there were good people in the world and it wasn't, much as it felt that way, entirely bleak. Meeting Tina had done me the world of good. I really wanted to visit her in her home. I really wanted to go for drinks with her. And that meant that I really was thinking, for the first time since Florida, about the future in a semi-positive light.

The next morning, as I pulled myself out of bed with slightly less effort than normal, I may even have heard a chirp or two. I tucked my T-shirt into my jeans, hoping Anita hadn't gone out. I really wanted to drill her about Tina. Although she was older, there was something about that woman I found intriguing. Maybe it was her confidence, maybe it was her good looks, maybe it was her glamour, but whatever it was, I had a little spark back.

Anita, being one of the first to arise, was either in the kitchen or back in her room, if she hadn't already gone out that is, I thought, trying the kitchen first. There were a couple of bodies sitting around the kitchen, but none of them was Anita.

"Any of you seen Anita?"

None had, so I went to check her room. Knocking gently on her door I waited for a moment, then knocked again, getting no reply. After the second knock, I was about to leave when I heard a noise inside. Putting my ear to the door, I listened for signs of life and heard what I thought was sobbing.

"Anita, are you in there?" I shouted, suddenly worried. "Anita!" I turned the handle, and to my surprise the door opened. I walked in and immediately heard a low moan coming from the bed.

"Anita, are you okay?" I said gently, turning to the light. When I turned back I saw that she was lying on her side, her eyes were open and she was staring at me. "Are you sick, shall I call someone?" I said, seeing how pale she was.

"No one loves me," was all she whispered.

"Anita, you are loved," I said, kneeling down beside her. "Shall I call someone?"

"I've taken paracetamols. No one... loves me," she said closing her eyes.

"I'm going to get you a cup of tea, hold on a minute," I said, standing. She looked so sad, I really didn't know what to say, so I left, thinking the tea might lift her spirits. I was gone no more than the time it took for me to make the tea.

"Here we go," I said coming through her door.

Anita opened her eyes and looked through me for a second before closing them again.

"Anita, I really think I should call someone" I said, placing the cup and plate on her side-table. I had turned to do exactly that when Anita's body went into convulsions.

"Anita!" I screamed, rushing back to her. "Anita!" I implored, but by now there was no response. Shoving my hands under her, I fumbled her into my arms, resting her head back against my chest. I could feel no movement, no firmness, it was limp.

"Help! Someone help!" I screamed, not wanting to let her down. I was afraid she would vomit and choke. Her face was ashen and I couldn't tell if she was breathing. "Dear God please no!" I prayed, screaming again at the top of my voice. But no one came, and I was left with no choice but to lie her back down, so I could run to the phone. All the way back from the phone, I kept saying over and over, "Please God don't let me be dead, please don't let her be dead!" I had seen death, I had seen Mary, and it couldn't, it just couldn't, happen to Anita too.

"Not Anita!" I implored as I ran back to her side. Her body was still and, for a horrifying moment, I thought she was dead. Not knowing really what the hell I was doing, I fumbled for a pulse. Feeling nothing, I yanked her up into my arms and screamed, "Anita, don't you be dead!" Suddenly, I felt movement. I didn't have time to celebrate before a violent convulsion hit her. "Hold on Anita, the ambulance is coming," I said, unable to do anything but hold her. She looked so fragile, so young. I closed my eyes and prayed to God she would make it.

I don't know how long it took for the ambulance to arrive. All I know was that when she left her room on the stretcher she was alive, and when a police woman came to speak to me, a week later, she was dead. She had swallowed 70 paracetamol tablets, making her death both slow and inevitable. There was nothing anyone could do for her.

"No one loves me," were the last words Anita had said to me, maybe to anyone. Anita had not died from an overdose. She had died from an absence of love.

Anita's death left me devastated. The graphic images of that morning were my constant companions. There were no filters to mask the horror. She had not gone quietly. She had died as she had lived the last years of her life – alone and in agony.

Grieving for Anita, as I was, I spent the next couple of days locked away in my room. I just couldn't bring myself to visit the rooms where we had spent time together. Nor could I face the endless questioning I knew would inevitably come from every other resident. I had done enough questioning of myself, and I just couldn't take any more. What if I had called the ambulance straight away? What if I hadn't been so stupid as to have gone and made tea? Relentless questions such as these now haunted me. How could I get over the fact that Anita had told me she had taken paracetamol and I had gone and made bloody tea? There was just no getting around it. Day by day more guilt heaped upon me. Why didn't I spot it? I asked myself this over and over. Getting through the day was hard enough, but with Anita gone the days simply overwhelmed me.

In February 1989, two weeks after Anita's death, things hadn't got any better. I remained, for the most part, a prisoner of my own making, hiding away from everything and everyone. I had already asked to be transferred, but was told there was little or no hope, given the current homeless crisis. I did wonder if leaving regardless was my best option. I had never felt such a weight across my shoulders. And it wasn't just the sadness, the apathy, the hopelessness – there was the growing anxiety I was feeling about practically everything.

It was in the midst of one of these anxiety moments that I went out to the kitchen in the middle of the night. The room had suddenly become claustrophobic and I needed to go somewhere. Walking in at four in the morning, I hardly expected to see anyone. Yet I was stopped in my tracks by the sight of a young woman slumped over the table. Although my gut instinct was to run a mile, I found myself asking, "Hey, you all right?"

There was no reply, only mumbling. I was about to leave when all of a sudden she raised herself up, like the living dead, turned and screamed, "Me lips! Me lips!"

She was high and her lips were badly blistered from pipe burns. Much as I wanted to leave, I didn't, as she was in such a terrible state. I took a deep breath and went to the sink, where I found a cloth and dampened it. "For your lips," I said, handing her the cloth. She looked at it for a moment, then waved it away. "Ah fuck off will ya. Get out of me face!"

I put down the cloth and left the kitchen. I could feel the tears welling. This was the end, I had had enough. I just couldn't go on living in this place.

The next morning I packed my belongings into two plastic bags and left. I was walking away from all the harrowing memories that had pushed me out. I walked, not caring in the slightest where I was. Cold as the wind was that was picking up about me, it felt better to be outside.

Turning a corner, I walked past a local coffee shop. Feeling into my pocket, I stopped and walked back, I had just enough to buy a coffee, maybe even a small bar too.

Inside, I brought my coffee as far away from the window as I could get. I didn't want to see the world busily passing by. I no longer felt a part of it. Stirring my sugar, I did wonder if people really lost their minds or just gave them up.

I sat over my coffee, for the most part keeping my head down. A couple of customers came and went as I sipped my cup to make it last that bit longer. After an hour my cup was finally taken and I stood to leave. Then I saw a woman from the shared accommodation walk in. Instead of heading to the counter, she took one look at me and went straight out. The strange actions of people no longer shocked me. If she had come in, stood on her head and snorted cocaine with her feet, it wouldn't have surprised me – nothing would.

Outside the street was quiet, and black water was running down into the drains from a storm that morning. I jumped across and walked to the opposite side of the street.

After a minute of walking I became aware of a silver convertible slowing down beside me. The roof was up and I didn't look that much to see who was driving. The car went ahead, pulled in and came to a stop. Thinking nothing of it, I continued. As I reached the car, a woman leaned over to the passenger side to get my attention.

"Hey Lisa! It's me, Tina."

I stopped and walked over.

"Hi, it's Tina, remember me?"

"Sure," I said nervously. I suddenly wondered if she had heard about Anita. "Um, you know about Anita?" I asked awkwardly.

"Yes. Do you want to go for a coffee?" she answered. "Come on, get in." She opened the door for me.

Tina took me to a nice coffee shop a couple of miles away. Over coffee and a sandwich she gently told me the story of how she had gone to the hospital and spent as much time as she could with Anita.

"In the end, it all got too much. I'll never forgive myself for not being there for her."

"You shouldn't blame yourself," I said softly.

"You were the one who found her, weren't you?" she said sympathetically.

"Yes, I called the ambulance."

"What are you going to do now?" she asked. I opened up and told her that I had no intentions of going back.

"I haven't really thought of it. I've a couple of friends, in Islington."

"Look, I'm only saying this because you were a friend of Anita's, but I've a spare room, if it's any use to you."

"But you hardly know me."

"I know Anita liked you, and I'm looking for someone to help with some cleaning. I don't know, maybe we could help each other out. That's what I was talking to Anita about that day. I really thought she was going to make it... I'm sorry."

"You okay?" I said, feeling her pain.

"Yeah... look, it's an offer. I can give you my number anyway," she said, going to her bag.

"No that's okay," I said stopping her. "If it didn't work out there'd be no hard feelings?"

"Absolutely! None at all. So, do you want to go get your things?"

"This is all I have," I said bending for my bags. "The rest of my stuff is at home." I was lying. I suddenly felt embarrassed admitting to her that I had so little.

"Where's home?"

"Far from here," I said clasping the bags in my hand. "Um, I don't have any money, maybe you can take it from my wages?"

"I would, but this one's on me," she said smiling. "Listen, I know it's early but how do you fancy going for a liquid lunch? There's this nice little pub close to mine, we could celebrate."

"Sounds nice, but like I said I'm smashed."

"Aren't you running a tab with me?" she said playfully.

Sitting in Tina's car, I was secretly glad that we were going for a drink. Although Tina chatted easily, I couldn't help the tension that was lodged in my stomach. I just wasn't sure I was doing the right thing. Then again, I told myself, there was always the squats.

Tina laughed loudly at my suggestion that her house was probably a mansion.

"It's comfortably modest," she said, explaining that although she often had friends over, it would just be the two of us. As she spoke she kept her eyes on the road, which gave me the opportunity to take a closer look at her. Staring at Tina when her eyes were upon you was impossible because she was beautiful to the point of being quite intimidating.

Turning away and staring out the window for a moment, I might well have pinched myself. What a rocket-ride the morning had been; one minute I'm walking the streets destitute, the next I'm sitting beside an ex-model who has just offered me not only a home but a job.

I looked down at my T-shirt, which had a little stain on it. It was the first time in days that I had worried over my appearance. Suddenly, the thought occurred to me that I might even smell. Shuffling in my seat, I really wanted to smell my armpits, but I was too afraid.

"Is it too hot?" Tina said.

"No, no, it's just, well... I'm nervous."

"Nervous! What the hell of?" she said, looking at me and laughing.

"I don't know... you," I said, laughing back.

"Me? You need a drink," she said. "You like cocktails?"

"I like Malibu," I replied, not knowing if that counted.

"Me too," she said, leaning across me to open the glove compartment. "You wouldn't mind lighting me one?" She pointed to the pack of smokes. "Have one yourself, if you smoke."

After lighting her cigarette, I went to pass it to her.

"You wouldn't mind placing it in my mouth, the bends are awkward here," she said, parting her lips.

"No, not at all," I said, reaching over and placing it between her parted red lips. She was gorgeous, she was sophisticated, she was sexy, and I couldn't help my body coming alive.

After a liquid lunch that extended well into the afternoon, Tina took me the short distance to her home. I was surprised at first to find myself driving into a pretty average housing estate, but once inside I instantly relaxed, seeing all the designer stuff and antique decorations. And just like she said, the back of the house had been extended into the garden to accommodate her dance studio and gym. Her kitchen was ultra-modern, complete with a breakfast bar. And the adjoining room was simply plush luxury, complete with a beautiful wooden home-bar. Upstairs, my bedroom was small and tidy, much smaller than the other two bedroom suites that completed the upstairs.

My settling-in period went a lot smoother than I had anticipated. I liked Tina, and I liked living with her and I even liked working for her. The work was mostly light; cleaning and running errands, just as we had agreed. For one whole month I cleaned and cooked and shopped and ran errands without one cross word thrown my way.

Running the studio, Tina had a lot of clients come and go. Friends too, mostly male, all admirers no doubt, but none very close, as far as I could tell.

"I like men making a fuss over me, but I've no intention of letting one of them tie me down," she said, one evening over a bottle of wine. There were many evenings like this, just the two of us, eating take-aways and chatting over a bottle or two of wine.

Although I hadn't seen anyone, I did telephone Grandad once, hoping to get to speak to Gavin. I wanted him, to pass the word onto Becky and Jen where I was staying. I knew once they knew where I was, one or both of them would eventually get around to tracking me down. Much as I liked Tina, there were times that I missed my old friends, especially Becky.

As it happened it wasn't Becky and Jen that tracked me

down first, it was Gavin. I opened the door to him and went wide-eyed.

"Can I come in?" he said. Tina was out for the morning, not that it would have mattered, I was sure.

"You want a coffee? A tea?"

"You got a can of something?"

"Sure, take a seat," I said, directing him to the kitchen island.

"Nice place this," he said as I passed him a Coke.

"Mum's split from John for good, they're getting divorced."

"Right," I said, wanting to add, So what, what does it have to do with me? But I didn't.

"You know Dad is living with Uncle Tom."

"No," I said, not really giving a damn.

"Yeah, the tart took him to the cleaners, gobshite."

It wasn't that I minded Gavin calling, he was my little brother after all and under normal circumstances I would have been happy to see him. But these weren't normal times, I still had open wounds and I still had nightmares. Being dragged back into the turbulent world of my family was something I just wasn't ready for. In the past month I had worked hard for Tina, as a way to thank her, but also as a way to forget.

Later that evening, I mentioned to Tina that I had had a visitor. She went and got two glasses and we sat down and discussed what Gavin had told me. I told her about my history with my father and how he now had to live with his brother. It wasn't easy opening up like this, but Tina had a way of getting you to talk, even if you really didn't want to.

Following on from our conversation, a couple of days later I was surprised when Tina came to me with the suggestion that I should make contact with my father. I guessed she thought it would provide some sort of healing.

"Tina, you've no idea what the man is like," I said, trying desperately to pour cold water on the suggestion.

"Yes, but he's vulnerable now, you mightn't get another chance. How would you feel if something happened to him?"

The question pretty much knocked the wind from me. "He probably wouldn't want to see me anyway."

"Well, there's only one way to find out. Come on, get your coat."

"No Tina, I don't think..."

"I'm the boss, get your coat," she mocked, making light of it.

I don't think there would have been another person on the planet who could have coaxed me into that car. But Tina was very persuasive, when she wanted to be.

Seeing my father again was really difficult for me. I was still really angry with him, and in truth I had no idea why I was standing on his doorstep. When he opened the door he acted like nothing had happened.

"Hi my name is Tina, I thought you should know that your daughter is okay and that she's staying with me at the moment."

"Right," he said as if he was talking to someone selling lines.

"It's a wee bit nippy, can't we come in?" Tina continued.

"Yeah, come on in," he said, with as much enthusiasm as a wet hanky. "There's nothing in, so you'll have to make do with tea."

"Listen, I fancy a drink, why don't you come back and see where Lisa is staying? I've plenty of wine, or there's whisky if you prefer."

When we got back to the house, Tina put on the works; booze, smokes, nibbles, music. My father danced, drank and ate as happy as you like. And when it came time to go, he called a cab, stepped out and pulled me to one side.

"I just want you to know your friend's a tart," he said.

Throughout the night I had treated his presence pretty much how I would if a Bengal tiger had been in the room. I had seen his claws and felt his teeth, and I knew eventually he would get round to stripping a limb or two from me – and there it was, after everything Tina had done. I was angry this time, not only for me but also for Tina. In the month I had lived with her we had become close. I had feelings for her, which in truth, weren't strictly platonic. It wasn't just her looks, it was everything. I might have fallen for her the very first day I met her or it might have been the second day in the car, whenever it was, I was more than smitten, I was crazy about her.

Obviously my feelings for Tina put me in quite a dilemma. And curiously, it wasn't not being able to act upon them that terrified me, it was her finding out. "That's sweet, but I'm not a lesbian," I could hear her say. And then there would be the pregnant pause, the awkwardness, the gradual melting of the friendship. Maybe I would end up losing my job, my home. Yes, I was afraid, and given where she had rescued me from, I was very afraid.

If there was ever going to be a time in my life that wasn't riddled by fears and complications, I couldn't see it. Even, when things were on the up, I could always trust my gender identity issues to put the lid on how far my positivity could go. With this giant shadow looming eternally on my shoulder, I could never really escape fully into happiness. Even in Florida, I'd had to leave a large part of my aspirations behind to allow myself a very specified kind of happiness, which was for all intents and purposes a happiness that had nothing to do with the happy-ever-after of romantic love. And while this may be possible, if not preferable, for some, I on the other hand had the great misfortune, given my circumstances, of being a hopeless romantic. I wanted the great love affair I had seen in the movies. I wanted the girl, the sun, the moon and the stars. I wanted to touch and to be touched. I wanted to love and to be loved. I wanted so much that was so far out of reach.

My father's visit had burst the bubble that was protecting me somewhat from my feelings for Tina. Not having the stamina to instantly construct a new one, I decided the best thing to do was to get away for a day or two. Anyway, I hadn't seen Becky in a while, so I really should just go.

"Tina, listen," I said, as I explained my plan, "I was wondering if you could give me the wages we discussed, it's been a month now..."

"Sure no problem," she said, cutting me off, "but it's very short notice. Tell you what, how about I give you enough to get there and back. Why don't you get your friends to come here, I've plenty of booze. I'd love to meet them."

"Um... you sure?" I said, a little thrown by the sudden change of plans.

"Of course! Don't be silly, you've told me so much about them. And, I'll get to the bank first thing Monday and sort you out, okay?"

"Brilliant! Um, my friend Becky might have a boyfriend."

"Look, the more the merrier as far as I'm concerned."

When I eventually hooked up with Jen, she told me that Becky was living a couple of miles away with a new boyfriend.

"You know how she gets, don't even bother asking, she won't come out with us."

"No, I was going to ask both of you back to a house in Tottenham."

"What in the shared accommodation?"

"No no, I'm staying with a friend now."

"What friend?"

"One I met through Anita, you remember the girl..." I suddenly remembered that Jen did know Anita and probably hadn't heard. "You know that girl Anita you knew her from the clubs?"

"Yeah, what about her?"

"Well she died."

"Of an overdose?" Jen asked matter-of-factly.

"She took paracetamol."

"Shit, she was okay."

"Yeah, yeah she was."

"So which friend of hers are you living with? I might know her."

"A friend called Tina."

"No shit!" Jen said, laughing.

"You know her?"

"Yeah! She's totally cool. I didn't know she was a lesbian."

"Jen, I told you I'm not a lesbian," I said, putting her straight.

"I know, but I don't believe you. You don't shag men, so what are you?" she said, not understanding how much she was cutting to the quick.

Jen and I took the next bus back to Tina's house in Tottenham. I hardly think that she noticed just how quiet I was. Her throwaway comment had really done some damage, and in my delicate state, there really wasn't too much undamaged flesh left.

As it happened, Jen and Tina knew each other well

enough from the clubs around North London. It didn't matter much that they did because they hit it off so famously any one would have been forgiven for thinking them the best of friends.

With the second bottle of white wine opened, it didn't take long for Jen to pull out a small bag of weed. "You don't smoke it?" Tina asked after I had refused a puff.

"No it's not my thing."

"Me neither, but I'm game for a giggle."

At first I was a little annoyed at Jen for introducing drugs into the mix with Tina. In the month that I had lived with her I had never seen so much as a tablet in the house, so of course, I immediately blamed their presence on Jen. After Mary and Anita, drugs were the last thing I wanted around me. It was as if Jen's presence had somehow soured the air. I was annoyed with her and I was, in truth, sorry that I had invited her especially when her visit was extended, especially when she hugged Tina warmly and promised she would return.

Jen was my friend, yes, but Jen was too connected with drugs. If I could have separated the two I would have been the first to throw my arms around her and welcome her. But Jen was an addict, and how was I supposed to do what a stay at the most expensive rehab couldn't do?

Monday came and my annoyance with Jen had all but worn off. I had worked really hard and I was looking forward to enjoying the fruits of my labour. Money in my pocket meant some independence for me, and this was better than anything I could purchase.

Between the clock in the kitchen and the watch on my arm, I must have checked the time fifty times, waiting for Tina to return. When seven o'clock came and went I assumed she must have got waylaid. I finished what I was doing in the kitchen and settled down in front of the TV to wait for her. I would have liked a drink to sip on, but I never went near any of Tina's drink without her invitation.

It was after ten when Tina finally arrived home. She came into the living room laughing and joking with a businessman, who was a lot older than her. She didn't bother introducing him to me, she just grabbed two bottles from the bar and took him straight up to her room, which was more in the nature of a second sitting-room, only it had a bed.

I continued to watch the film that had started, wishing I had taken my opportunity to ask Tina for my money. I was sure she would give it to me when she got a chance, but that didn't stop me from being anxious to have it. I watched the movie through to the end and went into the kitchen after to make myself a cup of tea. Tina must have sneaked in quietly, because when I turned she was already sliding onto a high stool.

"Pour me a chardonnay, would you love?" she said, pulling her white satin robe into place.

I placed the glass in front of her and passed her a cigarette.

"Did you manage to get to the bank today?" I asked, hoping she had.

"For what, love?" she said, lighting her cigarette.

"You know, for my wages."

"Oh yes, hand me that slim notebook over there, will you."

She slid her cigarette to the side of her mouth as she flicked through the pages.

"Right well from my account, you owe me nearly three hundred quid, give or take a bottle of wine here or there that I threw in as a freebie."

"Right!" I said laughing.

"Your tab for all the drink and drugs you've used," She said, sliding the book towards me.

"But I don't understand."

"What don't you understand?"

"You're joking, right?"

"Do I look like I'm fucking joking?"

"But I haven't used any drugs and I only drank what you gave me."

"Your friend, Jen had some Coke, didn't she? Don't you remember us agreeing that you would run a tab?"

"But I thought you were messing."

"Sweetheart, if there's one thing I don't mess about with, it's money people owe me."

"But it's not what you said Tina! I've done all this work."

"And you'll see where I deducted for that."

"But..."

"Listen, if you think it's not fair fine, there's the door, but you pay me before you leave."

"You know I don't have it."

"Why don't I send someone to see your dad and we can ask him to settle up?"

"He doesn't have it, none of them do."

"Well then, we'll have to find another way for you to pay me off, won't we?"

"What ways? How?"

"Don't you worry, there's plenty for you to do. For a start, I've a friend coming over tomorrow, she needs help with a bit of charity collecting."

Laying my head on my pillow later that night, I felt again the gnawing ache in the pit of my stomach that was all too familiar. My head felt heavy with the burden of trying to shift through what had just transpired downstairs. Trying to make some sense of it, I replayed the scene from the car over and over, trying to pinpoint the exact details of our agreement. I couldn't have got it so wrong, could I? No matter how many times the re-run played, I just couldn't get to the place Tina was. *No, you didn't get it wrong, you couldn't have*, I told myself, throwing my legs out of the bed. I hadn't got it wrong, I was sure of it. But this was cold comfort, because it left me once again waist-high in quicksand.

But if I was right, then what the hell was Tina playing at? I had feelings for Tina, strong feelings, and the last hour just didn't add up. The utter confusion I felt was too much for me; it felt like my brain was slowly being pulled apart. Why did this keep happening to me? The tears rose to the surface. I got back into the bed and turned to the wall. I kept my eyes open as my chest heaved out my sobs for Mary, for Anita and for myself.

In the morning, I headed for the kitchen with my eyes puffy and my mood as low as it had been on the first day that I entered that house. The thought had struck me as I walked quietly down the stairs that maybe I should make a run for it. But it was quickly squashed out of fear of Tina turning up at my father's door. I was now deeply sorry that I had taken her there that night. I wasn't sure if it wasn't all bluff, but not being sure, I was afraid to take the risk.

Entering the kitchen, I was surprised to see two large white buckets in the middle of the island.

"You ready to go?" a girl's voice asked coming from behind.

"No, I want to get some tea."

"Well, hurry up," the girl said, well wrapped up for the wet March weather. Her name was Fiona, and I had seen her a couple of times in the house. Tina had not mixed us socially, but I did have a little chat with her on one occasion when she came into the kitchen looking for water. I just presumed she was a dance client.

Fiona sat at the counter, picking flakes of paint from her fingers.

"So what are we doing today?" I asked, not liking the silence.

"Holding a bucket, if that's not too complicated for you."

"I'm going to get my coat," I said, throwing the rest of my tea in the sink.

The two previous times I had met Fiona she had appeared very bubbly and very friendly. This was like a different person sitting in front of me from the seventeen-year-old who told me she was going back to Northern Ireland after a gap year to study psychology.

When I came back into the room. Fiona was already standing with the buckets.

"Here," she said thrusting one at me.

"What are we collecting for?"

"Sick children. Anyone asks you anything, keep your mouth shut and send them over to me."

"Why would I have to keep my mouth shut?"

"Because your job is to hold the bucket. Now come on."

Going out the door, I knew deep down that the children would see very little of the money I would collect, if any. I knew it, but I didn't want to admit it. The knock-on effect of admitting I was being sent out to steal was too much for me to handle. What I should have done, at that very moment, was tell Tina and Fiona to shove it, but my mind kept telling me that if I left I would just be creating a far greater mess that I would have no control over. It seemed my mind was also conspiring against me, by fooling me into believing I had control when there was clearly none.

I got back to Tina's after the days collecting to find Jen sitting on the couch, totally out of it. I don't know if Tina had gone looking for her or whether she had just turned up, but either way I wasn't happy to see her.

"What are you doing here, Jen?" I asked, tugging a response out of her.

"I've moved in," she said laughing. "Her too," she said pointing limply at Fiona, who had just walked in.

"You moving in?" I asked, turning to Fiona.

"What's it to you," she said, walking through to the kitchen.

"You're not moving in," I whispered to Jen as I left her to follow Fiona into the kitchen.

Fiona had already had the money spread out on the kitchen table. Tina was leaning with her back to the counter looking straight at me.

"Good day Lisa?" she said brightly.

"Jen says she's moving in?"

"I thought you'd be pleased. Fiona's moving in too, so you'll have to bunk up with Jen."

"What's she on?"

"What am I, her keeper?"

"You putting that on my tab too?" I said, finally letting some anger rip out.

"Listen sweetheart, Jen knows the score, you get drugs from me, you owe me."

"What, are you like some lowlife drug dealer now?"

Tina stopped in her tracks and turned to Fiona, "Sweetheart, you going to let her talk to me like that?"

Next moment, Fiona lunged at me, caught the top of my head and dragged me down onto the island.

"What the hell?" I screamed as a searing pain shot through my forehead.

"You shut your mouth, bitch," she snarled, pressing my face into the cold marble.

"Let me up!" I screamed, trying to wrestle free.

"Let her up," Tina said, shutting the knife and fork drawer and coming beside me.

I pulled myself up and with fright backed myself up against the sink, seeing the large carving knife dangling from Tina's hand.

"Go on Fiona, show her what happens when you think you can do what you like."

I looked on in horror as Fiona rolled up her sleeve to reveal a three-inch knife scar. The sight of the red knotted skin punched a hole through my stomach. I was powerless by the time the cold blade ran playfully along my neck.

"You owe me, I own you. You think you can stitch me up, try it. You think about doing anything stupid like that whimpering fucker Anita, I'll use this on her, then you."

Tensing my neck, I looked out at Jen curled up on the couch and I knew that that Tina wouldn't hesitate slicing her.

"And after that I might even take a trip to your father. I know where he lives now, don't I?"

"I'm sorry... I'm sorry" I said, crumbling.

"You should be. Count yourself lucky I don't add the money you cost me losing Anita," she said, tapping the blade against my chin.

"Please Tina, I didn't do anything with Anita."

"She asked for your help and you made tea."

"It wasn't my fault, please," I whimpered.

"Wasn't it? Fiona, you'd know this, doesn't every minute count in those situations?"

"Sure does," Fiona spat, moving about the kitchen like a caged beast awaiting the master's orders.

I had nothing left, I looked up at Tina and sobbed, "Please!"

Tina lowered the knife and stroked my hair. "Oh it doesn't have to be that bad, we have fun, don't we Fiona?"

"Lots," Fiona grinned, leaning against a counter and biting her nails.

"Why don't we grab a bottle of wine and take it up to my bedroom, you feel like partying?" she asked, as sweet as ever.

I just couldn't bring myself to answer, so instead I just nodded.

"No? Wine not good enough? You want to try something better?" she continued, slapping me full in the face. "See how happy Jen is."

"Wine will be great," I said, choking back the tears.

"So now you want to party?"

"Yes, I want to party, I really want to party, please," I said, a lamb to a lion.

"Do I get my treat now, for being so good today?" Fiona asked excitedly. The aggression, the jitters, it all made sense now. She was obviously craving the same thing Jen was on – crack cocaine.

"Come on over here, sugar," Tina said, pulling a little plastic bag into sight.

Fiona walked over and stood attentively as Tina opened the bag and smeared a little across her own lips, inviting Fiona to come and get it, which she eagerly did. Tina had used Fiona's insecurities about being a lesbian to great effect. She was a master manipulator, she had to be, for how else could she stir a clever A-student from her bright future to this?

Divulging all my vulnerability to the one person you shouldn't, I had fallen headlong into the spider's web and now, just like Jen, just like Fiona, I was well and truly trapped.

CHAPTER 11

— ∞ —

In a matter of weeks, Fiona had gone from a bright star to a half-crazed crack junkie whose only function was to serve her habit by serving Tina. I, on the other-hand, had become enslaved through fear. Through homeliness, I had encountered varying amounts of good and bad in people, but never before had I encountered a person who dished out cruelty with such revelry. It was like she got off on it, as if the destruction of others sustained her. I don't know how the darkness had consumed Tina in the first place - I only know that at this time, it had consumed her completely.

Once the veil of pretence had lifted, Tina, in all her horrible glory, came into view; prostitution, crime-gangs, drug-dealing, blackmail, coercion, you name it, there was nothing too low for Tina. While, she had Jen under her roof, she was confident that the fear, the booze was enough to keep me put. However, as soon as she found out who Jen was, and that her family were on the lookout for her, Jen was swiftly departed. After that, I guess she saw it as imperative for me to get hooked on drugs as well.

"You going to take it?"

"No" I said, time and time again, knowing full well that I would have to sustain another beating for my refusal.

Looking back now on the game we played, I think in some twisted way, Tina enjoyed my final stand. She knew by now after a couple of months that I wasn't going anywhere, so this was just another of the little games she played. In truth, with a knife to my neck, there really wasn't very much I could have done but to take the drugs in that scenario, but I think Tina liked the feel of her fist against my flesh. She liked the standing over me and feeling her foot press into my stomach. She liked the grovelling, she liked the tears, and she liked the power she had to come and kneel beside me to kiss it all away.

After Jen's hasty departure I knew I wouldn't see her there again. As she couldn't rescue herself I had no such misconceptions about her rescuing me. I knew her family would find her eventually and take her off to rehab, and I hoped for her sake that I would never see her again.

By March my life in the crime gang had already caught up with me. Arrested for shoplifting, I was put on probation for two years. My twenty-first birthday had come and gone, and obviously living with Tina, there was no appropriate celebration. I kept the date to myself, not wanting to give her any more of myself than she already had.

I remember one evening after this, May had arrived and the sun was shining its light off the small cobwebs hanging over my bed. I went down and got a duster and when I returned I hauled the bed away from the wall. I swept the duster through the air and was about to shove the bed back with my leg when I noticed something written at the bottom of the wall: "Anita waz here."

"Oh my God," I said, sitting down on my bed. One by one the pieces all came together. That first night, when the truth came out, Tina had brought up Anita, but with the shock and the terror I didn't have the facilities at the time to pull everything together. But now, I could finally see the awful truth – Anita's suicide wasn't a cry for help, she wanted to escape. She wanted to escape from Tina and had swallowed 70 tablets to make sure she did exactly that.

However bad things were for me at the moment, Anita's mark on the wall told me things were going to get far worse.

* * *

For the next two years, I served my probation and served Tina at the same time. I managed, I don't know how, to avoid the law and to avoid any serious incidents with Tina. The abuse went on, and I guess in a twisted way it became a way of life for me. I relied on Tina for everything. And there were times when she was nice, very nice. As long as I was serving a function, and bringing in money for her, it was in her best interests to throw some scraps at me, now and again.

Suffering as I was from such mental abuse, I guess in many ways her methods institutionalised me into the dependence, into the abuse. I remember one three-month period in particular, when Tina was sent to Holloway for three months on a charge of handling. Before she went inside, she arranged for Fiona and me to live in a hostel she had dealings with. Suffering from a lack of food and security by the time she came to get us, we went back with her willingly. She had broken our ability to see a world outside hers, and she knew it.

In May 1991, when I was 23, my luck with the law finally ran out. I found myself in the back of a van in handcuffs, on my way to Holloway for three weeks. Looking out of the window, I thought of nothing. If I had thought back to my first time being transferred from the court's holding cell to prison, I would have noted how different things were. I had little emotion this time around. The sustained abuse I had endured over the years had all but kicked the emotion out of me.

* * *

Handling, theft, attempting to obtain property by deception, six counts in all, and I for one wasn't contesting it. It was ten months later, March 1992, and I was standing in the dock, this time beside Fiona.

Hearing that we were being held over until trial, wasn't the shock it should have been. *Do your time and forget about it* – doing the crime and getting caught was just part of the life I was leading. After three years of working for Tina I was well and truly institutionalised into a life of crime.

Sitting on my bed, the first morning in Holloway, I looked at my cell door knowing it was about to open. My previous stay had taught me the routine well. I knew how to walk, I knew how to sit and I knew when and where an attack was most likely to take place.

Breakfast, back to the cell, gym or education or work, back to cell. Lunchtime, back to the cell, dinner, back to cell, association (social hour), back to cell, supper, back to cell until morning. That was Holloway.

The first day went by without incident. Fiona and I were

on the same wing, which meant that we saw each other throughout the day, but neither of us made any attempt at communication. Although she had done some pretty deplorable things to me at the behest of Tina, I knew, at the end of the day, that she was as manipulated and abused as I was. I also knew that Fiona had her drug addiction to deal with. I'd imagined it wasn't going to be easy for her going through cold turkey in prison. Still, there was so much bad blood shared between us that I was glad she kept her distance.

Now whilst twenty-three hours of your time was tightly structured, one hour, called 'association', was not. This was the only time during the day when you got to socialise with others on your wing. You had the choice of watching TV or just hanging out in each other's cells. This was the one hour you really looked forward to when you had nothing but friends, but it was the time you dreaded when you had enemies.

Whilst inside, I was always looking over my shoulder. Tina had ways and means of getting to you, even inside, if she really wanted to. The question I asked myself over and over was, did she really want to? Fiona was the most likely tool she would use, and she hadn't once come within ten feet of me. Still, Tina was so volatile you just never knew when something would inspire her to give the word.

By the third day I had stopped looking over my shoulder, feeling the chances of a "message" coming from Tina had diminished significantly. It wasn't like I was going anywhere anyway, I said to myself, rationalising the reason why I could relax and forget about Tina, for the time being. And so, taking my own advice, I did exactly that.

"Do you know what's on tonight?" I asked a grey-haired woman who was taking a seat beside her, in front of the TV.

"Don't know love, they never tell ya," she said, bending to take up her knitting. "You knit?"

"No."

"You should, it'll keep you sane."

"Here we go," I said, as the TV was turned on.

"Shh, shh! " she hissed, telling me straight, that it was time to shut up.

I smiled and crossed my legs. She was allowed to have her idiosyncrasies, an extended amount of time inside will do that to you. I was about to lower myself into a more comfortable position when I found myself being hauled out onto the floor. It was my right shoulder that took the full force of my fall, but then came the pain in my back as a fist dug deep into my arch. Next my face felt the pain of being shoved into the hard floor. Struggling to free myself, I became semi-aware of a ring of shouts, whistles and cat-calls forming around me. And then suddenly the voices dimmed as the sirens began to wail. Knowing any moment the guards would be on us only intensified the attack. Managing to twist my body around, I pulled my arms up in front of my face. I already knew it was Fiona; I didn't need to see her, I knew it the moment I smashed into the floor.

It took four guards to drag Fiona off me. With the drugs and the adrenaline, by the time they arrived, she was half-crazed.

"She fucking owns you, you're nothing, she owns you, fucker!" she screamed.

"No one owns me, you hear, no one!" I screamed coming towards her.

"Get back! Get back!" a guard warned, placing her baton in front of me.

After Fiona was escorted off the wing, I went back to my wing. I sat down on my bed and cried my eyes out.

Fiona was given solitary for two days. The day after, she was back on the wing. She huddled with two other girls, and by the looks of them every one of them was a drug addict of one sort of another. Bribes, blackmail, services rendered, God knows how Tina managed to get the drugs in, but she did. In reality, she could have got to me on day one, but she waited, toying with me. She waited until I felt safe, and then in one moment she took it away from me.

After my attack, I knew life on the wing would soon become an endless wait for trouble. Not only was Fiona sent to the block, she was also put on report, which meant that luxuries were taken from her. One thing you could be sure of inside was the swift arrival of payback. I knew Fiona would seek revenge, I just didn't know how.

During the day, I worked to make up a little spending money at the end of the week, and I went to the gym. Four days had passed since the attack and Fiona hadn't even looked at me. I had made up my mind, the first day after the attack, to go to the gym daily – I suppose it was a psychological exercise to convince myself that I could have some control over my future.

Moving back to my cell after working out in the gym, I did feel a little strength growing, not only in my arms but also in my resolve. Next time she comes for me I would be ready. That was my mantra, that was what helped me push through the pain of every moment.

"In the gym again?" Gladys asked. She was the woman with the knitting. Everywhere she went Gladys took her knitting, and no one messed with her.

"Yeah, in the gym again Gladys. What are you knitting there?"

"Bonnets for the babies," she said, stepping into her cell, which was two up from mine.

I smiled at the thought as I walked into my cell.

It took a split-second for me to realise what had happened. First there was the sickening stench, which made my stomach convulse immediately. Turning to the door, I knew I had a few seconds to get out before lock-down to draw the guards to me. If I went now that's exactly what would happen. The guards would come, they would see the excrement covering my cell; the walls, the bedding, my clothes, everything. They would be sick just like me, they would want to know who did it, and they would then go to Fiona's cell. A split-second, I could do it, but then I thought, if I do this will never end.

The doors locked and I turned with my arm firmly pressed against my nose. I would deal with it myself, if it emptied all of my stomach and took me the night, I would deal with it.

The next day, I washed and dried my belongings as best I could without drawing any attention to them. I also went to one of the guards and put in a request for a transfer to another wing.

Later than night, I lay on my clean bed with a monumental decision cooking in my head – get hurt or get hard. I knew, in the world that I was in, being soft-natured was a liability. And I also knew that becoming hard meant more than a couple of weeks in the gym. It meant forgoing one's nature for survival. And maybe that's what it would take. If I was ever to free myself of Tina, maybe I would have to become as cold and manipulative as her.

Logical as it all sounded, I just couldn't shut down a small amount of resistance to the one thing that would guarantee my physical survival – the hardening of my heart. As the wing began to grow silent, voice by voice, I closed my eyes and asked God, in his infinite wisdom, to decide if there was anything in my heart worth the debate.

* * *

The next morning, I was woken up to the news that my transfer request had been approved. I had never before apportioned any thanks to God for any of my good fortune. Even the miracle of Florida had gone by unnoticed, but when I packed up my things and left Fiona and her cronies behind, God finally took the credit. Walking onto the new wing, I suddenly felt a piece of the world lift from my shoulders. And in that fleeting moment of uplift, I was made privy to an important truth; Just because you give up on life, it doesn't mean life gives up on you. When I had called, something had come through the darkness and listened.

Regardless of the amount of praise I gave up to God in those initial moments walking onto the new wing, by the next morning, all was forgotten. And yet, despite the severance of my conscious connection, the blessing continued.

Shortly after my arrival on the new wing, a girl named Carol popped in to say hello. A year or two younger than me, her story was like all the rest; a one-way ticket onto the streets via a dysfunctional home. And her charge sheet wasn't so different from the rest either – a litany of shoplifting offences. After a string of probation and community service orders, Carol finally found herself in Holloway serving a six-month sentence.

Carol and I hit it off immediately. Unlike so many of the other girls inside at this time, Carol was clean, which was, as in my case, a minor miracle. It didn't take long before we were spending association time in one or another of our rooms. I really enjoyed our time together. Carol was sweet and very unassuming. And it only took two days for our friendship to turn physical.

Thrown together in such unusual circumstances, many of the women, with boyfriends or husbands, developed romantic relationships. In Carol's case, she believed me to be her first lesbian relationship.

"I don't know what's happening, I've never even looked at a girl before," I remember her saying, cuddled up beside me one evening.

"Well, I'm not really a girl. I'm a tomboy," I said, feeling the pangs, but making light of it all the same.

Carol and I were only together two weeks when another miracle occurred – immediate release. As it transpired, the case against me was dropped due to lack of evidence, whilst Fiona had to stand trial and was convicted.

As I walked out of the prison gates the next morning, there was no mention of God upon my lips. No, God was neither being praised nor cursed as I walked out, of my own accord, straight back into the clutches of Tina, standing beside her car.

"Come on, get into the car!" she said, bracing her slim frame. She had been leaning against the car, shades on, feet crossed, waiting for me. Someone, I don't know who, must have tipped her off about my release time, so it was made all so easy for her. If there had been another car waiting for me, a friend, a family member, I might have had the courage to defy her, but there wasn't. I might have again called out to God, but neither my faith nor my will was strong, and so I remained silent. Fear still had its collar on me, and it had given Tina the leash.

"I told you I'd look after you. Someone had to go down, I

could have chosen you, but I choose Fiona. Now what does that say to you?"

"It says you care about me."

"That's right, I'm the only person in the world who cares about you, isn't that right?"

"Yeah, that's right." I didn't believe any of it, it was just the game we played.

The moment I entered the car was the moment, through the exercising of my free will, when I determined the course of my life. I could say that fear left me with no choice, and this is true, but ultimately the fear was of my own making. And although I didn't know it at the time, I ultimately had the power within to build up or tear down the walls of fear. I could have stood my ground, I could have been bold, I could have summoned the power within me, but knowing none of this, I did nothing. I was compliant and I was complicit.

Straight back I went into 'the life', and within a couple of months I was back inside for a week. Then out again and straight back into the life. And curiously, despite all the odds, I managed, unlike so many, to maintain myself within the chaos – I took my beatings, I suffered my loneliness, I endured my desperation, and I numbed my emotions, as best I could. I placed a thick metal mesh over my heart, over my mind and I went on, and I never gave up. I never gave up because somewhere deep inside was a certainty that my life wasn't going to end this way.

In May 1993, when I was 25, I was imprisoned for the fifth time. *You find me, once again, in a cell in Holloway, and I'm turning to you again for a miracle, because I'm low, I'm empty and I don't know how much more I can take.* This was the gist of what I said, staring into the darkness with a nine-month stretch ahead of me.

Even with my curtains open there was no light, and even

with the blankets tucked under my chin there was no warmth, and with only thoughts of what I might face in the morning, there was no peace. Five years of the life had taken its toll.

At 7 am, I would hear the wake-up bangs on my door. An hour later I would hear the lock being drawn back. Shortly after I would join the exodus being herded towards the canteen. I would find myself once again amongst the population of the toughest woman's prison in the country, and I would quickly get a taste of what my time was going to be like inside. If I found a saviour, a protector, as I had with Beth, then life would be bearable, but if not, Fiona, who had once again been sent down with me, would work endlessly to maintain her drug supply by make my life a living hell.

The next morning, I walked with my tea and toast towards a table. For me, this judgement morning was probably the worst of all the trials one faced inside. It was like walking on the edge of hell, never knowing if you were going to be the one singled out to be cast into the flames. And, on top of this, I knew a message from Tina was en route.

Knowing there wasn't anything else to do, I kept my head down and took my place at an empty table. And to my utter relief it remained empty. It remained empty right up to the day, a fortnight later, when I got word that I was being transferred, just as I had been nearly seven years before, to Cookham Wood open prison, in Kent.

Being in Cookham Wood again, crazy as it sounds, actually felt really good. My first stay in the facility had been as easy as prison can be, thanks to Beth, and besides that I really liked the idea of being so far away from London and so far away from Tina. It was the first time in five years I felt her clutch loosen.

It was two weeks after arriving in Cookham Wood that I noticed a girl called Jamie. She was tall with long black hair, olive skin and the most amazing deep brown eyes. Although I didn't know her name at the time, I had seen her before. It was a week or so after I said goodbye to Carol in Holloway. I had come to see Carol, and Jamie was sitting at a table with her mother.

"They're letting me out next week," Carol said quietly.

"Hey, that's good isn't it?" I said, registering her apprehension.

"Yeah, but well, I'll be going back to my old life."

"Okay."

"I have a boyfriend, and well..."

"Oh, so why didn't you say?"

"I don't know, you know how it is inside."

"Yeah, look, friends?"

"Yeah, friends."

"Do you know that girl?" I asked, glancing across at Jamie.

"No, why?"

"Just thought I recognised her," I said, lying. The truth was I couldn't take my eyes off her. Even in the midst of getting dumped, my main focus was Jamie.

It took me a month to get up the courage to approach Jamie, and to my delight we hit it off immediately. I don't know what it was, but there was a definite chemistry between us, which both of us felt.

"So what you in for?" I remember asking, soon after our friendship was established.

"Drug smuggling, I got four years."

"Shit."

"Yeah, still two years down, two to go."

"You might get time off?"

"Nah, not for drug smuggling. My solicitor tells me there's a good chance my citizenship will be revoked and I'll be deported back to the States after."

"Shit."

Although Jamie had been born in New York, her mother was born in Liverpool, which is why she had dual citizenship. Her father, who was out of the picture early on, was Romanian, which is why she had her gorgeous looks.

"You know your cell is one of the most boring, sorry excuses I've seen," she said.

"Yeah, well take it up with the governor," I said, teasingly.

"Don't you have anything to put up?" she said, pointing to the walls.

"Nah," I said, lying, because the truth was that I had a whole heap of sexy swimwear models and actresses under my bed.

"Why don't you have any skirts or dresses?" Jamie asked, rifling through my clothes. We were that friendly now, she knew I wouldn't mind this level of intimacy.

"I never liked girly stuff even as a child."

"You were like a tomboy?"

"Yeah I was. That's what they all said, my Mum and all, since I was small. I don't know, I was just always into more boy stuff," I said, feeling a great ravine open up in front of me. As I stood looking at Jamie, who had her back to me as she settled my clothes, I knew this was another do or die moment, another chance to take my leap of faith. All I had to do was to verbalise my feelings, that I was a man trapped inside a woman's body, but how do you do that when you don't understand it yourself? How do you explain to someone, when you can't explain it to yourself? The answer was I had no answers, and I had no idea how to leap into the unknown. Fear was all I knew, and fear is what I continued to abide by.

"Actually, I lied," I said, doing a U-turn with the conversation.

"About what?" she said, turning about with a serious look on her face.

"About these," I said bending under my bed and grabbing my pile of pin-ups.

"Wow," she said, shuffling through my stash. Amid the models and the actresses there were a few pretty boy bands to allow for a multiple of conclusions. Maybe Jamie would label me as a lesbian and run a mile and maybe she wouldn't; maybe she'd think of me as a messed-up tomboy with aspirations to become a swan; and maybe she'd...

"Let's put them up!" she said, shoving the pile into my chest. "Hang on, I'll get tape."

In an instant she was back with tape, and in another instant the posters were up, and in another instant I had turned my back well and truly on my leap of faith. Whatever Jamie thought of me it didn't seem to matter, because next she had her hands on my collar and was pressing her lips hard against mine, and I knew I would love her forever.

After our bodies parted we looked at each other, one trying to read the other.

"You know I'm not a lesbian," Jamie said, laughing.

"Neither am I," I said with a deep hidden sadness. Maybe this was as close to the truth as I was ever going to get.

"Do you care if that's what they'll think?"

"Do you?"

"No. I think we were meant to meet, so I don't care, it's how I feel. Is it how you feel?"

"Yes."

"Can we kiss again?" She came closer.

"Yes."

From that moment Jamie and I were inseparable. I needed her desperately, and she seemed to need me. Having a soft and gentle love in my life was spellbinding. Jamie had a way about her that made me feel not only wholly loved but wholly safe. Day after day we would spend caring for each other, and day by day I started to open up to her. Whilst I couldn't bring myself to speak about my sexuality, I could make amends, in my mind, by telling her the truth about my life with Tina. And whilst my whole relationship with Tina could have been summed up with the obvious question: "Why did you stay?" Jamie listened without judgement while I tried to make some sense of it all for her, for me.

I know it's hard for many who have never been in an abusive relationship to understand why people don't run from them, whether it be crime-related, as in my case, or domestic abuse, as in so many other cases. For me the simple answer was fear – not only of physical retribution, but of having to survive by myself. Five years of sustained abuse had rendered me childlike. It had stolen all my power and all my wisdom and was well on its way to draining every drop of love and humanity from me. And so, like a child, the only thing that kept me going was the hope that someday, by some miracle, things would get better – someday, Tina would stop being so cruel, someday Tina would treat me with respect, and even, perhaps, someday, Tina would love me. I built up my prison with fear and fortified it with the illusion of hope – hope controlled by someone else.

Day after day Jamie listened and guided me.

"You have to know it will never end. If you go back again

you'll either end up like Anita or she'll wind up killing you, you know this, don't you?"

Yes, I knew it, logically it made sense, but five years of blocking out the truth had made my logic somewhat twisted. The truth was I just couldn't imagine the possibility of an alternative life. My mind had been warped, my logic twisted, and I needed somehow to go deep inside to erase the enormous damage that had been done to me. Whilst Jamie couldn't erase everything, no matter how much she tried, with her love and her persistence the light slowly started to dawn.

"You know, I met her," I remember Jamie telling me whilst sitting together outside.

"No!" I said becoming suddenly uneasy.

"Yeah, in Holloway before I came here, so I know what I'm talking about when I say she's just a manipulative slag."

"Did you ever speak to her?" I asked hesitantly.

"She tried it on, as she does, and I basically told her to go fuck herself. Somebody like her wouldn't intimidate me, I've seen the likes of her and far worse. You've just bigged her up in your mind, that's all it is."

"Yeah, maybe."

"No, definitely! I'll be in here minimum another year, what are you going to do, go back to her?"

"No."

"No, that's right because she's only a stupid whore, right?"

"Right."

"I've been speaking to a few of the girls and they say the hostel on Holloway Road will keep you safe. We're going to get you there, away from her. Right?"

"Right."

The fact that Jamie had met "the enemy" so to speak,

and had stood up to her, gave her words an added punch. And the more she coached me, the more I started to piece together the fabric of another life. As yet it was a patchwork, but it was now visible in my mind's eye, and I could believe it was really possible.

Another thing that went a long way to instilling hope in me was Jamie's own past. Like so many of us, Jamie had been flung from a broken home into a world that preyed on the never-ending supply of teenage desperation.

"Yeah, we all have our tests, our trials, but this is it for me," she said. "I'm never going back to that life. That's why I chose to do my time here."

Again, like so many, Jamie had gone from dysfunctionality to the streets to drugs and to the wrong people. And before she knew it, she was on a plane to London with cocaine strapped to her stomach.

"Putting the distance between me and them let me see them for what they really are. And you can do the same."

"So what happens if you go back?"

"I have to go back, it's smuggling, I have no choice."

"So what happens?"

"I'm out of it, my Mum is going to help. I'm clean. I'm never going back. I'm worth something you know, and so are you."

"I don't know..."

"What? What don't you know? You know that's exactly what put you where you were. You let others tell you this and that about you. Fuck it! You tell yourself about you, no one else. You got to start loving yourself."

"But how?"

"Tell yourself, over and over, fucking lie, whatever, tell yourself until you believe it, because one day you will."

"I suppose."

"Here," she said, going to her pocket and pulling out a silver pendant. "This is for you, I got it when I was a child. It's a guardian angel."

"Wow, it's gorgeous, but I couldn't..."

"No, I want you to have it. It'll keep you safe when I'm not there."

I knew Jamie couldn't have had many childhood keepsakes, so her present meant the world to me.

So from that day until my release I had a guardian angel by my side, one I could see. For Jamie's part, she worked tireless to help me recover from some of the damage that years with Tina had inflicted upon me. Day by day, she worked to build my resolve to finally break out of the net that I was in.

The first thing Jamie helped me to do was to ignore all of Tina's calls and letters. And when she resorted to passing messages through other prisoners, Jamie would simply turn and say, "They're just words, don't attach any emotion to them and they stay just words."

And sure enough, little by little, day by day, with Jamie beside me, I began to feel the shackles of fear loosen from me. The time I spent with Jamie over the summer of 1993 were without doubt the most loving moments of my life.

And then, one morning with over three months still to serve, I got notified that I was being released.

Leaving Jamie was hard. Neither of us wanted to say goodbye, but both of us knew we had our own paths to walk. Jamie had another year in prison, after which, we both knew, the Government would send her back to the States. I, on the other hand, had to figure out how I was going to come back from so many years of physical and emotional abuse. Strongly as we felt for each other, we both recognised that the faith that had put us together, for its own very good reasons, was now pulling us apart.

CHAPTER 12

—⚭—

I was released from prison on the 15th of October, 1993. This time no one was waiting for me as I walked out into the cold uncertainty of a grey Friday morning. And much as Jamie's words strengthened me, I still walked with one eye over my shoulder, feeling the company of the many demons that had bedded with me for these last five years.

Still, there was that light of determination that Jamie had help light that one day I would walk straight, free from their influence. As I looked up at the sky, not a dot of blue could I see, yet somehow the grey wasn't its usual mix of gloom and depression. I had called out my demons, I had acknowledged their residence, and I had made an oath to myself that every day from here on I would work to cast them out, one by one.

As I sat on the train taking me back to London, there wasn't a headline about the Loch Ness Monster to distract my mind, there wasn't alcohol to dim it or denial and illusion to fool it. Looking out at the world speeding by, my mind was free to wander inward, which was neither a comfortable or a natural experience for me. Having had no peace for over a decade, my mind had willingly given in to every control and manipulation – anything to avoid the unacceptable reality of who I was.

Stepping onto the concrete of London, I could feel the rush of unease rise in my stomach. Despite my mantra that this time was different, there was always the jeering back-chatter that quipped relentlessly at my stupidity. Without Jamie by my side, standing up straight wasn't so easy. Between the swirls of my stomach and my head, I caught my breath long enough to understand that healing would neither come easily or come at once.

The first baby-step in the right direction came with my placement in a hostel run by the prison service. Going straight there meant I had four solid walls of safety around me. This hostel had strict rules to protect vulnerable ex-prisoners from the people wishing to pull them back into their old lives – people such as drug-dealers, pimps and crime-bosses – or in Tina's case, all three.

The room I was allocated was bright and welcoming. By force of habit, the first few nights I guardedly watched the door. It was easy to be so optimistic, so brave when Jamie was around me – not so easy when I was alone. I had in the past, out of sheer desperation, run from Tina, but each time she found me and the beatings I received had got worse with each escape. It soon got to the point where I was too afraid to run – the beatings were that bad. One minute she would be laughing with me, stroking my hair, and the next she'd put a knife to my throat. "Beg for your life, sweetie." It was all a game to her.

So it did take a while for me to sit easy, to just sit in a room and not worry about who was going to hurt you. But in time, as the weeks moved on, I did start to sit a little easier.

Although a sort of uneasy peace regarding my survival had started to stir within me, the days in the hostel were long and lonely. At this stage in my life I had no one other than Jamie. My family, Becky and Jen, had all fallen away, lost in their own worlds, and this made me miss Jamie all the more. I did what I could, with the limited means that were provided to me in the form of state aid, to keep the relationship with Jamie alive. I made the long trip to visit her as often as I could and I phoned her daily. When I wasn't visiting, writing or phoning her, I kept myself to myself, mainly in my room, either reading or watching television.

I remember sitting on my bed and watching the news of the Nobel Peace Prize being awarded to Nelson Mandela and Frederik Willem de Klerk for their work to end apartheid and build a new democratic South Africa. It made me feel happy to know that momentous positive change was possible. I lay back on my bed and closed my eyes. It was not in my habit to let myself think upon my future, but, I guess being so inspired, I allowed myself to dream a little. If a country like South Africa, with its tumultuous past, could change, maybe there was hope for everyone – even me.

* * *

A couple of days later, I braved all my fears and reached out for help in the form of counselling. I had no real idea just how emotionally scarred I was until I sat in front of my counsellor and looked blankly into her face. How do you start? Where do you start? I just didn't know. For over a decade I had longed for someone to come along and sit me down and explain the whys and wheres of my life. I reasoned that if only I could make some sense of it all, garner some meaning, then maybe, just maybe, I could endure, I could get through it and I could prevail. But there, sitting in the nice comfy room with its pale yellow walls and its pleasant-looking female counsellor, I felt only terror.

"How do you feel?"

"Uncomfortable and terrified."

"Of what?"

"I don't know."

But I did, I felt absolutely terrified that if I began to even scratch the surface I might very well fall asunder. I left the room feeling incredibly insignificant and frightened. How do you verbalize the traumas of your life to a stranger? How do you verbalize them to yourself?

After the session, which didn't last all that long, I went back to my room and sat on my bed. From within I could feel a great surge of emotion rising, but instead of forcing it back down I let it pass. I let it rise up and overcome me. I let the tears fall and my realities take shape. I saw myself as broken and frightened. I saw the years of trauma accumulated inside me. I saw the long hard road ahead. I saw the courage, the fortitude, the trust and blind faith that was required. I saw the many monsters waiting to pull me back down. I sat and I acknowledged it all. And while I doubted whether I would have the inner strength to fix myself, I resolved before I gave myself over to sleep that I would at least take the leap of faith necessary to find out.

The next day I phoned Jamie and told her that I had had my first counselling session. Jamie's words were so supportive. She made me believe in myself way beyond my own capability.

"How will I cope with it all?"

"One step at a time. Have faith."

In truth all I had was faith, because I had absolutely no idea how I was going to heal the wounds of my past. All the rejection, the insecurity, the abuse, the violence, the deprivation and harrowing senseless death, all of the traumatic events of my past had gouged out their own unique hiding place within me. I knew this as well as I knew that every one of these demons would have to be dragged to the surface in order to be cast from me. This terrified me. And yet even more frightening was my hidden battle with my identity – beyond all the trauma the reality of my gender identity terrified me the most. While I could imagine coming to terms eventually with all the traumatising events of my life, I just couldn't see how I would ever come to terms with my gender identity. Life had presented me with so many perfect opportunities to share my pain and confusion with people who had meant something to me, people like Becky and Jamie and even Leah in Florida, but every time when the choice was presented I let the fear silence me. I let fear make the choice for me, which, I see now, was always the wrong choice. The issue with my gender identity was now so enormous that I felt as if I was standing at the foot of Mount Everest knowing that I would never in my lifetime climb it. It was huge. It was daunting. And it had beaten me down and forced me to live a life in duality. It was a duality that was tearing me apart, yet all I had to do was open my mouth and speak the truth and I just couldn't do it. Not even to Jamie, not even to the love of my life.

And it was this, my inability to speak my truth to Jamie, which remains my biggest regret. There are many "What ifs" I guess in everybody's life. In mine, the biggest is, "What if I had told Jamie?"

As if in compensation for my inability to deal with my gender identity, I resolved to get my life, schizophrenic as it was, back on track with future counselling. I also resolved to do what I could to keep my relationship with Jamie alive. Christmas was approaching and I put all my positive thinking into what to get Jamie as a present.

"Why don't we get a love necklace, you know two halves of the same heart," Jamie answered, taking my hand.

"I could get it engraved."

"In Latin?"

"Okay."

"I just think it's romantic... special."

I did as Jamie suggested. She put on her part and I put on mine at the last visit before Christmas. How I wished I could spend the holidays with Jamie. I felt every one of those thousands of miles between us.

* * *

I got through the holidays as best I could. They were lonely and sad, but I got through them. It was a couple of days into the New Year and I was only three days away from my next visit to Jamie. I was so looking forward to seeing her, and as far as I was concerned the New Year wouldn't start until I saw her.

I was on my way out to buy some extra bits for the visit when a knock came to my door. I opened it and my blood ran cold. It was Tina.

"Surprise!" she said, smiling. "Did you miss me?"

Before I could close the door, the girl that was with her shoved her way in.

"You're going to come with us."

"No!"

"I've paid them all off, so don't think anyone's going help."

I still don't truly understand the power Tina held over me. All I know was that I was so scared of her that I walked out and got into the car and let her bring me back to her house.

"So did you miss me?" she said, toying with me. "You like my new pets?"

I nodded, looking at the two pit-bulls sniffing around my ankles. I could imagine her laughter as they gnawed at my legs. I could imagine her smirks as I crumbled once more at her feet. She was beyond my comprehension.

"What's that around your neck?" she asked. "Come over here and let me see."

I could feel the sharp rip at the back of my neck as the chain came off.

"You in love with that American bitch?"

"Give it back."

"You in love?" she taunted, holding the chain away from me. "Feed the dogs, I have to go out."

She left for an hour or so, leaving two others to watch me. Crazy as it sounds, I did exactly what she said. I fed the dogs with a can I found in the cupboard and I sat and waited, fear controlling me once again. And when she got back I stood up and looked at her.

"I fed the dogs."

"What did you feed them?"

"The can, the dog food."

"Come here."

I walked over beside her. It was either going to be a kiss or violence of some sort.

"Fucking dry food not canned food, you stupid bitch!" she said, punching me straight in the nose. I looked down at the splatters of blood hitting the tiles. "And wipe that shit up, you fucking bitch."

As I bent to the floor I could see her feet leaving the room. I cleaned up the blood, put a towel to my nose and walked out the back door. I knew I had to get back to the hostel, one way or the other, because if I didn't I knew I wouldn't go on.

From that day on, my days were limited largely to my room. The safety I had found within the walls of the hostel had been taken by Tina. I called Jamie later that day to find that she had had a call from her.

"It's crazy Jamie, you know what she is like, I haven't been seeing anyone. I'm not having an affair."

"I know you're not, it's okay."

But it wasn't. Tina's campaign to destroy what Jamie and I had was relentless. She phoned, she co-opted witnesses, she did everything to destroy the one good thing in my life. And little by little the dark seeds took root in Jamie. Being locked inside is not a natural existence for a human being. Insecurities, unrealities, paranoia, all can build and take hold. At the back of Jamie's mind also was the gaping question of how we could maintain a relationship, with her in America and me in England. And also, I guess even deeper in her mind was the question of her own sexuality. Jamie had always identified with liking men, so on the surface our relationship was an anomaly to her, one she just couldn't fathom. Her heart knew the truth and her mind couldn't get to grips with it.

And so, my regret, my biggest regret always, was not telling her. If only I had told her the truth about my sexual identity, it would have wiped away all her doubts and all her confusion. If only – but I had the choice and I gave it away to fear.

A letter came from Jamie in the last days of January telling me that the relationship was over. While I was sure Tina had played a significant part in the demise of the relationship, I know now I too played a part, probably the biggest part. The next couple of days were a veritable daze. Life had once again had pulled the ground from under me, first Tina, then Jamie.

But then, just like before, right at the moment when I really should have gone under, a tiny light glimmered – in the form of a new home. I was being given the chance to move into my own home with a permanency I had known since my childhood. And dark and obscure as it was, this new path opening up for me, it was a chance, one I knew I had to take.

CHAPTER 13

—— ⚬×⚬ ——

Spring 1994. It was just before my twenty-sixth birthday when I found myself taking definite steps towards a brighter future. While the wintry weather wasn't supporting my inner glow, I didn't care, because I was genuinely excited about this new path I had set my feet upon.

I remember turning onto this unfamiliar street, my view obscured by a blinding snowstorm, but I didn't care. I remember my feet stinging from the Arctic slush, but I didn't care. Seven inches of snow was causing travel chaos about me, but I didn't care. I had in my hand the key to number 33 Henry Road – my new home.

By evening, the skies had cleared and there was that crispness to the air that only snow can grant. The temperatures had dropped considerably, but I didn't notice - at least I didn't care, because I had a new warmth inside me – happiness. It was measured, this new happiness, it was small and it was fragile. It had to contend with my heartbreak, my fears, my hurts. It had to contend with the fact that I was totally on my own, cut off from every stitch, every fibre of my old life. It had to contend with all that, and yet this happiness I had simmered and sustained, enough at least for me to begin to want to formulate plans for my future.

In the first few weeks of my new life, I'd just sit at my small kitchen table and run my eyes along the brand new walls of my self-contained one-bedroom flat. The perfect, new walls, I guess, symbolised my hopes for my future. I knew the issue of my sexual identity was a bridge too far at this stage, but there were other blessings to be had, like peace of mind and healing. This is what I would tell myself as I sat on my new chair in my new kitchen sipping on a cup of hot chocolate and staring at the perfect structure about me that was my new security, my new serenity, my new hope.

* * *

While the winter cleared the way for spring, life at No. 33 continued being good. I kept breathing and I kept thinking, and miracles started to happen. Suddenly there were thoughts in my head that somehow lingered long enough to lead on to inspirations. And my biggest of these was to start a business. Even more miraculous was that next thing, I found myself acting upon it; I'm signing up for a eight week business course; I'm applying for a start-up grant through the Prince's Trust; I'm preparing my very own business plan; I'm standing in a brightly-lit office in front a panel of Prince's Trust Trustees; I'm delivering my presentation outlining my plans for the future; I'm opening an envelope, jumping up for joy, and reading that my grant has been approved; I'm jumping up for joy some more, buying my equipment, supplies and van; I'm going around London selling my contract cleaning service and actually winning customers; I'm doing the work and getting paid. And before I know what has happened to me, I'm just like everyone else, with a solid future in front of me.

Being so very occupied with creating my new life meant that I didn't have time to dwell on the loneliness I carried. Instead of drowning my sorrows, I sidestepped them by working to the point of exhaustion. I continued to win contracts, and I continued to prosper. I felt I was succeeding in banishing the darkness from my life, and little by little I felt my life was lifting out of the cracks. And with my new-found sense of security and direction came moments of genuine peace.

It was during one of these peaceful moments that my door buzzer rang (the flat came with a security intercom system which made me feel safe). I answered it and a voice said it was a delivery for me. I had set up a corner of my living room to act as my home office and I was awaiting a delivery of stationery. Every time a delivery came for me, I got a real sense of achievement; I enjoyed the fact that I was becoming successful and I enjoyed the fact that I finally had my independence.

I went to the door with a big smile ready. In the doorway a tall guy stood; no parcel. I looked at him and smiled, waiting for his explanation. But what came at me was not his words, it was his hands forcibly pushing the door open. Knocked back a couple of steps, I had hardly regained my balance when my heart stopped dead. I instantly knew what was happening – Tina was there, back in my life.

"So you thought I wouldn't find you, you stupid bitch!"

she sneered, coming for me with her hands clenched. My mutters of protest were stifled as her fingers clasped shut about my neck. I could feel the air thicken as she readjusted her grip. I could feel her breath, her perfume and a rush of her sick excitement as she bent her face an inch from mine.

"How's that feel?" she sneered as her sharp nails dug for my jugular. I could feel my legs give way as the terrifying thought came to me, was she going to kill me with her bare hands?

"Shut your mouth, bitch!" she said as the cold of a knife pressed my flesh. "You think I wouldn't find a stupid cow like you?"

"Please Tina, please…" I spluttered.

"You got money? I hear you do."

"Only what's in here," I said yanking my wallet out of my trousers. She could have it, she could have it all, I just wanted her gone. Dear God, I wanted her gone. As she rifled greedily through the notes inside, relief of sorts came to me, enough at least for my mind to switch back on. If it was only money she was after, it mightn't be so bad, I told myself in a desperate attempt to subside my panic. If I gave her what she wanted, I might get through this without her cutting me or worse. Dear God, make this about money and not revenge.

"Two hundred quid, it'll take more than that, remember you owe me bitch," she said, waving the knife in front of my face.

"That's all I have Tina, I swear!"

She hesitated as she suddenly became aware of her accomplice looking on with concern. By the look on his face, events were going a little beyond what he had expected.

"What the fuck are you looking at? Go see what's worth something!" she ordered as she pushed me back against the wall. "Don't fucking move!" Too scared to disobey, I stayed exactly where she left me; only my eyes moved to follow her as she wandered into the living room. It was only when my eyes began to sting that I realised I was drenched in the heavy sweat of fear. There wasn't enough time to think beyond this before she was back at me, this time with a crack-pipe in her hand.

"Tina, please, please take the money and go," I begged, knowing inside that this was never going to happen. She was too far into the game, too demented, too sick, too far gone.

"You ever stab someone?" she said coldly as a flame torched the end of the pipe. "Did you?" she continued after taking a long inhale. "Too much of a cry baby, I'd say."

"No," I finally said, gaining the courage to look her in the eye.

"The pipe or the knife? You choose," she said, holding the pipe out to me.

"Why Tina, why?" I cried, feeling the years of abuse collapsing on top of it.

"*Why Tina, why?*" she mocked. "You want me to slash your pretty face? You think that con slut of yours would want you then? Or maybe I should tell one of the girls to go have some fun with her, yeah maybe..."

"Stop it! Stop it!" I screamed. What was she? Didn't she have a heart? Wasn't there any light in her? I looked into her eyes, and there was nothing, they were empty – dead. I took the pipe from her and lit the end. I had seen this done a hundred times. I took as long an inhalation as hers and watch as the smile spread across her face.

"Again!"

I did as I was told, again and again, until I could feel the stampede of the cocaine reaching my brain.

"Nice place this, I mean for the likes of you," she said, taking her knife to the walls. "Well made are they?" she asked as she bashed at them with her heels.

"This is all I could find," the man said, coming into sight with an arm full of electrics. "Can I have a go?" he asked, his eyes suddenly mesmerised by the crack-pipe still in my hand.

"Get the kettle, idiot!" Tina said, turning her back on him and walking towards me. "You go out and get me more money and when I want it I'll be back for it, understood?"

"Yes," I said, feeling a wave of panic clamp my chest.

"Come on," she said to her accomplice as she walked toward the door. Passing the hall table, she casually picked up a vase, turned and flung it at me. As the pieces exploded about me, she simply walked out of sight.

I wanted to get up and race to close the door, but I was too afraid. Instead I simply listened and listened until I was sure the only sound inside the building was that of my own racing breath. I don't know how long I sat amongst the broken pieces, maybe just long enough to rub off the worst of the fear and the worst of the drugs. When I eventually found my feet, I walked over to the door calmly and closed it. I walked back through the hall, picking up what I could, disposed of them in the bin, went to the sofa and sat and closed my eyes, praying for oblivion.

When I opened my eyes again there was no daylight in the room. I got up and switched on the light in the kitchen. I had this terrible dryness in my mouth, so the first thing I did was to drink as much water as I could take. After the thirst was satisfied I continued drinking, thinking it would flush out any drugs still swimming in my system. I wanted it gone, I wanted every memory of Tina gone.

Futile as it was, I went out into the cold night air and

walked and walked, hoping to put some distance between me and the memories of what had just happened. On my way back towards my house, a strange determination overtook me. I quickened my pace, resolved now to go home and scrub every inch anew. Tina had come into my home and defiled it yes, but that didn't mean that I had to let her take it from me. She had taken so much already, but not my home. Late into the night I scrubbed and cleaned, the walls would have to be re-plastered in places, painted over in others but it was all doable, I had the skills necessary to make everything new again, at least on the surface.

It was the small hours before I finally got to bed. I was happy at least that Tina had not left her mark in my bedroom, as it made it easier to rest, to think, to pray. And I did pray. I prayed that the powers above would not allow my life to be taken away from me again. I prayed for my sanity. I prayed for my freedom.

When morning came, the full impact of the attack crashed down on top of me. I sat down knowing I would have to face the brutal truth of what had just happened to me. I knew in my heart that the time had come to make a choice between fear and hope. I could stay in fear and my life would keep repeating its downward spiral, or I could rise up into the unknown with nothing more than faith holding my hand. And so, with trembling hands I dialled 999.

It took a couple of hours for the police officers to arrive. Sitting quietly on my sofa, I went through the details of the attack. I knew every word, every disclosure could very well be putting a noose around me, but I went on with a quiet determination burning inside. All in all, it didn't take long, twenty minutes or so and the two young officers were gone. Closing the door on them, I felt relief and fear mix inside me. I was terrified of the ramifications of my actions, but I was happy also that I had found the courage to finally face up to Tina. Happy enough to get to the sofa at least before my head started to pound.

You've done the right thing, I told myself over and over, but no matter how many times I said it, it didn't seem to register. It didn't stop the pounding. It didn't stop the squeezing in my chest. And it didn't stop the cold fear that was running up my spine. Oh my God, I'm having a heart-attack, was all I could think as I felt the world go sideways. Tina coming back into my life in this manner must have been the final shock my system could endure before reacting with a full blown panic-attack.

In the days after the police visit, I was constantly on guard against Tina and subsequent panic attacks. My first attack had instilled such fear into me that I was absolutely terrified that I might have another. Maybe even more so than having Tina come back.

A couple of weeks went by and there was still no sign of Tina. I had got back to work, which helped to keep my mind occupied. It wasn't the working day I feared now, it was my time alone, because the panic attacks had returned and were now plaguing my life. Tina had yet again done her job well. In truth she didn't have to return to do me harm because her presence was all about me. And every time I suffered another panic attack, she took a little more of me away with her.

In an attempt to recover some ground, I decorated inside, but there were still knife marks on my door that couldn't be repaired, so I decided to replace the door altogether. I don't really know why, because it was the last thing I should have been doing, but I went around to see my father and asked him if he would like the work. The exchange between us was cordial. As it turned out he was happy to get the work and

I was happy to give it to him. It was the first time we had spoken since that night when he had partied in Tina's house with me. As it turns out his summation of Tina, rough as it was, was very accurate.

A couple of days later my father came around and did the job for me. After he sat with me, we had a chat over a cup of tea. We talked about the football, about the racing, about the weather, nothing heavy, nothing emotional, and this was fine with me. Before he left I gave him my new number and asked him to call whenever he felt like it.

And so, with his money in his pocket, my father said goodbye, presumably to head straight to the betting shop. He never did get himself back on his feet financially. He remained a compulsive gambler for the rest of his life. He never did call again either, but that was all right too, because at least I knew the animosity was gone, and for that I was grateful.

* * *

Strange as it might seem, having my father come around and fit the new door had a positive effect on me. Whilst I wasn't under any illusion that my life was in any way rosy, I was a little more determined to make things better. For now, that meant finding something to take me out in the evenings away from the panic I was experiencing. And so I signed up for singing lessons.

I remember distinctly the first time I visited the neat little town house in that area of Greater London called Swiss Cottage. I was nervous. I thought I could sing, but then again most of us do! Walking into the narrow hallway, I was immediately blown away by the famous faces lining the hall. Shirley Bassey, Lisa Stanfield, George Michael and so many more had all gone down this same hall. Maybe this should have made me turn and run, but it didn't. I walked into the small back room and went straight up to the piano and gave it my all. Leaving the modest home, I took with me a pocket full of positivity. I returned home, put on the kettle and waited for another panic attack.

It didn't come.

* * *

A year into my singing lessons, things were much improved. Tina hadn't returned and my panic attacks were far less scary and far less frequent. It was 1995, and with the spring I had turned twenty-seven. My business was going from strength to strength, which was a blessing, but in spite of everything I was beginning to feel lonely.

My life at this point was devoid of family or friends. I had by and large got used to this, but the absence of love in my life wasn't so easy to accept. I hadn't heard from Jamie, though I thought of her often. I imagined her back in the States beginning her new life. I imagined her meeting someone else and being happy. If I could only have imagined the same happiness waiting around a corner for me, I might have been able to keep the pain at bay, but I couldn't – I really couldn't imagine a person in my situation getting too many chances at love.

Twenty-seven years of my life had passed, and the way I made sense of it all was that I was a man trapped inside a woman's body. At this stage, I had no clue how a thing like this could happen, nor had I any notion of being able to do anything about it. I was trapped, as far I was concerned, with an outside that didn't match the inside, trapped by a secret I couldn't tell, trapped away from love.

* * *

By the summer of 1995, I had started to make some tentative reconnection with my past. Becky and Jen had found out where I lived and made a visit. After that Becky, more than Jen, would come around every now and again. Still taking drugs, their lives, it seemed, were as chaotic as ever. Becky was the mother of two children, and they had only recently been returned to her after being taken into care for a period. Now, with my life a little more stable, I tried to help her as much as I could.

"Becky, I'll sort something out for you, you need to get off them, you know that?"

"Yeah, yeah I do."

"For the kids, for you."

"I know. I want to. Just let me sort some things out and I'll come back."

"And you'll let me take you?"

"Yeah, yeah, I promise. Thanks for the money."

"For the kids, yeah?"

"Yeah, look I'll be back in a couple of days."

But it was a couple of weeks before I'd see her again, and then we'd play out the same conversation, over and over. At the end of the day, Becky was my friend, so I just kept trying.

About this time, I also started to reconnect with my sister Karen. We had met each other at our uncle's funeral and this was when I found out that she had finally left Marc. She was now in a new relationship with a guy called Greg, who was so much better for her. Having instantly hit it off with Greg, I was happy when Karen invited me over for a visit. It not only gave me the chance to reconnect with

Karen, it gave me the opportunity to meet my niece and two nephews.

Having made the initial connection with Karen and her family, I put in the effort to maintain the relationship. By the Christmas of 1995, my business was still doing well and I had continued with my singing lessons, but I was lonely, and in truth I liked the comfort of being around family. And so, with an armful of presents, I jumped at the chance to visit Karen over the holidays. By now, Greg and I had become firm friends, so visiting was a pleasure. I was happy when I heard the news that they were planning to get married. After Marc, Greg was exactly what Karen needed, so yes I was happy for them, very happy.

After exchanging presents and having something to eat, we all settled down to have a couple of drinks. I don't recall why, but eventually we hit on the topic of America. After I had told them all about my time in Florida, Karen began talking about his Auntie Rita in America.

"I'd love to go back," I said in all honesty.

"Why don't you go to New York? Auntie Rita would love to have you," Karen said excitedly.

"Don't be daft," I retorted, brushing it off as one of those throwaway remarks people come up with while drinking.

"No I'm serious. I'll ring her now," she said, rising from the couch.

"Are you serious?"

"Totally."

"But... I've got my business, and..."

"And you've got someone who can take over, right?"

"Yeah."

"Well! You can take a holiday can't you?"

"I suppose..."

"Done. Now shut up, it's ringing."

After making the initial introductions, Karen passed me the phone.

"What, this January? But I couldn't."

"Why not? I'd love to have you, we're practically family, aren't we?"

So two weeks later, I was on my way to New York. And the minute I put down the phone was the minute the realisation hit me: New York meant one thing, Jamie. I would be able to see her face to face and to tell her the truth, that I still loved her and I had always loved her. Perhaps the trip was meant to be, perhaps after all, Jamie and I were meant to be.

No matter how hard I had tried to forget her over the past years, I just couldn't. No matter how hard I had convinced myself I was over her, I wasn't; she was always there in the back of my mind. And if I had dared to delve into my heart to find out how I truly felt, I would have come back with the answer that there was still unfinished business between us. I still loved Jamie, and I couldn't help getting more excited with each minute that passed by on the flight. I loved Jamie, and by the time the plane landed, she was all I could think of. I had to see her.

In the back of a New York cab on 5th January, 1996, I thought about my forthcoming meeting with Jamie and unleashed my imagination. Rita's daughter, Renee had agreed to take me there. As it turned out it wasn't so far from their home in Manhattan to Jamie's mum's house, so there was nothing at all for me to worry about. I had decided not to make contact beforehand; I didn't have a number and with the holidays a letter would take too long anyway. Still, I didn't worry, I sat back in the cab and let my imagination run away with itself. Deep in my gut I knew Jamie would be there. I knew we would meet, I just knew we would.

By the time the cab stopped outside the townhouse in Lower East Side I had met Jamie many, many times in my head. Leaving my imagination running in the background, I waited for Rita's door to open. And when it did, to my delight Rita and Renee were as lovely as I had imagined.

It was quickly settled that Renee and I would go to New Jersey to meet Jamie the next day. But the following morning I woke to an eerie silence; it was the first day of one of the worst blizzards in US history. Parting the curtains, it took me a couple of seconds to get my head around what I was looking at. This wasn't New York, this was the Arctic. On my first visit to America I'd been met by a hurricane, and now on my second I was facing this. I was afraid God was trying to tell me something.

"Sorry honey, it doesn't look good, there's a lot of snow out there and the forecast isn't good. There's already been a train crash," Rita said, turning away from the small TV that was propped up on the kitchen counter.

"No that's okay, I totally understand," I said, taking a seat at the table.

"Maybe tomorrow hun. You want some coffee and pancakes?"

"Lovely, maybe we'll go tomorrow, yeah."

"What's tomorrow?" Renee asked, walking in, still dressed in PJs.

"The trip to New Jersey," Rita said, putting a steaming cup of coffee in front of me. "You want pancakes or cereal, Renee?"

"Mum, it's New Jersey, not California!"

"It's bad, hun."

"It's only snow! You get snow in London, don't you Lisa?"

"Sure, but if your mum thinks..."

"No, she's just... you know..."

"You know what?" Rita asked playfully.

"Look, we can wrap up, we'll even wear snow boots to make you happy, won't we Lisa?"

"Well, it's not up to me," I said politely, but inside I was begging for Rita to say yes.

"Mum, seriously it's only snow, and we promised. Look, if the lines are not running, we'll come straight back. Okay?"

"Okay."

I was never so glad in all my life to hear the word 'okay'. I left not caring a jot about the blizzard. I was in love. It had been love at first sight, I couldn't control it and I couldn't contain it. I didn't know what reaction I would get, if she was there at all, I didn't care – I was in love.

What the hell am I doing? I was thinking as we finally approached Jamie's door. Renee and I looked like a pair of climbers coming back to Everest base camp after a day losing to the mountain. The daylight had already vanished and still the snow wasn't finished. Over 20 inches had fallen so far that day, and still it was coming down. I wiped away the snow from my face, tapped out the snow from my boots, smiled at Renee and rang the doorbell. The only good thing about the weather, I thought as we waited, was that it increased the chances of Jamie being at home, that is assuming she still lived there.

As the light from the hall spilled out upon our faces I held my breath. It was Jamie. She opened the door and had to double-take. What a sight I must have been.

"Oh my God. Oh my God, I don't believe it!" she said, staring out at us.

"Surprised?" was all I could think to say.

"Oh my god, what the hell!"

"Can we come in? It's kinda cold out here," I joked.

"Of course, oh my god, come in, come on in."

"Jamie, who's at the door?" a voice asked from inside.

"It's a friend, Mom."

"Tell them we're having dinner and it's blizzarding outside in case they haven't noticed."

"It's okay Mom," Jamie said. She closed the door, suddenly looking awkward.

"Is this okay?" I asked.

"No really, it's great to see you. Who's this?" she said, turning to Renee.

"Oh sorry, this is my cousin, Renee."

"I didn't know you had family here?"

"Cousin in law, through my sister Karen."

"Oh right, right, well nice to meet you Renee."

"Yeah you too," Renee said, taking off her hat and gloves.

"Jamie, your dinner's getting cold," said a young male head, popping around the door.

"That's okay, you go ahead Frank, I won't be long."

"Friends of yours?" Frank asked, coming out into the hall.

"Yeah, from London."

"What's going on?" said Jamie's mum, coming into the hall.

"This is Lisa, the friend I told you about from London."

"Right, how are you Lisa? You know there's a blizzard out?"

"I know, I'm sorry I should have called, let you know."

"Well you're welcome to join us, we're in the middle of dinner," Jamie's mum said. She seemed to be getting over the shock of two total strangers landing on her doorstep in the middle of a blizzard.

"No that's all right, you go ahead, I just wanted to say hello."

"You can stay, it's fine," Jamie said, more politely than excitedly.

"No really, it took longer than we expected and it's late, we better get back."

"Okay, well I'll see you out. Go on back in Frank, don't let your dinner go cold."

Jamie smiled at us politely, waiting for her mum and Frank to go back in.

"Is Frank your boyfriend?" I asked quietly.

"Yeah, yeah he is, we've been together a while now. I wanted to..."

"No that's okay. I'm happy for you, really. Anyway, we better make tracks. You take care of yourself."

"Yeah, you too, you okay?"

"I'm great, better, have a nice house and a little business and family, I'm good."

"Glad to hear that, good to see you."

And with that the door shut on us. Not as I had imagined, not at all. Gutted. Mangled. Heading back out into the snow, I was heartbroken.

"Wait! Wait!" a voice came behind us.

We both turned to see Jamie running through the snow. "I have chains, I can run you back to Manhattan. Come on!"

Seeing Jamie running through the snow meant the world to me. I knew then that I hadn't imagined it all. I knew then that I meant something to her. I knew we meant something to each other. I knew that there was still unfinished business, no matter if life had got in the way of it.

On the drive back, Renee sat in the back and put on her headphones. She was clever and had figured out there was something unspoken going on between Jamie and me. Sitting up beside Jamie and being so close to her somehow made all the distance, all the complications, just slide away.

We chatted and we giggled, just like old times.

"So how long are you and Frank together?"

"A couple of months."

"Is it serious?"

"I don't know, maybe."

"Like us?"

"Maybe, no, maybe, I don't know. It's different, that was there and this is..."

"What?"

"I don't know, this is, I guess, the real world. Anyway, how would we work, you there me here? Some things just have their place, their time."

"So you love him and not me?"

"I like being with a man, I guess that's the simple truth of it."

"I understand."

"What we had was special, and I often think of you, but like I said we have to be real."

"No I understand, and I'm happy for you."

Jamie was right. We had to be real, she needed a man and I needed to tell her the truth about me so she could truly understand the nature of her feelings for me. But I couldn't. I didn't. And so we parted under a veil of half-truths. I let her run away from the confusion of her feelings. I let her run back to the security of the familiar, to Frank. I let her go because I let my fear overpower my love. It was me, not Jamie, it was me who let her go.

CHAPTER 14

When I arrived home from New York, I felt the shadow of
depression descending. The discovery that Jamie had moved
on hit me harder than any record-breaking blizzard. I had
dared to dream, and as usual I had got trampled for it. And
what had I to pick myself up for, a life-long companionship
with loneliness?

Trying to imagine a brighter side to my darkness, I
plunged myself back into my work, my singing and the
tentative relationships I was rebuilding with my sister and
Becky and Jen. While Karen's path had definitely taken a
turn for the better, both Becky and Jen's paths had become
ever darker. Both had moved on to crack cocaine, both were
addicts and both were walking a very hazardous path. And
this terrified me. I had already seen the horrible realities of
drugs first-hand, and I didn't want to see Becky and Jen go
the same way. The sad truth was, I was overjoyed every

time I opened the door to either of them just to find them alive.

It was a couple of weeks after arriving back from New York that a knock came on the door. I had by now got over my fear of opening it. Tina had been out of my life long enough for me to believe she would never darken my doorstep again, and this, if nothing else, was a bright enough reason to get up in the morning.

Another knock. Too late for it to be a delivery, maybe it was Becky. I turned the latch. Close enough - it was Jen.

"Happy New Year" she said, walking past me.

"It's February, Jen."

"Yeah, Happy New Year, you been up to anything?"

"I was in New York."

"Yeah, get anything nice?"

"I didn't do much shopping. You want a cup of tea?"

"Coffee. You got anything to eat?"

"Sandwich?"

"Nah."

"Pasta, fry, what would you like?"

"You know, I fancy a kebab, haven't had one in ages," she said, rubbing her hands anxiously.

"You okay?" I asked, picking up on her anxiety.

"I told you, I'm hungry."

"Look, can I make you a sandwich?" I said turning to the bread bin.

"I don't want a sandwich" she said abruptly. "I already told you, I fancy a kebab."

"You really okay?"

"I haven't used anything in over a month, if that's what you mean."

"No, I know, wow that's great," I said, both of us knowing it was total bullshit. "Fine, let's just go and get a take-away."

"I had to hitch, can I wait here?" she said, taking off her jacket.

"Sure, you want chips?"

"Yeah, and Coke?"

"There's a bottle in the fridge, help yourself," I said, putting on my coat and heading for the door.

"You got any new videos?" Jen called after me.

"Yeah, under the telly," I shouted back.

"I'll pick one, for when you get back."

"See you!" I replied as I closed the door.

I knew Jen was having withdrawals and I knew she was hurting. Maybe this time I would be able to get through to her, I thought as I ordered our meal. We'd have something to eat, something to drink, watch the video and then I'd talk to her about rehab. Maybe we could even think about going back to Florida in the summer. Yeah, maybe that would be just the thing to tell Jen, if she had a goal, just maybe...

These were the thoughts filling my head as I walked the short distance back to my apartment.

"Here we are! What film did you pick?" I called from the hall.

Getting no answer, I walked straight into the living room. "Jen?" After this I went to the bathroom and knocked gently at the door, "Jen, you in there?" Still no answer. "Jen?" I called again, pushing the door open gently. I was immediately gripped by the most horrible feeling. She wasn't there. She wasn't anywhere. Maybe she'd gone to find me, I told myself, putting the bags on the kitchen table and preparing to head back out.

I retraced my steps in the hope that we had just missed each other. I couldn't think of anywhere else she could be, so I went back to the apartment, thinking she might have stepped out for a moment and was back now waiting for me. But she wasn't.

I let myself back in and sat at the table. I was worried now. I would have liked to say it wasn't like Jen, but with drugs anything was possible. I had a pile of food on the table and no appetite for any of it. *I'll put it on low. Maybe she'll turn up*, I thought, putting the food into the oven.

I was about to turn on the TV when I glanced over and saw my filing trays had been disturbed. Strange, I thought. I headed over to the space in the corner of the room that I had designated as my office. Rounding my desk, I saw my briefcase with the key in it and immediately my heart sank. I knew there was no point checking if my money was still inside, but I did it anyway. Food money, petrol money, work float, all gone.

"Why didn't you just ask, just ask Jen?" I shouted, sitting on the couch absolutely destroyed. It wasn't the money, I would have given her that. I had never refused her, and I never would. No, it wasn't the money, it was the trust. She had stolen the trust, the drugs had stolen the trust. Either way, I couldn't help feeling the senselessness of it all ripping our friendship apart.

I looked over at the TV. Maybe she had taken the videos too; I didn't bother to look. I knew our relationship was over, I knew I wouldn't see her again. I felt that deep inside, and sadly, a number of years later, I found out I was right. Jen, like so many perfect souls, just didn't make it. She succumbed to drugs having barely passed her thirtieth birthday. Family, friends, money, status – nothing could save her.

I never did know what drove Jen to look for sanctuary in between the cracks. It never did make sense to me, and I suppose it never will. We all have our demons, I know this, and maybe it's just the case that the brightest souls have to fight the darkest ones.

* * *

My immediate reaction to being robbed by Jen was despondency. I was already feeling low over Jamie, so Jen's betrayal hit me hard. The only bright spark shining on my life at this time was the continuing success of my business and the intermittent contact I had with family. Through Karen I had slowly begun to establish contact with my mother. The relationship had by no means healed at this time, but at least it was a start.

As 1996 moved on, I slowly began to put much of the hurt Jen had caused to the back of my mind. My mood was also lifted in no small part by a renewed correspondence between me and Jamie. Out of the blue a letter arrived which was to be the start of a steady stream of communications between us. Although the word 'relationship' was dropped from our conversations, I couldn't help feel it lingering between the lines. I knew, from what Jamie wrote, that her relationship with Frank was still going steady, so, given how I felt about her, the sensible thing would have been to break off contact. Anyone who has suffered unrequited love knows it ain't no fun, but what could I do? I loved Jamie and in the back of my mind a voice kept telling me that she loved me too, and by some miracle the faith that twisted us apart would one day bring us together again.

* * *

Throughout the rest of 1996 and the whole of 1997, life took on a familiar pattern. There was my work, my singing and the renewed relationship I was enjoying with my family, especially my mother. My father was still, by and large, a no-show in my life, but from what I heard he was doing okay, and of this, I was glad.

Come 1998, a new focus entered our lives and it was a happy one – Karen's wedding. It was a June event, and all the family were invited. I couldn't help wonder if everyone would show up. If they did, it would be the first time since the breakup of the family in 1982 that all of us would be together.

As it turned out, all of us did gather to celebrate Karen's wedding, and what's more it went off without a hitch. Everyone was civil, everyone was happy, and as the night went on, even happy. I think a lot of ghosts were laid to rest that day. Although we were never going to be the model family, we were, as it turned out, a family, and that was reassuring in its own way.

* * *

It was shortly after the wedding that a new dream started to formulate. I had watched the band at the wedding and suddenly remembered my childhood dream of performing on stage. I knew I had a good voice and all the years of singing lessons had given me enough confidence to believe I could front a band. Why not? What did I have to lose? I liked the idea more and more. I was still very lonely, so not only would singing in a band give me a chance to do something I loved, it would also help me occupy a lot of my lonely times.

The idea was well set in my mind, but I couldn't see any way it could happen for real, how I could get myself into a band. The singing lessons were a solo exercise. I knew no one in the band scene, so the chances of me getting into a band were slim.

And then along came Amanda. She was a songwriter, and amazingly, she was a customer of mine. It turned out that she had a band and lots of songs, but no singer. I really couldn't believe I was hearing all this. "I can sing!" I told her immediately. We got on well and shared similar tastes in music, and so, there and then, we decided to start a band.

1998 was coming to a close when the band finally took to the stage. I had enough confidence by now to end my singing lessons - five years, it was time. My aim in life now was to rebuild my life and my confidence. My work, my family, my band, this was what I had, and it was enough. I went on convincing myself. The truth was, it wasn't enough, because my aim had always been to find happiness through love. But at this point in my life, I just couldn't dwell on this. Out of self-preservation I had to delude myself a little. The alternative, dwelling on the problems my sexual identity posed, were just too painful.

Extraordinarily enough, while I was continuing to block out thoughts of my sexual identity, the Universe, if you will, was giving me yet another opportunity to face these mighty fears. Because, as it happened, not only had Amanda and I our love of music in common, we also had gender identity issues in common.

It was not so long after getting the band together that Amanda spoke about her transgender situation. We were sitting having a drink together when she told me about her hormone treatment and about the fact that she was awaiting a realignment operation. It may seem strange, but I didn't jump at the chance to tell her about my situation.

Looking back now how Amanda came into my life, I do feel now that there was a higher purpose to it. Yes, through music Amanda played a part in my process of healing, but perhaps more specifically I feel that she was placed in my life to give me another opportunity to speak my truth. Like all the other kind and loving people who had appeared in my life at dark times, Amanda was yet another opportunity, another gift presented to me, and as with all the other times, the gift came and went unopened. Mentally and emotionally I just wasn't healed enough to open up and trust someone. Amanda and I played side by side for nearly two years, and not once did I even hint at my gender identity. You see, it was fear, a debilitating and paralysing fear, and it was very much preventing me from clearing the past and moving on to a totally new direction in my life.

What I didn't understand at the time was that by holding onto fear I was leaving myself wide open to all the negativity the world had to throw at me, and boy was there no end to that. I had by and large living in a self-imposed prison, as it was at home alone that I felt it the most. During the day I was living a functional life, but when I wasn't playing with the band I was very lonely. It was becoming increasingly difficult for me to keep depression at bay, but thankfully, I had healed just enough to realise that.

The fear of losing control over my hard-won sanity now pushed me into counselling, and started me attending weekly sessions. It probably was these weekly sessions that pushed me into the lesbian scene. If I had been totally honest with my counsellor, who knows, I might have wound up having my gender reassignment years earlier instead of digging myself deeper into the hole of self-denial. I was lonely, I longed for love and I was terrified of the prospect of a life without it, so I fooled myself into believing that I could find love by hiding in plain sight.

When 1999 rang in, my New Year's resolution was to

totally dedicate myself to my integration into the lesbian scene. In my heart I knew I was a fraud, but I was so lonely I was willing to try anything. I was so convinced that a lesbian relationship was my only solution that I jumped straight in with both feet – two left feet. Only after two disastrous relationships and a number of non-starters did I eventually learn, to my cost, that there is nothing to be gained by lying to yourself.

In truth, I might as well have taken a machete to my self-esteem, because by the time I came to my senses it was nearing an all-time low. All I wanted was to find love, and all I got was one disaster after another.

I'll spare you the pain of hearing about all my failures and summon it up with my last lesbian affair, with a girl named Kate. Kate was bisexual and the image of Jamie. On the face of it she was very nice, until I found out that she was into crack cocaine in a big way and into cheating in an even bigger way. I would like to say there was some silver lining to it all, but there wasn't, not a glimmer.

The new millennium was nearly upon us and I just couldn't figure out why I was a magnet for so much disaster. I was totally blind, at this point, to the direct link between my inner denial and my outer catastrophe. What if life had allowed me to find some semblance of happiness in the illusion I was trying to create for myself? I probably would have taken it and subjected myself to a half-life.

Of course hindsight is great, but back then at best I was confused, and at worst I was bewildered. Most definitely I was despondent and for certain I was losing interest in life a little more every day. I was worn down by it all: my sexual identity, my loneliness, the constant presence of fear in my life. And the new millennium was really upon us.

Largely unmotivated to make any arrangements, I

considered going to bed early and missing the whole shindig. No matter how hard I tried, I just couldn't whip myself up into a frenzy. And if it hadn't been for a phone call from Becky, I might well have followed my plan for an early night.

By now, Becky had two children, girls of four and 10. They were lovely children and the news of them coming to stay over Christmas was enough to dust off a couple layers of gloom - enough anyway to take me out Christmas shopping. I knew Becky had a good heart, but with her problems with drugs I also knew that it couldn't be easy for the children. Thinking of children kindled the Christmas spirit in me, and the more I shopped for little presents the more I looked forward to their visit.

Having Becky and the kids over for Christmas gave the season meaning for me again. As I watched her children open their presents, I had fond memories of my own childhood. As for Becky, there was no obvious signs of her using, she told me she was clean, and as I watched her play with her kids, for the first time I started to really believe her. Maybe there was something to this new millennium after all.

I had such a wonderful time with Becky and her family over Christmas that I practically begged her to come back for New Year. I really didn't want to spend it in bed and I really didn't want to spend it alone. Becky had been the one constant in my life, she was my best friend, and apart from Jamie, I really couldn't think of anyone else better to spend it with.

"I'll leave the kids with my mum and come back, okay?" she said.

"Sure," I said, trying to hide my disappointment. How many times I had heard those words.

"No, I'll definitely be here. Why don't I come early and we can go to the supermarket together?"

"Okay," I said, without any extra enthusiasm.

As it turned out, miracle upon miracle, Becky did return and we did, as she had suggested, spend the day in preparation for the big night. With everything prepared, we finally sat down in front of the television all ready to ring in the new millennium. By the time Big Ben chimed I was over the moon. It had been a great night. We had drunk, we had feasted and we had laughed, about everything in our lives, the good as well as the bad. We had hugged and we had danced like old times. We had a ball.

The celebrations went on into the early hours and by the time I went to bed I had a very large grin upon my face. In the morning, after a healthy lie in, I got out of bed thinking about the day ahead. Maybe I'd go for a drive, I thought, staring at myself in the mirror. Becky's mum had said she would keep the kids for a couple of days, so I could think of no reason in the world not to keep the celebrations going for as long as we could. Life had been so hard on both of us, we deserved this little respite of happiness, I told myself, heading out of the bathroom. We could find a nice out-of-the-way pub and stop for a bite to eat. But first a good old fry up, just like Mrs Burke used to make, I thought, making my way into the kitchen.

I had just about co-ordinated everything to perfection and was hoping to hear some sound of life from Becky. I made a fresh pot of coffee, laid everything on the table and went to fetch her.

"Hey sleepyhead, you hungry?" I said, tapping gently on the door.

"Come on or I'll eat it all," I added, getting no answer. "Becky?"

I peered around the door. "Becky," I said again, walking over to the bed. It was empty. "Becky, you in there?" I said, going to the bathroom door. Still no answer. Looking in, I saw she wasn't there either.

"That's strange," I said to myself coming out of the bathroom. "Maybe, she's gone for a walk. Maybe..." I stopped myself, suddenly feeling something wasn't right. I went back into the bedroom to check if Becky's things were still there. I looked under the bed, in the closet. They were gone. All gone.

"Oh God, please no, good God no, please let this not be happening," I said, pulling out the book which contained my money. "No."

Feeling my world tumbling, I looked for my keys. Maybe I could get to her mum's before she spent it all, I told myself.

My car was gone. "Oh no, please tell me... no!" I said, looking out of the window. She had taken the car as well. Becky, my car and my money were all gone.

I sat on the couch and held my head in my hands. I spent the whole afternoon trying to convince myself that any moment now she'd arrive with an explanation. It was too much for me to take. I prayed for it not to be true, but it was.

Eventually, giving up on the idea of Becky returning I had the idea of ringing her at her mum's. I held my breath as the phone rang. I had no idea what I would say to her mum. I held my breath as a voice came on the line. It was Becky.

"Becky, please tell me you didn't take my car and my money."

"What if I did?"

"Becky!"

"Oh shut up, you have everything and I have nothing, you can get another bloody car. What can I do?"

"I want my car back."

"You can't, it's gone, and if you open your fucking mouth I'll have you seen to. Do you understand?"

"Becky, you can't do this, I'm your friend!"

"I don't give a fuck if you think we're friends, I don't, so don't think I do."

And with that the phone went dead.

* * *

The next few days went by in a haze. The more I thought about my life, the more I wished I could blot out everything. Despite all my trying to convince myself to the contrary, I knew I wasn't happy. I knew my life was shallow and unfulfilled. And I knew that here I was again, dealing with the fallout of abuse. On the surface, much had changed, but how much underneath, how much had changed there? I questioned how much progress I could have actually made if it could have been wiped away so easily, all in one night.

* * *

A week later, I didn't feel any better. Nothing, not even music, seemed to be able to lift the gloom. I was sitting watching the television when I suddenly felt the most horrible wave of hopelessness empty me. It was as if all the hurt I had suffered had come back to visit, bringing with it a wish to die. It wasn't long before I was wanting to close my eyes and never wake up. I wanted the pain to end. I wanted it all to end. No matter how hellish things had been in the past, the thought of ending it all had never entered my mind, but now it seemed I was being stalked by the demon. I wanted love, and no matter how much I convinced myself it just didn't seem possible. And I also wanted peace, and peace seemed possible only with the taking of my life.

The suicidal thoughts gathered pace over the coming weeks, but at the very moment when I truly had reached my life's end my mother, of all people, came firmly back into my life. She landed on my doorstep and brazenly announced that she was staying for the weekend. I looked on in amazement as she bustled her way past me and plonked herself on my couch. I still didn't believe in angels at this stage, but my mother's arrival back in my life at the exact moment when I most needed someone was nothing short of miraculous. And what's more, after that weekend she turned up again and again until she was something of a regular in my life.

Month by month throughout 2000 the relationship between my mother and me continued to build. She was lonely, I was lonely. And together two lonely souls found some comfort. As it turned out, some comfort was exactly what I needed to hang onto life. My depression ebbed and flowed over the first half of the year, but come the summer I finally felt it falling behind me.

The re-establishing of my relationship with my mum allowed me to take the momentous decision to move back to my home town, after fifteen years. The years I had spent in Islington trying to rebuild my life had in reality been spent focusing mainly on survival. I had never got beyond the need for safety and control. I had continued to ignored the real root of my loneliness and dissatisfaction with life – my gender identity. While I thought I was grounding myself into a better life, in reality I was still stuck. There was an illusion of healing, but this was not real. The final straw that broke with Becky's betrayal had shown me that. And yet I still really didn't understand that my denial of who I really was had created a wound that would continue to fester for as long as I allowed it to.

Our family coming together for Karen's wedding had been a turning part in all our lives. It went by quietly, but I felt a healing of sorts had taken place. It had taken a long time, but I finally felt ready to make peace with my past. I felt ready to come home. And so about a month after returning from a holiday with my mother, I was on my way back to my roots in Enfield. I was 32 years old.

My move back home came with a fresh determination to fix the multitude of problems that seemed to dog my life. Arriving at my new home, I had to hold tight to this determination lest it should crumble at the sight of my new home. The council house I was allocated was run down compared to my previous apartment. The area was blighted by unemployment, crime and drugs – not exactly what I had hoped for, but still I felt the move was right for me.

In an attempt to separate myself from my past in Islington, I gave up everything; my job, my band, everything and everyone I had come to know over the 15 years I had been away from Enfield. The only exception was Jamie. Our relationship, strictly speaking a platonic one, had continued, the letters and cards continued, and still, between the lines, I believed the love continued on.

Her most recent letter about her break-up with Frank had for me brought things to the surface. For a spell, my imagination went into overdrive, but soon after another letter arrived that instantly turned off the ignition – she had a new man in her life. Although it hurt to think what might have been, I still looked forward to hearing from her. She was always in my heart, no matter whether I wanted her there or not. That was something I would just have to figure out how to live with.

The shock of losing Becky put a distinct stain on my happiness. And instead of dealing with the pain head-on, I buried it right next to the truth of my gender identity. And so, side by side, they lay pounding on my self-esteem, making it impossible for any true happiness. For how can happiness exist without self-acceptance and self-love? Both are the foundation from which true happiness springs and that's exactly what my life lacked, a solid foundation. I had worked so hard to bring mental well-being into my life, but as it turned out, without a foundation all my building came to nothing with the first wave.

In an attempt, once again, to rebuild my castle, I decided to dedicate myself to the education I had missed. Without qualifications, I knew my chances of getting a career was a non-starter. At this stage in my life, all I wanted was what everyone one else seemed to be striving for – happiness through material success.

To this end, within a matter of weeks I had enrolled in a two-year course to gain credits towards my ultimate goal of obtaining a degree. The plan was to retake my GCSE exams and go on to college to obtain a Higher National Diploma, which would be my stepping stone to my degree. It was another plan, and to my mind a good plan, and as it turned out, come 2003, I was well on my way to achieving my goal. In order to fund my studies, I worked hard doing part-time administrative and sales jobs for various companies. My dedication was starting to pay off, and before long I had earned enough money to not only to support my studies but to buy my home from the council.

The wind of change brought about by my new goal was strengthened by the continuing presence of my mother in my life. Two years had passed now, I had passed all my exams and was now on my way to college. And once college started, a further fortification was added by a nice new circle of friends. On the face of it, life was good. But not good enough to put aside the loneliness caused by my hidden male gender-identity.

Nevertheless, in an attempt to push the loneliness aside, I once again became the life and soul of every party. And being students, there was never a shortage of these, especially given the fact I had at my disposal the perfect party venue – my home.

It was in 2003, at one of these parties, that I first met Natalie. She was a neighbour who had recently broken up from her boyfriend. She had two small children whom she supported on her own. Although she was in her late thirties, five years or so older than me, she gave the college girls a good run for their money. And not only was she beautiful, she was so much fun. A perfect match, two happy party people.

Perfect yes, as friends like Becky and I once were – that's what I immediately told myself. But after a few drinks I forgot my own guidance and unashamedly started to reciprocate the attention I felt she was laying on me. We danced and we drank and we giggled, and by the end of the night we pretended to smooch, although I doubt it felt like pretence to either of us.

Over the next couple of weeks Natalie and I continued to spend time together – she'd pop in and we'd chat over a couple of glasses of wine. Eventually, we took the relationship to the next level. I knew all of Natalie's relationships had been with men – I guess she was trying something different – but I knew, happily, that it wasn't a real lesbian relationship.

Being with a woman again brought so much joy into my life. I woke up to hear the birds singing once more. I had so missed having the companionship of a partner. All I had ever wanted, in truth, was to love and be loved. So, really I was more than happy – I was absolutely thrilled. When you've been denied love for so long it isn't hard to plunge yourself into a relationship. I didn't bother with all the fail-safes that most people might consider when starting a relationship. I wasn't afraid of being hurt – I was afraid of not being loved.

Having Natalie in my life made me want to spoil her. She struggled with money and so, when I could, I was thrilled to help her out. I wanted to take her out and show the world that like everyone else, I could be loved. I wanted to and I would have, but Natalie preferred, just as Helen had done, all those years earlier, to keep the relationship a secret. Of course this hurt deep down, but then again I wasn't exactly being honest with her.

And so, yet again I found myself unable to open up about my gender identity. By now, it had grown to be such an enormous issue in my mind that I just couldn't find the courage to acknowledge the truth. As far as Natalie was concerned she was in the middle of a lesbian relationship, and for her own reasons she didn't want to acknowledge this either.

My relationship with Natalie continued into 2004, by which time I had started my Higher National Diploma in Tourism Management. As part of the course I had the opportunity to work in New York for the summer. Some of my classmates suggested that I apply with them to work at Tomahawk Lake Water Park in New Jersey. And to this end I did a crash course to get a certificate for lifeguarding. Come June, I found myself on my way to America once again.

Being so close to Jamie stirred up the old feelings once

again. But this time both of us were in relationships. Natalie hadn't wanted me to be away from her for so long. She had come to rely on me both emotionally and financially, so the break was difficult enough for her. Natalie was not Jamie, I knew this deep down, but our relationship was developing and I wasn't going to dishonour this, so I took the decision not to visit Jamie. I knew it would ultimately only bring both of us pain, which we'd both had too much of already.

The summer delivered lots of fun. It was great being back in America, and work at the water park was terrific. I came home raring to get stuck into the final year of my diploma. I was also glad to be reunited with Natalie. I had missed her, which boded well for the future, I thought.

As it happened, it seemed Natalie missed me too. Before long the days between our seeing each other drew closer, and eventually hardly a day went by without us seeing each other. I think both of us were getting more serious about the relationship, which could only be a good thing, I told myself. I had, for some time, wanted Natalie to come out into the open about our relationship. I understood that she had the children to consider, but after so much time, this argument really was wafer thin.

"But if we come out, and say we move in, then I'll have to rely on you for more, not only for me but for the kids too," she argued.

"Yeah, well that won't be a problem, I'll be finished soon and be earning."

"I don't know, it's a big thing..."

"I know it is. I'm not saying it isn't."

"Okay. Look, there's this bill I have, its two hundred quid, can you help me with that?"

"What, immediately?"

"Yeah, I want to get it off my plate as soon as possible."

"But I have the mortgage and I have to pay fees."

"This is what I mean!"

"That's not fair Natalie."

"Forget it!" she said, storming out.

I felt bad not giving Natalie the money, but to my relief, she came around later and told me not to worry about it. All made up, we spent a lovely evening together curled up on the couch chatting over a couple of glasses of wine.

The next morning, I woke up not remembering anything. I looked at the clock and jumped.

"Where you going?" Natalie moaned.

"I'm late for college."

"Oh fuck it."

"I have to go," I said, searching for my wallet. "You see where I put my wallet?"

"No, try your trousers. Can you get me a coffee?"

"It's not there!" I said emptying out my pockets.

"Look on the floor, maybe it fell out. Can't you get me a coffee, I've such a headache?"

"All right," I said, down on all fours. "There it is!" I proclaimed, reaching under the bed.

"I'm dead late, but only for you, I'll make coffee," I said, opening my wallet to check if I had my student card.

"Good, make it strong," Natalie said rising up on her elbow.

"My money, for the mortgage, it's missing!"

"Didn't you pay it?" she said smiling. "Why don't you come back to bed?"

"No, I'm serious, it's gone!"

"Well, if you spent it that's your own fault. How was I to know it was the mortgage money?"

"What the hell are you talking about?"

"Tracey and Kev came around you remember?"

"Yes, and?"

"And you decided to buy some gear."

"No, no way, there's no way."

"You calling me a liar? For Christ's sake you can't remember what you did, you were so out of it. I told you not to and you told me to shut up."

"No, that's not what happened, it can't be."

"You call me a liar once more and you can forget it, forget everything. I'm not taking responsibility for your drinking. If you can't remember things then maybe you shouldn't drink!" she shouted, getting out of the bed. "You know what, fuck this, I don't need this shit."

I went to the bathroom and got into the shower. It was true I couldn't remember a thing other than Natalie's friends coming over and opening up another bottle of wine. After that, as Natalie said, I remember absolutely nothing. I scrubbed my face, feeling a sickening feeling rise in my gut, and before it could be interpreted properly I felt Natalie's arms slip around my waist.

I didn't question Natalie's version of events after that. The relationship continued, as did the drinking and the spoiling. I never stopped to question her motives. Again, having no fail-safes in place made me extremely vulnerable. Whatever Natalie wanted, I gave her. Every time I refused her anything, she always found a way to get around me. And her way was to hook me in emotionally to the point where I would do anything to stop her leaving me.

* * *

By the time 2005 arrived, more and more payments were being missed and more and more days from college as well. What was also being missed was the fun and love from our relationship, because the more I became dependant on her emotionally the more controlling she became. Knowing she had me emotionally hooked, she used this power to get what she wanted. And what she wanted was money. Just like Becky and Jen, she had a cocaine habit, which she skilfully kept hidden from me for well over a year after the relationship turned sexual. She also liked to drink and she also liked to be driven, which placed me at risk of getting into trouble once again with the law.

The more I became dependent on Natalie, the more my life started to unravel. It was starting to look more and more like Tina all over again – though I wouldn't allow myself to see this at first. As my situation worsened I found myself experiencing the same panic and anxiety I had suffered with Tina. And just as it was with Tina, the more vulnerable I became, the worse Natalie treated me. The fact that I was nothing more than a meal ticket to her became blatantly obvious. The years of psychological damage I had suffered at the hands of Tina came back to overwhelm me; in truth I was easy pickings.

Eventually the relationship turned violent, and by then any sense of self I had rediscovered had well and truly disintegrated. Once again I found my life cascading downwards and once again depression, anxiety and hopelessness were right there beside me.

Gripped with depression, it became impossible for me to function. My college went first; with only six months to go, I dropped out. Next went my jobs and finally in 2006 my castle fell. Without that solid foundation of self-love and acceptance, my new life never stood a chance. I had 'vulnerable' written all over me, scrawled in indelible ink. I was a sitting target just waiting to be run through.

I remember sitting in Natalie's kitchen with the repossession notice in my hand, the tears pouring down my face.

"It's your own fault, so you might as well get that moan off your face," she said coldly.

"What am I going to do?"

"You'll move in here. I'll claim for you until you find a job."

"I just can't believe this is happening."

"Oh get out of my face will ya, you're pathetic!" she said, waving at butter knife at me.

I looked over at her, making her sandwich, moving to the beats from the radio without the slightest bit of care for my situation. And in that moment I knew that I could run or I could die. I know it sounds profound, but I believe now that I was being given the opportunity to see clearly the outcomes of two very different options. It wasn't easy running away once more into an unseen future, but as soon as I had made that decision I felt an immediate sense of relief.

CHAPTER 15

—⋈—

I left soon after, took what I needed and wound up in a shelter for abused women. Four to six months in one shelter and then I moved on, and the next two years of my life were like this until my final transfer, which came in 2008. On this occasion, I found myself in Stevenage, about 50 miles from my old home in London. Living such a precarious life had done nothing to heal my many issues. And so by the time I arrived in Stevenage I felt pretty much dead inside.

The first thing I noticed about Stevenage was how friendly the care workers were. There was something different about the atmosphere here, nothing you could put your finger upon, but something different nonetheless.

The shelter offered protection not only to women but to their children, so the atmosphere was very holistic. I remember the first weekend of my stay a barbecue was organised in the garden and I sat on my own watching the children laugh and play. It reminded me of my own childhood out on the streets of London. Little made me smile those days, but seeing the children so happy, I came close.

"Come on, it'll all be eaten," a voice said from behind me.

I looked up to see one of the care workers, Rachel, smiling down at me.

"I'm not hungry."

"It's all home-made, come on."

At Rachel's insistence I got up and went over with her to fill a plate. After which we sat down together.

"Hmm, it's good," I said, chewing on a chicken leg.

"Told you," Rachel beamed, "Sarah! Over here," she continued, catching a young woman stepping into the yard.

"Hi there," Sarah said, smiling down at us.

"This is Lisa, why don't you get a plate and join us?"

Sarah came back and we chatted about nothing in particular, which suited us both I think. After Rachel left, Sarah and I chatted on and despite my enormous lack of trust in anyone, I couldn't help liking her.

I was to learn later that Sarah had three young children with her in the shelter. She had finally run away from an abusive relationship when her husband had tried to strangle her with the phone wire. Every one of the women in the shelter had their own story to tell, and none was any better than Sarah's.

After our initial meeting in the garden Sarah and I just gravitated to each other. She reminded me so much of Jamie, not in looks but in her gentle nature. She had a warmth and serenity to her, which was extraordinary considering her brutal past. Over the course of my four-month stay in Stevenage, Sarah and I developed a close relationship. The shelter provided a retreat from the torments of a world that had nothing but darkness for every person there. Its rambling cottage gardens were filled with berries and apple trees. How gentle it all was. How civilised. How kind and caring.

I remember, one perfect morning, going out into the garden with Sarah and filling baskets with apples and berries.

"I think we'll have enough," Sarah said, peering into my basket.

"You know I haven't the foggiest how to make apple pies."

"I'll show you, come on, they'll be ready for lunch. We can have a picnic."

Apple pie and summer picnics with gentle people was all that was needed to rescue my sanity and soul. Every day I spent at the shelter was a day when a little more darkness dissolved from me.

"Yummy, what a lovely smell," said Rachel, walking into the kitchen.

"Why don't you join us," I said, proudly showing off the pie I had made. Rachel came out with me, while Sarah went to gather the children.

"You know I really have no clue who I am," I said, suddenly overcome with emotion. I don't know if it was the normality of it all, but something was stirring my soul and my emotions were in the mixer.

"I don't think you're the only one who feels like that. You'd be surprised the people who feel exactly the same way. And most of them are out there walking around pretending to be together, but really they aren't, they're as lost and confused as you are. The only difference is you've already had your crash to the bottom and now you're at a place from which you can start to discover yourself."

"Yeah, I guess, sorry for the..."

"No, it's perfectly normal, it's very good actually, keeping going, bawl your eyes out, you're acknowledging the fact that your focus now is on discovery yourself. Kinda exciting in a way."

"Yeah, I suppose."

"You know, it's a really good place knowing you haven't a clue who you are."

"Is it?"

"Yes, it takes a long time to discover who you are and sadly most people don't even get started. You're actually now in a much better place than most. Granted it in no way feels like that, but you are. And you've got so much more support around you than you could ever imagine."

I smiled, not really taking in too much of what she was saying.

"It's nice here isn't it, good for the soul," Rachel said, relaxing and looking out at the garden.

"It is nice," I said, feeling an enormous weight lifting from my shoulders. I look on at the children playing in the warmth of the blazing sun and felt a pinch in my heart. I so wanted to be happy, more than anything I wanted to be happy, and I realised there and then that if I was to give myself the slightest chance of happiness I would have to put all the betrayals behind me and open up to trust.

I didn't understand that day the subtle nuances of Rachel's words. It was only upon reflection that her words truly started to resonate with me. I was to find out a few years later that she firmly believed in the presence of angels – which makes total sense now. Soon after both Sarah and I left the shelter, Rachel established a library filled with literature about angels. I'm sure to this day that the shelter in Stevenage is helping people in more ways that they can begin to understand. I'm convinced that the positive energy filling every inch of the shelter was a result of a host of angelic presences serving to heal the souls of some of the most vulnerable women and children.

* * *

Summer 2008 was the date I left the shelter and moved into my brand new apartment. Once more I found myself in a new home which provided me with the opportunity of a new beginning. The house which was found for me was in the town of Welwyn Garden City in Hertfordshire, 25 miles north of London. Shortly after I moved in, Sarah got her own home, which was close enough for us to continue our fledgling friendship, although I suspected that she, like me, felt something more than friendship.

From the start, our relationship was of a gentle nature – friends who trusted each other. Sarah spoke a lot about spirituality and had a very open mind. I often wondered what she would make of my situation, my mixed-up sexuality. I liked her a lot and felt I could trust her, but here again I was too afraid to muddy the water with talk of sexuality. I guess I was afraid to lose her friendship. A crazy notion, I know now, but without the clarity that comes with self-acceptance the prisons we build for ourselves are very convincing.

It was about two months after moving into my apartment that Sarah left for a two-week holiday in Spain. We had been spending a lot of time together of late and I really missed her while she was away, so I was delighted when she rang, having just arrived back, and asked me if I fancied a night out in London. The invitation made me feel wonderful, because it showed that she had missed me too. Deep down I guess I had feelings for her, but I was doing my level best to suppress them because I just didn't want to have a romantic relationship with Sarah when I thought it would be a non-runner from the very start.

Putting all negative thoughts aside, I got ready for our night. We had arranged to meet at a well-known bar. I was there first and rose the instant I spotted Sarah coming into the busy lounge. She was bubbling over from her two weeks in the sun. She was also very tanned and very beautiful, which I desperately tried to ignore.

After a couple of drinks Sarah and I decided to take a stroll through the West End. Turning on to Compton Street, we suddenly found ourselves in the middle of a very flamboyant gay festival. The atmosphere was electric. A flotilla of brightly-coloured bodies occupied every inch of the grey concrete, turning its gloom into a cacophony of sparkling joyfulness.

Down the street now, bodies coming from the four corners, there was a chance Sarah and I would get separated, so I instinctively grasped her hand and led her through the swaying crowd. Same-sex couples, laughing and loving, were everywhere to be seen. In the back of my mind, I wished I had the self-love to be so free. I turned to Sarah, still holding her hand, and she smiled back at me. I felt a rush of energy, and I knew there and then that there was something more than friendship between us.

After our night out in the West End, Sarah and I began to spend even more time together. I think both of us knew from early on that there was an attraction between us, and I suppose both of us were afraid of it. Afraid or not, the power of the attraction overtook us one evening when we were having a drink. I'm not sure how it happened exactly, but one minute we were laughing, loosened up by the wine, and the next minute we looked at each other, just like the movies, and kissed.

That kiss took our relationship into new territory for Sarah and old territory for me. In my mind, I knew I didn't want history repeating itself, but I just couldn't help myself – the heart wants what the heart wants.

And so once again, the whole complicated issue of my sexuality was waving in my face again. And once again, I tried my best to shove it right back into the recess.

* * *

The first few romantic weeks with Sarah were wonderful. She was such a free spirit, and being around her opened up a whole new world of angels and magic to me. Sarah believed that there was so much of this world that we just couldn't see. She believed whole-heartedly in angels and fairies and all the magic and enchantment that went with them. Whilst I didn't exactly buy into it all in full measure, I was happy to quieten my scepticisms for her sake.

All the talk of angels and otherworldly entities was certainly playing on my mind one particular night in August. I had gone over to Sarah's apartment and after a pleasant night in front of the TV, she went to bed with her daughters and I remained on the couch. August had brought with it the warm sultry evenings that couldn't help conjure the feeling of magic.

Feeling the heat, I shoved my head out the window and instinctively looked at the sky. It was a beautiful star-filled night. Taking in a deep breath, I focused on a star that seemed to be sparkling at me and made a wish to see an alien.

"That's strange," I giggled to myself, walking back in. I

wasn't sure where that had come from, it wasn't exactly the typical thing you'd wish for in a sky full of wishes. Still amused, I laughed out loud as I snuggled upon the couch. Wow, Sarah was really getting to me. I turned over enjoying the randomness of it all.

Later that night, I woke up in the early hours with the full memory of a dream still playing in my head. I don't know if it was the heat or the wine or something else, but either way I couldn't recall having ever had such a vivid dream before.

In the dream, I was in a strange land walking alongside what I can only describe as pillars of glimmering light, but it wasn't just light, it was beings, extra-terrestrial if you will, in all their strange glory. The landscape, although total alien in its appearance, seemed oddly familiar to me, as did the beings.

The dream felt so real, I was very excited to tell Sarah all about it the next morning. And as she entered the living-room, I was just about to do exactly that when she stole my thunder, "You'll never believe what happened last night!"

"What?" I said, rubbing my head and thinking how cute she was in her PJs.

"Honest to God, there were thirty or so lights in the sky last night."

"What kind of lights?

"I don't know, round, pulsating, and then they came together in formation. It was amazing, incredible, I can't believe it!"

"What, like UFOs?"

"Yeah exactly, it had to be, definitely, they were definitely spacecraft."

"You're pulling my leg aren't you?" I said, smiling.

"No, no! I swear. I'll call the girls, they can tell you."

"The girls saw them?"

"Yeah, we all did!"

"Why the hell didn't you wake me?"

"I don't know. I was so caught up..."

"This is too strange, you won't believe this, but last night, I made a wish that I would see an alien and then I had this crazy dream. I can't believe you didn't wake me!"

"Sorry."

"So the aliens were outside in the sky last night?"

"How do you know the aliens aren't angels? Maybe they're us but in the future, maybe they're family."

"Are you serious?"

"Why not? Thirty lights doing manoeuvres in the sky! Why not, isn't anything possible?"

"Seriously, you're having a laugh."

"No, I mean it, it's very possible. I believe it. Who says aliens are one way and angels are another. Isn't it possible there is more to it than that?"

"I guess," I said, mainly to keep the peace.

Although the concept of aliens was in no way new to me, I think there is a big difference between talking about aliens, or angels, for that matter, and really believing in their existence without a doubt. Maybe our rational minds are programmed to disbelieve and it takes a process of deprogramming, if you will, before such a concept finally sticks. Maybe it's a process of expanding our consciousness in a way that allows us to conceive the inconceivable. Whatever the explanation, at this point my mind was somewhere between disbelief and belief – I neither truly disbelieved or believed. I doubted – a lot.

"It's mad all the same that I made that wish and had the dream. Strange I'll give you that."

"See! You're saying you made a wish and they appeared, that's as crazy as what I'm saying."

She had me there. I went to the cupboard and took down the coffee. Suddenly, I realised that I was feeling a heavy pressure on the crown of my head. 'All this crazy thinking is giving me a headache now,' I murmured, pouring the water into two cups. Taking a deep breath, I consciously allowed my rational brain to kick in, which felt much more comfortable. Having a laugh was one thing, allowing yourself to dive into a black hole was another. I didn't like the discomfort that came with that, so I opted out – quietly.

After my coffee I turned on some TV to further anchor me into reality and after that I went for the afternoon paper, only to find the whole town was engaged in UFO mania. Even the local paper had dived right into that black hole I was talking about. It seemed the whole town, having seen the extra-terrestrial show in the sky, were now firm believers. Having heard the story a thousand times from practically everyone I met, I raced back to tell Sarah. By now her three daughters were electric with the news.

"What, you too?" I said in mock disgust. "Seriously, I think I'm the only one who didn't see the aliens. Bugger this! Come on girls, if I can't see one, I'll be one," I said, jokingly.

Taking me up on my offer, the girls did a great job. Twenty minutes later I walked out onto the street complete with a green face, black eyes and two antennae sticking out of my head. It was great fun, and everyone laughed at the sight of me, even Sarah, although she scolded me for not taking the UFO appearance seriously enough.

Although the whole affair did descend into quite a joke at the time, what Sarah had said about the angels being aliens stuck in my head for some reason. And it wasn't until after my ASDA awakening that the significance of the event became clear to me. I often wondered after why I didn't see the lights like everyone else had that night, especially as I had made that wish and had had that vivid dream. Over time I have come to the conclusion that the event was to be like a seed, planted to flourish at a time when I would have the clarity of mind to see that my dream was in fact as real as the lights in the sky were.

At the time, I disregarded my dream in the wake of all the physical excitement that everyone else enjoyed, and yet through it I had a unique and personal encounter which only took on the same reality of the physical evidence when I expanded my consciousness enough to view it in a new light.

* * *

It was shortly after the "UFO" encounter that Sarah, out of the blue, sparked up a conversation about a friend of hers, Lucy, who had gone through a transformation – male to female. The moment I heard these words, a heaviness came to my chest. I didn't know what to say. I couldn't say anything, so in panic I made up an excuse about being hungry and fled to the kitchen. A heavy portion of self-love had been removed as a result of being in the wrong body. And if any sustainable healing was to occur I knew I would have to face my reality head on – even if that meant running the significant risk of rejection. It was now or never.

Walking back from the kitchen, I could feel the fear rising. I paused before entering the living-room and closed my eyes. "Go away, I want you to go away now," I told the children, commanding my fear for the very first time. After a couple of deep breaths I walked back to Sarah and sat down beside her. "Sarah, you know you were talking about Lucy. Well I want to tell you that I've always felt that I was a male, not a female."

And there it was. Forty years it had taken, but the truth, finally, was out.

"You know, I already knew," she said. "That's why I brought Lucy up. Do you want to talk about it?"

Did I ever! We talked and we talked until I had told her absolutely everything. I kept nothing back; everything came into light that night. We went to bed together that night in each other's arms, and for the first time in my life I felt the glow of completeness.

Now Sarah was never one for letting the grass grow under her, so the very next morning she had me sitting in front of my local doctor discussing my options – one of the happiest moments in my life.

"You might want to take some time to think about things," he said.

"No, I've had enough time, let's get this done."

There wasn't a flicker of hesitation. I knew instantly what I was going to do. I was going to go through with the gender realignment operation in order to have the male body I so desperately needed.

Leaving the doctor's surgery, I looked at Sarah and we both smiled. I felt like a bright light had consumed the darkness and finally my life had so many wonderful possibilities.

"Thanks for doing this," I said, cuddling up to her in the back of a cab.

"You know, I don't always tell people this, but sometimes I have premonitions and last night I dreamt that one day you'll end up telling everyone about your life."

"Do me a favour!" I said, laughing it off. While I had shared so much with Sarah, I just didn't want to bring the darkness of my life with Tina into our world.

"No I'm sure of it, maybe you'll write a book."

"I'd rather forget most of my past not remember."

"Well, you should keep a diary at-least. It's a good way of marking the progress you're making. It helps me anyway."

"Maybe."

"No, seriously you should."

"You always this bossy?"

"Always, and you should."

Although I had absolutely no intention that days of writing either a diary or a book, as it turned out, eventually I did both. I have no doubt Sarah had psychic abilities, just as I have no doubt that Sarah came into my life for a specific purpose, which was to guide me towards my physical transformation.

* * *

A week after the doctor's appointment my head was a spinning-top as the fullness of the picture came into view. I knew I would have no option but to sit down and tell my family not only about my gender identity but about my decision to transform my body.

After a couple of days' deliberation, I decided to tell my mother first. Although I didn't relish the thought of telling either of my parents, the way I figured it was that my mother would be the easier of the two. The truth was, much as I dreaded telling my mother, the thought of telling my father was making me physically ill. And so, before I allowed myself to be talked out of it, I got on the phone to my mother and arranged for her to visit the following weekend.

The days leading up to my mother's visit were anxiety packed. I was so wound up that I barely let the poor woman in the door before I was dragging her to the table for a talk.

"Mum, I need you to sit down, I've something to tell you," I began.

"Oh Lisa, what is it? I don't like this," she said taking her seat nervously. "I knew by your voice on the phone there was something wrong."

"No Mum, nothing wrong, I just need to tell you something."

"Now you're really making me nervous."

"No its okay. I really don't know how to tell you this, Mum."

"Oh for heaven's sake, just tell me!"

"I've been to a doctor."

"Oh my God!"

"No, no! It's nothing like that. I'm fine."

"Oh don't! What is it then?"

"Okay, well you know the way you always said I was a tomboy?"

"Yes, yes, a proper little tomboy is what we called you."

"Yeah, well it's a bit more than that Mum. You see the truth is I've never felt like a girl."

"Go on."

"I've always thought of myself as being a boy trapped in the wrong body."

"Is that possible?"

"It is, it's called transgender and now I want to get it fixed."

"Fixed?"

"Have the right body, a male body."

"Well I've never heard of that, so I don't know what to say. I really don't. Is it dangerous?"

"No, no, not at all. It'll be done by proper doctors in proper hospitals, through the NHS."

"Is that so? Well they'll take care of you then, won't they?"

"Yes, yes they will. So you're sure you're all right with it Mum?"

"I only want the best for you and that's all I've ever wanted for all of my children. And you know thinking about it, you never were girlie, were you?"

"No I wasn't. You know if I'm getting the new body and all I think it makes sense for me to change my name too."

"To what?"

"Lee."

"Oh, that'll take some getting used to. But, Lee, Lisa... it's not so different and if it makes you happy..."

"It does Mum, it does."

"And I'll have to call you son now, won't I?" she said, smiling.

"Thanks Mum, you have no idea how much this means to me," I said, reaching over to give her a hug. "What do you think Dad will say?"

"Doesn't matter what he says, it's your life. I'm just sorry you didn't say anything before now. Maybe if things had been different..."

"No Mum, I don't want that. The past is over. I only want to look forward, okay?"

"Okay, Lee," she said, smiling and taking my hand. I looked at her and smiled back, feeling my heart bursting with happiness.

It was not long after telling Mum that I arranged a similar meeting with my father. Although I fully expected his reaction to be somewhere between indifference and outright hostility, I knew I had to go through with it.

"You feel like you're a man?" he asked calmly, after hearing the news.

"I do. I always have."

"Right, well if that's how you feel you have my full support."

"I do?" I said, trying to remain upright.

"Yes, you have my support, and I also want you to know that I think what you are doing is brave, very brave."

"Thanks Dad," I said simply, although the exchange wasn't in any way simple or superficial. In as few words as these, I had found my father again.

Leaving with my father's blessing had me walking on air. There was now nothing in my way; I was finally going to have the peace of mind I so yearned for. Of course I was frightened about the procedures, and the doctor made certain not to hold anything back from me. I would have six operations over a period of two years. Each would be as complicated as the last and would be buffered by a painful period of recovery. He explained: "The only people on the planet who would willingly put themselves through such an ordeal are people who are truly desperate to align their body to their gender. There must be no mistakes. Before anyone gets the go-ahead for the procedure, they have to agree to at least a year of rigorous psychological assessment and preparation. Do you understand what we're talking about?" He looked across his desk.

"I do," I said, feeling the sweat dampen my trouser seat. "Thank you, you don't know what this means to me."

"I wish you well with it all and if you've any questions or concerns you can always come back and talk to me. And you should know that at any stage you feel it isn't right for you, you can just call a halt to it."

"Oh, that won't be happening."

"Okay. Well I'll send out the appropriate paperwork and

get the ball rolling. You can expect to hear something in a few weeks."

It wasn't long after this that Sarah and I decided that our relationship was destined to continue only in friendship. It was as if the reason for us being together as a couple had disappeared overnight. I had a new direction to my life and she had hers. However, true to her word, Sarah supported me right through my year of counselling. She also guided me straight through the doors of university. She knew I wanted to get the degree I had always wanted and she literally took me by the hand straight to my enrolment.

Yes, it was because of Sarah that I enrolled in a university, and it was because of Sarah that I was so buoyant that day in the Asda car park, when my life did another giant loop upon meeting Candy.

Looking back on it now, I see that Sarah came into my life for a reason. She was like a guiding angel, only here in the physical. I also see now how finally speaking my truth to Sarah was such a pivotal moment in my life. It was the moment my life jumped onto the path of happiness.

Within a matter of weeks of seeing my local GP, I got my referral to a counsellor who specialised in gender transformations. After a number of different referrals, I finally ended up attending the gender identity clinic in Hammersmith, London.

Slowly but surely, I felt the bright person I was born to be emerging from beneath the many layers of darkness that had kept life so dimmed for so long. Truly, I felt wonderful. And for the first time in my life, I felt incredibly fortunate and incredibly optimistic about my future – not part of my future, but my whole future.

Before Sarah faded from my life, she did me one more great service. She acted as witness to my request to legally change my gender and name. Together, we sent off the forms and then I waited. Finally, a couple of weeks later, the envelope arrived. I picked it up and turned it over. I could feel my heart pumping with excitement as I opened the letter. And there it was, the official confirmation that I was Mr Lee David Carter.

I took a deep breath and ran my finger across the words. It was real, and it felt amazing. I took the letter to the kitchen table and sat with it for a moment. I now knew I would do something with my life.

It wasn't long after getting my name confirmed that I received word that I had been accepted into university. I would commence my studies the following year, September 2009.

As this date came ever nearer, I was so busy with everything that I hardly noticed Sarah gracefully bowing out of my life. There was no incident, no words, it just happened, I guess, as it was intended to. I have no idea if Sarah was consciously aware, at the time, of the role she was playing in my life, either-way I'll be forever grateful for having had Sarah in my life.

CHAPTER 16

It is September 2009 now, two weeks since I started college and two weeks since what I like to call, my spiritual awakening in Asda's car park. For some reason I can't get the events of that morning out of my head, and it's driving me crazy. I'm sitting at the kitchen table with the number Candy gave me, out in front of me, and that's driving me crazy too.

"Oh sod it!" I said. As I dialled the number a number of thoughts raced through my head, but it was the fact that I was one giant step closer to buying into every crazy notion that spilled out of Candy's mouth that took pole position. Was I crazy? "Oh sod it," I said, putting the phone down. This was no small act of lunacy I was about to take. I had spent my life hiding from opinions and yet here I was about to dangle myself over the pit of the outsider.

Breaking free from what society expects of you is no easy

thing. You have to accept that most of your family and friends won't accept your path as a viable option. They will view it as a copout at best and as total madness at the very best. Having gone through what I had been though, I should have been the last person on the planet to consider taking the alternative path in life, yet here I was two weeks later, having made that call, sitting in front of Candy listening to her chat easily with a spirit guide named Jeff.

"Are they here now?" I asked, referring, as you do, to the angels. It was like this for a while. There were days when I believed what she had said, that angels were all around us, and there were days when I thought both of us were barking mad.

"Of course, and they will be, especially Archangel Michael," she answered. "It's usually Archangel Michael who gets the ball rolling. He's the one who helps mostly with the initial healing phase. I know you've had a difficult past by the way, but it's okay, I don't need to know the details."

"I've had issues but I'm sorting it now. I'm going through the process of transformation, getting into the right body."

"I can see that. How's it all going?"

"I'm doing hormone therapy at the moment and then I'll start a series of operations."

"Call on Archangel Michael when you need support and start meditating. You need to rebalance your lower chakras."

"My whats?" I asked, totally lost, which was no big thing around Candy.

"You can look it up on the Internet. Ask for guidance and you'll be sent to the information that's right for you."

"What, it'll just pop up?"

"Pretty much. You don't think beings that have been

around just about forever would have a problem with the Internet do you?"

"I guess not," I said, more than a little perplexed. It was all so much to get your head around. When I was with Candy it all seemed almost plausible, but inevitably the moment I left her the doubts invaded. And it slid like this for quite a while.

While the jury was still out on the angels and all, what I did take on board wholly was meditation. The fact was, not only did I enjoy it, I found it very calming, which given my past was only a good thing. I also, as she had advised, found a video that gave a step-by-step explanation on how to rebalance the chakras. After a couple of goes, I got the hang of it and soon meditation became a part of my morning and evening routine.

I was a month or so into meditation when a curious thing happened; I started to sense a presence around me. At first I thought it was auto-suggestion, but then in addition to the strange feeling of having company, I started to find feathers again – sometimes beside my bed and sometimes at my front door. It got to the stage where I would almost expect to find one on the doorstep each morning.

Another positive in my life at this time was undoubtedly the Internet. I had no idea how small the world had become and how easy it was to connect with people from all over the planet. And for me this meant I could instantly strengthen the connection I had with Jamie. Suddenly we were able to chat whenever we wanted, and suddenly we were becoming much closer again. The rekindling of the special bond between Jamie and me allowed me, finally, to take the plunge and tell her the truth about my gender identity. And to my immense relief, she was totally supportive.

Having Jamie in my corner was a great source of comfort

to me. And whenever I worried about university or my operations, I knew she was there for me. It didn't take long before we were communicating with each other daily. And it didn't take long for me to wonder whether our story had one more twist in it after all.

This thought was well and truly stoked into a fireball during a chat, a couple of days later, with Candy. At this stage coffee with Candy had become something of a regular occurrence, and wide and wonderful as our conversations were we had never touched on my love life, so I was somewhat taken aback, to say the least, when she matter-of-factly said that I had a soulmate in America. I was by now getting used to being shocked by Candy's otherworldly insights, but this declaration well and truly floored me.

Upon leaving Candy, the only thing on my mind was Jamie. I couldn't help myself, Candy had kicked in the floodgates and the warm gushing water was swamping me. On this revelation, I didn't have to stretch for belief because all it did was confirm what I had always known deep down. And now, with my transformation in the works, there really was the possibility of blue skies ahead.

As I lay in bed that night, sleeping proved difficult. My head was working overtime putting plans together. I knew I needed to finish my degree, and anyway America was not an option while the operations were taking place, not anything permanent at least. Timing was never on our side, it seemed, but I had a feeling that somehow, one day, it would all work out. The only thing I had to worry about was patience. But that was so hard when all you wanted was to be with someone. Still, patience was what was required, so I resolved turning over one last time to set my sights a little farther into the distance. I would finish my transformation, my degree, and then the road would lead to Jamie. I was sure of it.

Another of Candy's revelations that day was her utter insistence that I would become involved with the media in some shape or form. Obviously, this one went right out of my head once Jamie was mentioned. I didn't buy what she said here, I really thought this one was a dude.

"You're having a right old laugh," I said, spreading some jam onto my scone.

"As you know hun, I don't do fortunes, but that's what I'm being told," she said, getting up. "I'm popping out for a fag."

"Hold on a minute. Are you serious?"

"It's nothing to do with me, that's what I'm being told."

"But why? In what way? Has it to do with my singing?"

"Hold on," she said, turning her head to the side. The sight of her doing this always made me uncomfortable. It was her way of tuning in, or so she said.

"No, nothing to do with music, though that's very good for your soul. No, it's to do with your story, your transformation."

"I'm going to go to the media and talk about my transformation?"

"Yes."

"Now I know you're having a laugh."

"Don't you think it might help others?"

"I'm not doing it, forget it! What about everyone in university?"

"What about them?"

"They see me as Lee, and I like that. I don't want people looking on me differently. I like my life now."

"And you should. Look, you can do as you like, no one's going to force you hun. Like I always say, we were given free will, so you do as you please," she said, putting her bag over her shoulder. "Back in a mo."

I'd spent forty years hiding my story, my truth, so telling my story to the nation would be a close second to a torturous death. She is having a laugh, I told myself, driving back home through the cold December evening. My past had taken great big chunks out of me that still weren't healed, so the very thought of sitting down and opening up to the world made me physically sick. Besides, I just didn't trust the media. What if they spun my story, made me out to be a laugh, an oddity or even a freak? There were just too many concerns, too many fears and too many present dangers. In truth, I was so disturbed by the whole media thing that I had to spend the entire evening convincing myself that there was no way on earth I was going to comply with the request – faith or not.

With the turning of the calendar to 2010, immediate thoughts of my first operation, a double mastectomy, came to mind. Six months to go and my physical transformation would begin.

Come the middle of January I was back in university. I was glad to be back. I liked the routine. I like the classes and I liked the time in between when I could read my messages from Jamie.

It was late January when I logged on this one time and found a message from a girl called Fiona. At first I had no clue who she was, but then upon going to her page light bulbs started to flash. No! It couldn't be - could it? The picture was familiar. I could see the resemblance. Oh my God, it was her, it actually was Fiona – the ghost from my past life with Tina.

I hadn't given her any thought since I escaped that life,

and now here she was. My immediate thought was to delete the message without opening it. What if she was still involved with Tina? What if it was just another scam? What if Tina was still out for revenge? All these questions moved my finger towards the delete button. But then, for some strange reason I paused. And against all better judgement, I opened it.

The message was short and simple. She wanted me to know that she had turned her life around, that she was, at this moment, studying to be a doctor of psychoanalysis in Trinity College Dublin, as she had always wanted, and did I want to call to have a chat?

To say that I found it all a little strange would be a gigantic understatement. There was no apology, no remorse, no regret, just a friendly, matter-of-fact, 'hey knew you once, want to reconnect?'

I had Fiona's number in my pocket for a couple of days before I finally decided to make the decision – call her or dump it. The fact that I hadn't dumped it already led me to believe that maybe I should call her. Candy had introduced me to the concept of synchronicity. You know, things happening out of the blue that appear to be more than a coincidence. Things like these tell you your angels are at work. I was starting to believe in the angels more and more, so I was always on the lookout for signs to strengthen my belief. And to my great delight I was finding them, so this is why I wasn't so quick to tear Fiona's number into shreds, the simple truth was I wasn't sure if it was synchronicity at work or not.

And so, seeing the piece of paper I had in my hand as one of life's little challenges, I shut off the sirens and went ahead and called Fiona. I had no idea how this was going to go - it wasn't as if we could recount the many happy times we had had together – but still I went ahead and called.

After an initial awkwardness, Fiona came out straight to tell me how she had finally made her escape from Tina. Hearing the horrors of it all made me realise that I really couldn't hold any grudges against her. Was she really that different from me? Both of us had got mixed up in a darkness that nearly consumed us. And thanks be to God, both of us had lived to tell the tale.

In Fiona's case, things had really got dark for her. She eventually escaped by moving to Ireland, but not before Tina had left her in a pool of blood in her kitchen. Fiona had made the mistake of complaining once too often and had received multiple stab wounds to the stomach for her punishment. She was very lucky to be alive. After fighting her way back to life, she had left hospital and fled.

I myself never saw Tina again. I'm told she is now serving a life sentence for murder.

After my conversation with Fiona, I sat on my bed thinking everything over. Both our lives were such cautionary tales. I wondered if maybe this was the reason why I was being gently guided towards telling my story. People face such challenges in life, I doubt anyone has come through to maturity without a series of war wounds.

During the conversation I didn't tell Fiona about my experiences with the angelic realms, but I did tell her about my gender transformation. It felt good talking about it. I felt a sense of pride that I was finally opening up about it.

* * *

By the time spring arrived, Fiona and I had developed a fledgling friendship. I wouldn't say it was a very close one, but we were on good enough terms for her to invite me over to Ireland during my mid-term break. After some deliberation, I decided to take fear out of the equation and take the plunge. I was over worrying about my exams and my operations, and in truth a break was exactly what I needed. And besides, the trip was to coincide with my birthday, and I kind of fancied the thought of doing something special for that.

With my red hair and fair complexion, it would be easy to surmise that I was a son of the Emerald Isle, while in fact, the truth was I had never been to Ireland. As I looked out of the small window at the few straggling clouds clearing I could see that a beautifully clear day was emerging over Dublin.

Turning away, I looked over my shoulder. Towards the back of the plane, there was an elderly man with his head stuck into his paper. Amazingly enough, apart from the two of us the plane was totally empty. I turned back as my attention was grabbed by the pleasant air-hostess announcing our approach.

And to my surprise, a giant knot twisted in my stomach. What in God's name was I doing? My sirens wailed. Too late now. I could feel the thud of the wheels hitting Irish soil. It was the 14th of April, 2010, my thirty-second birthday, and the day that the Eyjafjallajökull volcano decided to erupt, not exactly the slap of encouragement I needed!

Coming face to face with Fiona, given our tainted history, was awkward to say the least. Fiona herself seemed unfazed as she greeted me warmly into her apartment in Rathmines, in the centre of Dublin City.

"Come on, come in," she said, ushering me in. "God it's great to see you." She gave me an unexpected hug. "How was the trip?"

"Fine, good."

"You had no problem finding me then?"

"No, none at all," I said, feeling more awkward by the second. Here was I intending to stay a whole week and here we were struggling at small talk.

In truth, we had nothing in common other than a really bad portion of our lives that neither of us, if we had any sense, would want to bring up. As for Fiona, she genuinely appeared happy to see me. Either this or she was a terrific actor who was up to no good. Perhaps she had Tina stashed away in one of her closets. I didn't know what to think. I only knew all my senses were screaming for me to get the hell out of there.

"Cup of tea?"

"Perfect," I said, nodding. Having landed myself in the concrete, I would just have to make the best of it.

Having survived the morning, I was surprised to find out that Fiona had arranged a night out to celebrate my birthday. But before this, she told me she had a few things to do, which left me free to have an afternoon of exploring. And to be honest, the birthday night was genuinely a nice surprise but I was secretly delighted to escape the small talk, which by now had become truly painful, for both of us, no doubt.

And so, from Rathmines I hopped on a bus to O'Connell Street, the city's central thoroughfare. And from there, I walked up along the Quays, over the famous Ha'penny Bridge and through what the locals call Merchants Arch into the very arty district known as Temple Bar. It was nice to wander the unfamiliar. I felt a certain liberation coming upon me. I guess what I was feeling was a prolonged period of uninterrupted happiness.

After going in and out of the usual sorts of shops, I found myself down a side street staring into the window of an angel shop. I knew Ireland was known for its spirituality, but I thought that was more in the way of the regular Catholicism, so it really was a pleasant surprise to find such a treasure without having looked for it.

With a rather large smile on my face, I pushed through the door and stepped inside. The first thing that met me was the delicious exotic scent, and the second was the warm welcome from Maria, the owner.

"Well, you're very welcome to Ireland," she said, beaming, after I told her where I was from. "Let me give you a little something." She rooted under the counter. "There you go, Archangel Michael. You keep that with you and you'll always be protected."

"Wow, Archangel Michael! You know I pray to him."

"Well there you go, he's a firm favourite over here."

"You know it's so airy or something in here," I said, feeling almost lightheaded.

"It's all the angels love. You know you have them about you?"

"What? Can you see them?"

"I can. I have the gift, always have. You don't have to worry because they're looking after you."

"I'm going through some major changes in my life."

"And you've already acknowledged the angels and asked them for help, haven't you?"

"Yes, yes I have."

"Well then, that explains it. It's a comfort isn't it? You know, I can't imagine life without them."

"I can't see them, but I have a sense of them and yes it is, it is a big comfort."

"And they love it you know, they are such good sports, family I call them. You know there's a field not so far from here, it's well known as a place where angels dance."

"Really? People can actually see them?"

"Some, not all, but if you believe that's all that matters."

"Did you always see them?"

"Pretty much. Would you want to come light a candle with me? There's a beautiful little church just up the road."

And that's what we did; we went and lit a candle together. I was going to be a full man soon, and my outward appearance would very soon match my inward reality. I lit a candle and prayed for guidance and protection. I knew that for the next two years my life would be dominated by my physical transformation. I knew the five operations I would have to undergo would put tremendous stress on me, both physically and emotionally. I knew complications during either one of them would put my life at risk. And I also knew that there was no going back – no reversal later. There was no going back, only forward, so I needed all the guidance and protection that I could get.

After saying goodbye to Maria, I headed back to Fiona's feeling uplifted. Fiona too was in a very good mood. She had booked a table for us at the well-known Knightsbridge Tavern Inn. Which didn't disappoint, and treated to traditional Irish fare and dance we had a really good time. A couple of Fiona's friends had joined us and by the time we left the inn we were all ready to extend the night and go clubbing.

I was well aware that Fiona and her friends were lesbians, but as I had told Fiona about my sexuality I assumed there would be no ambiguity there. I assumed, but unfortunately no sooner had we got onto the dance floor than I was proved wrong.

"I'm straight Fiona." Awkward as hell, but it had to be said.

"Who cares? Live a little."

"It's just not my thing, okay?"

"Okay, suit yourself, what do I care?"

Yes, awkward, and I still had another four days to go. When I woke up the next morning all I wanted to do was to put myself back on the next plane home. I really had to dig deep to keep myself from running out of the door.

As it turned out, hopping onto a plane was going to be a little more difficult. The eruption in Iceland had sent a massive ash cloud across much of Europe, leading to widespread airport closures, including Dublin. I immediately took this as a sign that I was meant to stay in Dublin and that I was meant to be with Fiona, regardless of how uncomfortable I was feeling.

Fiona walked into the kitchen yawning.

"Good night," she said, heading straight to the kettle.

"Yeah, it was great," I said, trying to sound convincing.

"What do you feel like doing? I just feel like crashing for a while."

"I think I'll just head out and explore."

"Grand. You know, I was thinking the press would really go for your story, have you considered contacting them?"

"No," I said, although I was curious why she would bring the media up. Maybe there was a divine purpose to the visit after all.

"I have a contact in the UK, a friend that works with Max Clifford. Do you know him?"

"No," I said, taking my cup up and walking closer to her.

"Well, he's like the cream of press agents. Do you want me to contact him?"

"I don't know."

"Why don't I, what have you to lose?"

I was sitting in Ireland with someone of whom I had only negative memories, grounded by a volcano. There had to be a divine plan in action.

"Yes, why not," I said, ignoring the burning in my stomach. I didn't have a good feeling about it, but I really thought it was one of those moments when you just have to close your eyes and hold on tightly.

I left Fiona to do what she wanted to do and I headed straight back to the angel shop. I felt really nervous about mixing Fiona, the press and my life story all together and I couldn't think of anywhere else I wanted to go.

As I pushed my way through the small front door, I was immediately spotted.

"Ah, they're still around you!" Maria shouted from behind the counter.

It felt good being there, like I was meant to be there. After another lengthy chat about the angels we said our goodbyes and I never saw Maria again, though I kept her card with me, in my wallet, throughout all my operations, and still to this day, Archangel Michael comes everywhere with me.

When I arrived back later that afternoon, Fiona opened the door with a huge smile on her face.

"They've taken the bait!" she said excitedly.

Her choice of words immediately set alarm bells started ringing.

"They want to see you in their offices on Friday, you're going home on Thursday, right?"

"What did you tell them?" I asked nervously.

"Just about your operations, about your going from female to male. You know, I think it would be best if I went over with you, seeing as I made the introduction and everything."

I didn't want Fiona to come over; I wasn't even sure if I wanted to take the meeting at all. What did I know about press agents? All my worries about the press suddenly flooded my mind. I felt the ground turn to sand and I didn't like the feeling at all. I was losing my grip. Events were suddenly unfolding that didn't resonate well with me. I really wasn't enjoying the experience and I didn't want Fiona to come over with me.

I went to bed that night and prayed for guidance. In the morning Fiona rang the airlines and was told that in all likelihood Dublin Airport would remain closed for another couple of days. I made the decision there and then to take the ferry back to the UK. Due to college commitments Fiona couldn't do the same, so my immediate problem of her coming with me was removed.

Boarding the ferry back to the UK gave me a giant sense of relief. It felt to me like I had escaped the lion's jaws. With the last of my money, I bought a drink and sat in the lounge, which was packed to capacity. I found a space and sipped on my drink watching some children playing. While I was relaxed, others about me wore faced totally frazzled by the unexpected disruption to their lives that the volcanic ash had brought. I watched the children and was brought back to my own childhood, and how happy I had been until my mother had left and puberty had arrived.

The first of my operations was now only ten weeks away, and I knew I had a story to tell. I knew my story could touch others in a way that might bring them some relief from their own torments. I knew speaking publicly about my transformation was the next step for me to fully acknowledge and accept myself and my truth. Maybe coming to Dublin was divinely guided after all, but so too, I thought, was my hasty retreat.

The coach journey back to London was long and arduous.

I really should have slept, but I just couldn't, given the decision I now had to make: go or cancel.

The next day I made my way to Bond Street. The way I looked upon it was that if I really wasn't meant to make the meeting, I wouldn't have been so lucky as to get one of the last places on the ferry. Despite, this reassurance, I was feeling very nervous as I walked into the swanky office and up to the stylish receptionist and introduced myself.

After a short wait, a beautiful young woman came up to me and introduced herself as Anna. Full of smiles and enthusiasm, she led me into her office, where we stayed chatting for some time. She asked questions, listened and took notes. I answered her as honestly as I could. After she was done, she walked me back to the lobby, smiled and offered me her hand. "We'll be in touch," she said sweetly, and with that she was gone.

Walking out, I honestly felt a little deflated. I don't know what I had expected, but I guess I had built up the idea of talking to the press so much that failing a full on assault by the paparazzi, I guess I was bound to be disappointed. Maybe I had taken this whole press thing a little too far, I thought, heading down the stairs to the tube. Perhaps just being willing to speak publicly about my experiences, about my transformation, was enough. Maybe it was a test, conquering my fears, and all that. And suddenly my disappointment turned into relief. I did feel proud that I had summoned enough courage to place myself in that office. I did feel proud at how far I had come. And I was relieved now that it turned out to be no big thing. I had enough big things in my life - did I really need anything else?

The next day, a Saturday, I woke feeling a renewed sense of curiosity about life, the universe and everything. And so after breakfast I leapt onto my laptop, eager to browse as many alternative sites as I could find. I had so many questions that I felt the excitement of a child in the midst of a great treasure hunt. The only trouble I had was balancing my spiritual search with my university studies. I was equally dedicated to both, so I had to shoulder quite a heavy load, a load that in ten weeks' time was to have a couple of tons added to it. Maybe mixing in the media at this stage of my journey was one step too far. Maybe it was a blessing that nothing tangible had come out of the meeting. I took a moment away from the screen to digest the thoughts that had just come into my head.

What man supposes, God disposes. Two weeks later I got a call from Anna. As it happens, after our meeting Anna had a production meeting with a number of her colleagues and as a result, the proposal of my transformation being documented came about. Anna stressed that nothing was definite, that there was just the possibility of the documentary being commissioned. I listened to everything she said. When she was finished, I said okay, great, thanks, and hung up.

It sounded all so up in the air, it felt, in truth, more like a gentle kiss-off. And if it wasn't, well, the way I looked on it, if it was meant to happen it would, and if it was meant to happen it would be okay. I was finally learning to trust.

I had not heard from Fiona since returning, but curiously enough I got a phone call from her that very evening. In the back of my mind, I did consider the fact that Fiona probably knew as much as I did, if not more, about what was going on with the agency.

"Wow, BBC or ITV, I bet they'd pay big money for that," she said excitedly.

"I don't know about that. It wasn't mentioned."

"No, but they'd have to. You'll probably get tens of thousands."

"Doubt that."

"No, you'll be like one of those reality stars, you'll get shop openings and everything."

"There's nothing definite Fiona, Anna made that very clear."

"Ah they have to say that. Come on, it's Max Clifford, you're going to be famous Lee, so don't forget who helped you."

"I won't," I said jokingly.

"You know others would look for a percentage for getting you a deal like this, but I wouldn't. You know, let's say you did make it big, you know how you could thank me?"

"No?" I said totally bewildered by the whole bent of the conversation.

"I want to have a baby."

"Sorry?" I said, almost falling over with the curve we had taken.

"By artificial insemination."

"Oh," I said, words failing me.

"I can get it done in Harley Street, but it costs five thousand, sterling."

"Oh," I said, the penny finally dropping.

"And, you know it's a lot of money, if you don't have it."

"It sure is," I said, not knowing whether to laugh or cry. How, had I been so stupid! I knew it. I felt it. Never again, I vowed, would I do anything that didn't sit well with my own inner-guidance.

A couple of days after Fiona's disclosure, I got a call from Anna asking me to come to the offices to do a teaser tape. A well-known production company had signed up to do the necessary preparations for the commissioning process. In an instant, it all had seemed to have progressed so far that I felt uncomfortable letting Anna down. I should have said no, but suddenly swept up in it all, I said yes.

It was a sunny afternoon that found me back in Bond Street, this time up on the roof in front of a camera. I was very nervous, but somehow I found the nerve to talk openly about my transformation as well as my experience with the angels. I don't know if the production team expected that additional twist, but to me it just didn't feel right speaking about my physical transformation without talking about my spiritual transformation and all the assistance I was getting from the angels.

After getting a hold of my nerves, I relaxed and starting to enjoy myself. And by the time the evening wrapped up I felt feeling excited about the prospect of doing the documentary. The guys from the production company were very friendly, and it felt good working with them. Of course I really hadn't really considered the impact it would have on me, not only during the transformation but afterwards. Nevertheless, I waited anxiously for news all week. I waited and I waited, and I heard nothing back.

Eventually, tired of waiting, I called Anna, only to be told that I would hear as soon as they got word back from the TV stations. I waited some more and then some more and then I gave up. I was very surprised that things had not turned out as I had expected. And therein lay another great lesson for me, never to have solid expectations in matters of the divine. I wasn't entirely sure what had led me to those plush offices, but I was certain that whatever had really transpired was ultimately for my good.

As it turned out, the documentary that Fiona had been pinning her hopes on never materialized, so that was that.

With all the distraction of the media out of the way I was again free to concentrate on my forthcoming exams and operation, now only a matter of a couple of weeks away.

CHAPTER 17

My first operation, a double mastectomy, was scheduled for July 2010, and the months leading up to this were filled with both trepidation and terror. I continued to meet with Candy during this period, and little by little she taught me how to listen to the guiding voice within, which I came to understand was my higher self. She explained that I was on a journey, a process of healing, physically, emotionally and spiritually. She told me that the connection I had with Archangel Michael was there so I could call upon him for strength and protection any time I needed it. I knew, without being told, that this healing would be both arduous and lengthy, but I knew that at the end of it life would begin again totally anew. I was thankful to have the real-world guidance that Candy provided, but as she herself had said, many times, there would come a stage when I'd have to let go of the reins and go it alone.

Preparing me for such an eventuality, she suggested that I should get into the habit of speaking properly to my guardian angel and to Archangel Michael, not just in prayer but in daily life, as you would friends or family. At first, to be honest, I found it a little surreal, but as time went on, to my own amazement I started to feel a real relationship forming with them. I didn't feel that they were in some far-off magical realm, I felt, quite often, that they were standing right next to me, just like any regular person, only I couldn't see them. One thing was for sure, I didn't feel as alone anymore. It was comforting. It was very comforting.

I also started to get into the habit of listening more to my own intuition, my gut feelings – if you will, my heart. Although I had always thought of myself as having a good heart, the harshness of my past experiences I was sure had taken its toll. Being in survival mode for so long, coupled with the steady stream of betrayals, would harden any heart, I told myself. I was slowly coming to terms with my past, slowly finding forgiveness for myself and others. Slowly moving steadily along my path.

Out of the blue, a month or so before my first operation, I got word from the council that a larger house was on offer for me. Jumping at the chance, two weeks later, with all my belongings in boxes, I opened the front door of my new home. I was overjoyed.

The next morning, I stepped out onto my porch feeling absolutely wonderful only to find a small card at my feet. On the front of the card was a heavenly scene and on the back was written "Bringers of the Dawn, New Beginnings". I hadn't told anyone that I was moving, so I immediately took it as a "welcome home" message from the divine.

I was by now growing stronger by the day, and more confident in myself. I knew deep down that something extraordinary was happening to me. I could sense change in the world, though I understood it not at all. The more I believed in myself and my divine assistance, the happier my life seemed to get. I may not have understood, but I certainly believed. Going through the life-altering process of transformation while at the same time studying full time was an enormous weight for a fragile mentality such as mine. I shouldn't have been able to cope with everything, yet I lifted my burden with grace and ease. I was transforming not only my body, but my mind and spirit, simultaneously.

At first, getting my head around the fact that the angelic realm was real was a hit and miss affair. Some days I felt it was very real and some days I felt like I had a screw loose. I think it's a case of waiting for your mind to catch up with your heart. The curious thing was, on the days when I found myself questioning my sanity something would inevitably happen to steer me back on course Everywhere, it seemed, I was encountering people who spoke about the angels; the hairdressers, park benches, the library, even college, everyone seemed to be talking about angels. It really was quite extraordinary.

I remember going to talk with a university administrator named Danielle about juggling my exams and my operations. It was early May 2010, and my end of year exams were less than a fortnight away. I sat down in front of her, I guess, with anxiety written all over my face.

"You okay, Lee?" she asked immediately.

"Yeah, I'm just a little worried about everything. You know if I don't pass, will I have to resit them? And what happens if I have an operation?"

"Why don't we have a cup of tea?" she said, rising to put the kettle on.

"No not for me... oh okay. Oh, don't mind me. I'm not really sleeping and well last night... well... what am I like?" I said, hesitating.

"Go on, last night?"

"Well, last night, this is going to sound mad, but anyway, last night I said a prayer and as soon as I finished I looked out my window and there was this bright blue light outside."

"Like a UFO?"

"No, much smaller and closer, like just across the street, above the treeline."

"What was it doing?"

"It just kinda hovered and then disappeared, like a light being turned off."

"Like an orb?"

"Yeah I guess but much bigger."

"Well I totally believe in all that."

"You do?" I said happily.

"Wait until you hear what happened to me. You remember the really bad storm we had in 1987?"

"I do," I said coyly, not telling her that I remembered all too well the morning I was released from Cookham Wood Prison. "The cyclone."

"Is that what it was?"

"Yeah."

"Well, that night I was fast asleep, in a caravan of all places, and next thing I know I was awoken by a strong tugging on my blankets. I looked up and saw an old man standing over me. Well, I nearly blew the roof off myself."

"Who was he?"

"I don't know. He had a long white beard. All I know, one minute he's standing there and the next minute he's gone. He vanished, and I mean vanished."

"You think he was a ghost?"

"I think he was an angel."

"Really?"

"I do. I think he was my guardian angel, because you see, I got out of bed and got dressed, obviously shaken by the whole thing. I remembering hearing the wind howling outside and feeling the gusts shaking the caravan. Only someone out of their mind would go out in it and yet that's exactly what I did, I just felt compelled to go outside. Next minute a tree crashes down, smashing into the back of the caravan where I had been sleeping."

"Wow, so he saved you."

"Yeah, if I hadn't woken up and gone outside I wouldn't be here."

"Wow, that's mad isn't it? So you really believe in angels?"

"I do. I really do. I wouldn't be without them."

"Yeah, I'm doing meditation and trying to talk to them, but to be honest sometimes it feels kinda overwhelming, like I'm losing it."

"I know. It's natural to question yourself but I guess the more you recognise them in your life the more commonplace it all becomes. "

"I suppose."

"Just keep praying, especially to Archangel Michael."

"That's mad you said that, because that's who I was praying to right before the orb appeared."

"You see then, you've absolutely nothing to worry about."

* * *

The night before my first operation had finally arrived, June 29th 2010, and I couldn't sleep. The sterile environment of the hospital frightened me. I felt alone and uncertain about what lay ahead. I had been warned that the recovery would involve considerable discomfort, and I was very worried about having to going back to university in the September only to face another operation in the November. It really was a lot to get your head around, and probably not the sort of stuff you really should be concentrating on hours before an operation. But I couldn't help myself. I could feel the worry getting the better of me and nothing but to worry me further. Having lived with anxiety and panic for so long, I knew exactly where this was all leading, so immediately I started praying to Archangel Michael. And almost immediately, I felt a sense of perfect peace wash over me. All the worries evaporated and I fell off to sleep happy in the knowing that everything was going to be okay.

And I was. The operation lasted a little over three hours in all. There had been some concern whether I would lose one or both nipples, but in the end it all went as well as had been hoped. As I came around, in the male ward, it felt like my body had been ripped open by vice-grips. The pain was beyond imagination, and I was immediately filled with terror. I just didn't know how I was going to get through this operation, let alone four others. With tears rolling down my face, I closed my eyes and prayed for strength. I took a deep breath and managed to pull the cord for assistance. Shortly after a nurse came and arranged a shot of morphine.

Despite the incredible pain, which seemed endless, I remember looking in the bathroom the next day and feeling a wash of joy overcome me. I looked at my chest all bandaged up and felt an unbelievable sense of completeness and triumph. For years I had gone through the physical and emotional discomfort of bandaging my 36D chest and I knew, looking in the mirror, that all that had now come to an end. I felt blessed and humbled by the whole experience, because I knew for certain that I had not gone through it alone.

In the midst of my transformation and my studies, my curiosity was focused on finding answers to those age-old questions, such as who exactly is God and what exactly is his role in our lives? I had been born into a Catholic family, so it seemed logical that my first port of call would be Christianity, but in order to gain a firmer foundation spiritually I extended my research into the other major religions of the world. And here I found that no one religion had anything over the other. Basically, in their own way they were all saying pretty much the same thing. None really satisfied the burning thirst for the truth that was growing more and more inside.

Accepting the angels into my life triggered a stream of supernatural events. It was like a green light had been flashed on in the angelic realm, and now every opportunity was sought to provide me with further signs and validations. I remember, a little over a month after my double mastectomy, I was sitting by the banks of a pretty little canal, enjoying a coffee with friends, when out of the blue a middle-aged woman calmly walked up to the table and excused herself.

"I hope you don't mind me intruding for a moment," she asked gently, "but I must tell you that I can see wings on your back."

"I've been told there are angels about me," I said, reddening slightly. Let's face it, it's not a conversation you fall into easily with friends looking on.

"Yes there are, and I just felt like I should mention it to you. Mostly I work with horses. I'm what you call a horse whisperer."

"Like in the film?" offered one of my friends.

"Yes, animals are spiritual beings just like us. Well, I'll let you get on. I just felt I should tell you."

"Thanks for that."

"Not at all. It was nice meeting you all."

And with that she was gone. I shrugged it off and we got on with our conversation. But secretly, I was delighted to have met the horse whisperer. It was yet another sign that I was doing okay.

On the way home, I noticed what I can only describe as a small curiosity shop. I walked inside and was immediately hit by the heady smell of incense. I walked past a rack of wind chimes and past box after box of stones and crystals.

"Oh hello," a chirpy voice said from behind the counter.

"Hello," I said lightly. "What kind of shop is this, if you don't mind me asking?" Because to me it looked a lot like Aladdin's Cave.

"I like to call it an oracle shop. Oh how wonderful!" she said, suddenly clasping her hands, "You've angels all around you, do you know that?"

"Can you really see them?"

"Yes, yes I can."

"Earlier today a woman said I had angel wings on my back."

"Oh yes, that's probably your guardian angel. Sometimes people get fleeting glimpses of their wings or head. Others see them as shimmering lights or sparks of light at the extremities of your vision. I see them usually as translucent beings much like fairies you could say."

"People keep telling me I've angels around me."

"That means they are sending you a clear signal that you are being protected and guided."

"I'm going through a big transformation at the moment."

"Well there you go. Isn't it a wonderful thing to know that we're never alone and that when we really need them our angels will always be there for us."

"Have you always been able to see them?"

"Yes, always. You could too, everyone has the ability to see angels, babies and young children see them all the time. It just takes practice and patience to develop clairvoyance."

The thought of having angels around me all the time really fascinated me. And hearing it so often, I slowly began to process the whole concept that I really hadn't the faintest idea of what was really going on in the world. I began to wonder if every religion verified the existence of angels and if so many seemingly sane people not only believed but experienced angels on such a regular basis, why then was it such a big thing, in the light of so much evidence, to truly accept the role angels played in our lives?

I was also fascinated with the fact that no matter how much I wanted to fully believe in their existence, routine doubts seemed to keep clouding my mind. It was like there were these foreign thoughts that just floated into my mind for no other reason than to wreak absolute havoc with my belief system. I even began to imagine some external force working to derail my infant steps into spirituality. Finally, I decided that if it wasn't an external force messing with my state of mind it had to be my own rational mind and my ego. Either way I found it a daily battle to settle with the idea that the angels really were a constant loving force in my life.

From birth, I figured, we had been wired in a way that presented a very limited view of what was real and what was not. And so, confronted with my heart-based yearning to believe whole heartedly in angels, my mind went into revolt. Heart against mind, this tug of war was something that caused me great distress, until I decided to trust in the fact that getting beyond the rewiring in my brain was all part of the process of spiritual growth.

A big lesson I took on board was that the less I worried about my progress, the easier everything became. I stopped trying to think rationally about everything. I stopped trying to understand anything. Instead I just took a deep breath and started to relax into the great unknown. I surrendered to the process, and to my astonishment things continued to improve for me. And on the days when I felt anxious or fearful, I prayed and I meditated and things just flowed much more easily than they ever had.

A big change in my life I began to notice was the type of people I was attracting. Gone was the wash of negativity that surrounded me for so long. The new bright and light people who continued to surround me were like a mobile therapy unit. Day by day, these wonderful people helped me to regain my belief in mankind. And day by day I felt a little happier in myself.

I knew I had a long way to go to truly reclaim my self-identity and to be able to step out in total confidence, but I also knew I was on the path that would eventually lead me there. The fact that I was going through my physical transformation was a source of immense relief and joy for me. I knew that once I was standing in the right body I would have the solid foundation I needed to wholly focus on healing my emotional and spiritual self; mind, body and spiritual, it all made perfect sense to me now.

* * *

With my exams and my first operation behind me, I set my sights on spending the remainder of the summer in healing and in study. An intense desire to find out the truth about my spiritual nature now gripped me, and I was excited about having more time to delve into the great unknown.

Opening my laptop up on a shining Saturday morning, my mind contemplated for a moment how vastly different my life was now. In my darker days I had been so consumed with the slog of survival that I couldn't have conjured a single thought about my spiritual nature or true purpose here on earth. But now, with my survival guaranteed, with my self-acceptance on the rise, I find myself with the mental and emotional stability to open my conscious mind up to the notion of infinite possibilities. Removing the boundaries imposed on me as a child and adolescent, I could now lay my mind open to receiving and accepting vastly different concepts and truths. And I found it most curious that I felt a little giddy at the very prospect. How had this happened to me? How had I changed so dramatically? It was truly miraculous.

It was moments like these that sent my heart fluttering and my eyes watering. It was moments like these when I truly felt a little in awe of the scale of it all. I had changed so much. I had received the most wonderful miracle – a chance to live life to the fullest, the way it was always intended to be.

My excitement for life was increased in no small measure by my growing expectation of the unexpected. I would walk out of my door and fully expect to receive some message of encouragement from the angels. Sometimes I would get a physical manifestation, such as a feather or an unusual encounter with another person. Sometimes it was through a random thought or song and sometimes it was through my research; sometimes I would find the exact answers to questions I held. It was very exciting, incredible exciting.

And then, out of the blue it got a lot more exciting when

I got a call from Anna, the publicist, asking me to go on the popular ITV's 'This Morning' show. Four months had passed since I last spoke with Anna, so her request sent a small volcanic eruption off in my stomach. Doing a documentary was one thing, but going on live national television was something very different, something more akin to absolute terror.

In truth my natural inclination was to put down the phone and run off to Alaska or some such remote hideaway, but with Candy's revelation about the media banging in my head afresh, I found myself saying yes. Yes, I would go on the show and yes I would talk openly about my gender transformation and my own personal experience of feeling I had been born in the wrong body.

If getting the phone call about the show was a volcanic surprise, then finding out that I was to appear in a matter of days was a cause of another eruption. Nevertheless, it happened. In the early morning of 7th of August, a car came to bring me to the studios.

Pulling into the silent studio car park, I felt my stomach somersault over and over. I felt physically sick. I felt trapped into doing something I wasn't comfortable with. I looked about me, wondering if there was any way out of it. And luckily, I guess, before I could think any further, the door opened and a smiling female face stuck her head in the door.

"Come with me Lee, we'll get you straight to make-up," she said. True to her word, the young assistant whisked me through a series of corridors straight into a brightly-lit room where another smiling face was waiting for me, literally with brush in hand.

"This your first time on television?" she asked knowingly.

"Yes it is, can you tell?"

"Everyone is nervous the first time. Do yourself a favour and relax. Think about enjoying the attention."

As a teenager, I had created the persona of someone who liked attention. I was the class clown, the life and soul of the party, the one who seemed without a care in the world. But in truth I was shy and insecure. Isn't it curious how our outward projections can be at such odds with our inner realities? I don't truly know if I had ever enjoyed attention, as I had used so many devices to shadow my withered self-esteem.

As the liquid foundation skimmed across my face, I decided to take the advice that was given. I gulped in a few deep breaths and to my surprise I started to feel my nerves subside.

Being a Friday, the show was hosted by Ruth Langsford and Eamonn Holmes. I had seen them many times on TV before, and I was a little awestruck, to say the least, when I finally found myself sitting in front of them. I had worried about my voice trembling or my body breaking out in a sweat, but to my great relief I found myself strangely settled.

As it turned out, I really had nothing to worry about. Ruth and Eamonn were the most gracious hosts I could have imagined. There was nothing sensational about the interview; on the contrary, it was an honest enquiry into my personal experience of gender transformation.

Leaving the studio, I felt a rush of pride in my achievement and also a great wash of gratitude for the spiritual beings that I knew had been with me during the interview. I was grateful for their support, for their trust and for their guidance. Amazingly, the doubts and anxieties that had plagued me all my adult life were nowhere to be seen. I felt, deep down, that I was meant to do the interview.

I knew it was a tremendous moment in my life, the moment when I finally removed the shackles of self-loathing and stood up in front of the wider world to be counted.

The incredible shot of encouragement doing the interview gave me sustained me in the weeks that followed. I felt more courageous, about life in general and in particular about my second operation.

* * *

My second operation, a phalloplasty, to provide me with a penis, took place in November 2010. It was the longest of the six operations, a gruelling 12 hours. I awoke from the operation to see someone leaning over me. Groggy and blurry, it took a few moments for me to registered that it was my surgeon, Dr. Ralph.

"All done. I've given you a big one," he said, smiling.

At first, I couldn't really register what he was saying. The first thing I noticed was that my left arm was elevated in a holdall.

"It'll have to stay like that for a while, and when you get out you'll have to keep it in a sling," explained Dr. Ralph.

"For a couple of weeks?" I said, not remembering what exactly I had been told.

"For a couple of months, maybe three, maybe four, we'll have to wait and see. Sitting and walking will be awkward too for a while, but that should all heal a little quicker. So what does it feel like?"

It took another moment for me to take in what he was asking. I concentrated on the area between my legs and felt the presence of my penis for the very first-time. I looked back at him and beamed, "Amazing, right, complete". To that he nodded and left, happy with himself.

At this time, only a dozen or so previous cases of complete female to male transgender procedures had been carried out in the United Kingdom, so my operation was by no means routine. My recovery was not routine either. While my recovery from the mastectomy was very painful, it was in no way debilitating, like the recovery from the second operation. I had, like my surgeon had warned, a lot of difficulty walking, bending and sitting, and everything was made even more complicated and uncomfortable by the fact that my arm was in a sling. Still, the fact that it was my left, not my right, at least enabled me to continue with my lectures and studies. Although this was extremely difficult, especially during the first month, I found the strength was within me to get through it all.

What helped enormously, of course, was knowing that the angels were right there going through the healing process with me. I continued to meditate and to have my daily chats with them and it really helped. Whenever I felt my emotions swelling, I would go into myself for a moment, ask for a little extra strength and before long I would feel my emotions calming.

Throughout this period, I continued to find feathers in unusual places, left there, I supposed, to give me that extra boost, at just the right time. I know there are people who will read this and discount this out of hand, while others will understand, having experienced the fact that once you acknowledge angel messages, they only increase.

Personally, I don't think angels have a thing for feathers other than the fact that it's pretty much a universal association. I guess they are just an easy method for getting the two-way communications going. As for me, as soon as I acknowledged this form of communication, I immediately started to receive others. From time to time I noticed repeating numbers on clocks, signs and number plates and the likes, and the thought popped into my mind that maybe these might be another form of communications. I had not at this stage heard of angel numbers being a very popular form of communication. And again, just like the feathers, as soon as I had copped on to this communication method the frequency of occurrences increased dramatically.

During my four-month rehabilitation period the number of angel communications increased so dramatically that for the first-time it really started to drill into my head that something extraordinary was happening in my life, even beyond my physical transformation.

In addition to the feathers and angel numbers, I continued to see orbs and began again to smell floral fragrances. I also continued to attract people to me who, like me, had first-hand experience of angels in their lives.

One of the people I encountered during this stage of my journey was an incredibly brave cancer patient called Claire. As a result of her battle with the disease, Claire had a myriad problems with her health. The gruelling chemotherapy treatment she was undergoing had made her very weak and very sick, yet despite her hardship, she remained unbelievably upbeat about life. I remember meeting her in the hallway and asking her how she was feeling.

She looked at me and smiled. "I'm not alone you know," she said, moving to the side to let a group of doctors pass. "I don't know if you'll believe me, but every time I step out of my house to come to the hospital, I find feathers on my doorstep."

"From the angels," I said, finishing the sentence for her.

"I knew you'd get it!"

"I do, because it happens to me too."

"And during the treatment, I know that they're with me. And you know, no matter how sick I get or how bad it seems, I never feel down about it. People can't understand my attitude, but I'm that way because I know that my sickness is just part of my path and anyway I already know I'm going to get through it."

"Wow, that's exactly how I feel about what I'm going through."

"You're very brave," she said sweetly.

"Come on! Look at what you're going through," I said, embarrassed with the comparison.

"I wish everyone could know what we know. No one has to go through anything on their own. I wish everyone in here could know the comfort we have."

Claire was the brave one. She had such an incredible outlook on life. She was in herself proof positive for the existence of the angels. She just didn't talk like everyone else and she just didn't think like everyone else. There was something very deep going on with Claire. She was so connected with another world that it gave me great comfort to realise that it wasn't just me, that there were many people just like me who were at different stages of waking up to this truth.

I continued to meet Claire throughout my transformation as she continued her battle back to health. I never worried about her because I felt that just like me she was being lovingly led back to health by her own special team of angels and guides. Some say there are more angels than stars in the heavens - I don't know how true this is, but I totally believe that there are more than enough loving beings available for every person on his planet. And I believe that they watch and wait for their invitation to come into our lives and once this invitation has been extended they jump into their role with such love and dedication that no one, no matter how dark or desperate their lives may have been up to that point, can help but have their lives altered dramatically.

And the change, once underway, doesn't, in the scheme of things, take long. Just look at how quickly my life had changed. In the twinkling of an eye I had gone from an abusive life fuelled by self-loathing to a loving, joyful life filled now with self-love and self-acceptance. What grace can change a life so completely, so satisfactorily? This can only, in my opinion, happen by the grace of love, a love so complete that it inspires you to look inwards to find the same love waiting within.

CHAPTER 18

───✕───

It was with the same sense of joy, the joy that comes from having a wider perspective of who you are and what you are doing in life, that I welcomed in 2011. And with the New Year came a growing sense of knowing that there was a grand purpose to everything I had gone through up to this point in my life. I had no clear idea what that purpose might be, but I suspected it was far bigger than I could imagine.

What I did know, for certain, was that my third operation would take place in May, and that would take me that one step closer to completion – as I saw it.

Inwardly, I could feel myself evolving. There was nothing solid that you could place your finger on; it was more a knowing that something fundamental was shifting within me. The previous winter, with a growing urge to break out of my familiar surroundings, I applied for a work placement in America, in Connecticut. As it happened, my studies in

International Tourist Management presented me with the perfect opportunity for travel. In fact foreign study was an essential element of the course.

And so by the end of January, everything was set up for me to spend the spring abroad; all that was needed was the visa. My previous trips to the US had been in many respects life-savers, so I was really looking forward to having the opportunity of spending time in the US again.

Waiting for word back from the embassy was a matter of course, I felt. Given the roll that I was on, I was fully confident I would be on the plane and heading for Connecticut within the fortnight. So when the letter came through the door I practically ripped the thing open.

"What? No, this can't be," I muttered to myself, reading the word 'REFUSAL' over and over. I was shocked. I could not believe I had been refused. It was the first major setback I had received since my Asda awakening. I just didn't get it. Immediately, my mind was swamped with thoughts that maybe I had done something wrong. I searched for an answer, all the while blaming myself for having done something to upset my angelic team.

Shaken by the derailment of my plans, I decided to defer my foreign placement for a year. I had no idea, at this stage, that events such as these occur for good reasons. We all, I believe, come to this earth with a blueprint upon which we have already agreed. While we can of course, through the exercising of our free will, deviate from our path, in the long-run it is a blessing to be put back on your path, even if it feels, at the time, a tad rough. Having said that, I have to admit that this wasn't one of the easier realisations to get to grips with.

I couldn't for the life of me figure out what had gone wrong. I never stopped to ask myself what had gone right.

It's not natural to think like this, let's face it.

Still, a month on I started to get over it, helped in no small part by an extraordinary dream I had one night. This dream was very exotic, filled with the sights and sounds of Egypt. I found myself in a temple. The light was only candle light, but I remember running my fingers over a hieroglyph of an eye on the wall. I could feel the heat, smell the exotic aroma and feel the sensation of touching the ancient stonework. What was even stranger was that everything seemed so familiar; it wasn't like a dream at all, it was more like a memory.

When I got up the next morning, the dream was still so fresh it was like I had just returned from Egypt on holiday or something. I got up quite intrigued by the experience and headed off to university.

When I got there I did what I normally did - headed into my lecturers, went to the library and used the computers to chat with Jamie, but all the while I just couldn't shake the lingering feelings of my dream. And by the time I arrived home that evening there was nothing in my mind other than Egypt. For the next couple of weeks Egypt was consuming my every thought, and I couldn't figure out why.

In an effort to discover an explanation for all of it, I went online and found myself reading all about the Eye of Horus and the association with the Third Eye and Pineal Gland. I read and read all about Egypt. I just couldn't get enough of it, and I didn't know why.

By March, my appetite for all things Egyptian was just as strong. I told myself I had to ease off, as it was getting close to both my exams and my next operation, so one lunchtime, in an effort to get on top of my studies, I went to the library to do some exam revision. Sitting at my desk all alone, I dug my head into a book. I might have been there a half an hour or so when an extraordinary-looking figure appeared and greeted me with a broad smile. I looked up into the bronzed face of a very tall monk.

"Anything interesting?" he asked, in an accent I couldn't readily identify.

"Not really," I said, closing the book to give him my full attention.

"You mind if I rest for a moment?"

"No, not at all," I said, gesturing for him to take the seat opposite.

"I'm from Cairo, have you been?" he asked.

"No, no never," I said, taken aback. Cairo, Egypt – quite a coincidence.

"Well, you'd like it. Did you know that there are angels all about you?"

Yes I do actually, well, so I've been told," I said, hardly believing he had just come out with that.

"Yes, you have them close by you. You know you are very lucky to have such a strong connection with them."

"I know I'm being looked after."

"Yes you are. Here, I'd like you to have this," he said, pulling out a small bottle. "Holy water from Egypt."

"Wow, are you sure?" I said, truly flabbergasted.

"Take it. You know angels are a very big part of my culture."

"No, I didn't know that."

"See, I always carry this with me no matter where I go," he said, taking a small card from an inside pocket and handing it to me.

"Archangel Michael! You're not going to believe this, hold on," I said, rooting in my back pocket. "I've the exact same card," I said, handing it to him. It was the card that Maria from the angel shop in Ireland had given me.

"So you know?"

"I know he's around me and supporting me."

"I think you should go to my country. I think you will like it there."

Even with all my self-doubting, I had to admit that this meeting had to be more than coincidence. Was I being guided to go to Egypt? It certainly felt like it.

* * *

On April 8th 2011, I was facing my third operation, the removal of the womb and the reworking of my urinary system to allow me to urinate through my penis. I was both excited and terrified by the changes that would take me one step closer to having the body I so desperately needed. I was also terrified, because I knew I was orchestrating a change that could never be undone. I was recreating myself, going from a female to a male body - recreating if you will my physical existence. And for someone coming from a society which leads you to believe that you are insignificant in the face of an almighty God, going through such a change was a step that could be only taken by totally readdressing my relationship with God.

While others may view my gender realignment as flying in the face of God, I knew that ultimately it was my choice. My free will had led me to a place in my life where I felt ready to make the change. The support of the angels all about me eased all my worries in this regard. Why would I get such love and support from them if I was doing something so wrong? This basic logic helped me to set aside all the niggling doubts that had surfaced as a result of my upbringing.

Like the two previous operations, I knew this one would

be no walk in the park, nor would the six-month recovery time be very pleasant. It was a week before the operation that the nerves really set in. I meditated and I prayed, especially to Archangel Michael, to give me the strength to face the operation with bravery. I thought about Claire and how she faced her battle with the greatest of faith and serenity and it made me see that my hardship was temporary and all for my greater good.

By the time the day of the operation arrived I felt the strong presence of my angelic team around me and knew I was in the best of hands. And I was I awoken from the operation to find tubes coming out of my stomach. I no longer had a womb or a vagina, so for the next three weeks I had to use a catheter.

After a couple of days I was sent home, instructed to have complete rest. With tubes sticking out of me, there really wasn't much else on the agenda. Three weeks passed, and I went to Harley Street to have my tubes removed. After everything was fixed up, my doctor, a male in his fifties, smiled at me. "Right, there's a pub across the road, off you go and have two pinks then come back here," he said.

"You want me to drink alcohol?"

"Yes. whatever beer you fancy, two pints should be enough and then we'll see how everything is working."

"Okay, well I'll see you in a bit," I said, feeling a massive brick forming in my throat. It took all my strength to make it out of the office without breaking down. My mind flashed to the times when as a small child I would stand watching my father shave, watching him stand up straight to go to the toilet, watching him do all the things men do, and so wanting to be just like him. I know it may sound a little weird, but the difference between sitting and standing, when it came to the toilet, was such a big thing for me. I wanted to stand just like my father, just like every other man, just like I felt I was meant to. And now I was two pints away from, well, standing. I know it sounds weird but trust me, having lived as I had in the wrong body, this weirdness was something I was going to celebrate.

And so, I did as the doctor ordered, two pints and I was back in his office.

"Ready to go?" he said.

Something you don't hear every day, but I was, I was so ready. It was the strangest feeling ever, standing, yes standing, on my own two feet, and I was overjoyed.

Everything, thanks be to God, was in good working order, as they say. There were no infections and I was free to go. As soon as I got outside I rang my mum to tell her. "Mum I can now urinate through my penis, no more sitting down," I said. Again, not what you hear every day, but by now she was well on board with my transformation and was truly happy for me.

I felt more like a man that day than I ever had. Although there were still another three operations to come, I felt that the persona of Lisa, the female, which I had had to carry for over forty years had finally slipped away, allowing Lee to finally emerge. There was still a long way to go, not only with my physical transformation but with my emotional and spiritual transformation, but that day, standing upright, I knew I had turned a major corner. I was well on my way.

* * *

Although I was still in considerable discomfort, I managed to get through my second year exams, which left the summer wide open for me. My next operation was not until October, enough time for me to take a breather from everything that was happening in my life.

It was about this time that I really started to notice nature again. I had loved being out in nature as a child, a love that sadly dispersed with the darkening of my days. There was a river close to my house, so I started taking myself out and just sitting there doing nothing except watching life in all its glory. My life, at this point, being still centred on my physical transformation, I could sense an inner change happening as well. I was beginning to become much more aware of my surroundings, much more aware of the world, and much more aware of my connection, not only to nature but to every living being. I was surrounded now by people who were open to spirit. And it seemed that everyone I met was in their own way playing a part in my spiritual growth. No doubt, in turn, I was playing a part in theirs. I still had no clear idea what exactly was happening to me, but I suppose, at this point, it was enough to know that a change was happening, whether I understood the ins and outs of it or not.

In hindsight, not having the documentaries go ahead was a blessing. With life you cannot expect things to happen in the order you desire. Things happen when they are meant to happen; when the time is right and the divine beings know you are ready. And in truth, at this stage of my life, sitting by the canal contemplating the greater meanings of life, I wasn't ready. I needed to allow myself time to heal, and I needed time to grow spiritually. I was exchanging one body for another and upgrading an outmoded consciousness. I was being reborn, you could say, not only physically, but emotionally and spiritually.

That summer of 2011, sitting by the canal, I was worn down and on occasion I had a little cry to myself. It wasn't that I was unhappy, on the contrary, but you know any change is hard and hard as my physical change was, I think it was the spiritual changes within me that were taking the heaviest toll. Going through a spiritual awakening is nothing short of monumental, and no one should underestimate just how much courage it demands. And often, without physical guidance, it can be confusing and largely misunderstood. Very few of us have been prepared for such a life-altering experience, yet with a little knowledge and a whole lot of faith every one of us will be led gently to the emergence of our true nature, for we are all divine and we are all destined, in our own time, to take the path that leads us to knowing ourselves.

One hazy summer day I went for a wander through the side streets of a neighbouring town. I had been there once or twice before, but never had I taken the time to explore it until now. And winding my way down the narrow side streets and alleys I was thrilled to stumble across another angel shop. Who knew there were so many spiritual shops dotted here and there just waiting to be discovered? Like a moth to a flame, I found myself stepping inside, to have my arrival announced by a set of beautiful chimes which I banged into.

"Oh hello," A voice came from behind the curtain.

"Sorry about the chimes."

"No they're in strategic places, nicer than a doorbell don't you think?"

"Much," I said as I approached the smiling woman, who I guessed was the owner. Her name was Amira, she was in her thirties and with silky black hair and soft olive skin very beautiful.

"I sneak outside, every now and again, to throw my face up into the rays, it's good for the soul, you know," she said.

"Yeah, I was by the canal earlier. What's that smell? It's very distinctive."

"It's called Kyphia. It was traditional in my country to burn it at dusk but I like to burn it all the time. It was used for healing and purification, at rituals. You can buy some if you like."

"I might, I'll have a look around first."

"Please."

"What country are you from?"

"I was born here, but Egypt is my home, my father's from Cairo."

"Egypt! Go away!"

"Yes, from Cairo. He grew up very poor, even lived on the streets for a time, but then faith smiled on him and things got better, very much better."

"Wow, you know I was homeless too. I had my life turned full circle by faith and well, by the angels, if you believe that?"

"This is a shop dedicated to the angels."

"Yeah right, of course," I said, getting the joke.

"Angels are very big in the Egyptian culture. Have you been there?"

"No."

"Well, if you go, you will see boats sailing the Nile with angel names, right on their side. You know I think you will go."

"Do you?"

"Don't you?"

"Maybe, I've been having dreams..."

"Then you will go!"

"You will go. You know, I also see you doing something with the media."

"Oh don't say that!" I blurted.

"No, why?"

"I was meant to do some media stuff and it well, it fell through. But then I went on the telly, on the Morning Show."

"I don't watch TV, but no, I see more, I think the angels are taking care of it."

"Perhaps," I said, thinking she was probably picking up on some old messages.

Amira and I continued to chat for what seemed like hours. She took me into the back, where we had a cup of tea. Talking with her was easy, and I felt a real connection with her. She went on to tell me that she really was clairvoyant, and indeed she was, because a couple of weeks later I found myself with an itch that just wouldn't go away, and it was called Egypt.

The holidays were coming to an end and I thought to myself, right, it's now or never. So I booked a flight for the following week. And to top that, a day or so later I got a call from Anna asking me to meet a journalist from The Sun newspaper. As before I was told not to get my hopes up, but the way I saw it, if it was meant to happen it would happen.

A couple of days later, I went ahead and met the journalist and answered all her questions without reservation. I tried as best I could to talk about my spiritual journey as well as my physical transformation, but to be honest it just didn't seem to resonate with her. She was polite in her efforts to dig for triviality, which I guess was fair game as it was her job. I left the interview slightly perplexed by the whole affair and wondering what purpose was being served by it all. Still, the ways of the divine are often shrouded, for good reason I guess. And so, blinded as I was I put all thoughts of the whys and wheres away and turned instead to thoughts of Egypt.

Right before my trip, I went to stay with my mum, who was by now living in the lovely seaside town of Clacton-on-Sea.

"Why do you want to go to Egypt, Lee?" she asked, surprised, as this was the first she had heard about it.

"I can't explain it Mum, I just feel drawn to go there."

"You remember Malcolm James from the old place?"

"Yeah, he's the one that stowed away on a plane trying to get to Egypt."

"That's right, all over the news it was."

"Don't worry Mum, I have my ticket."

"No, but isn't it strange a boy of fourteen doing something like that? You wonder what got into his head."

"I guess there are a lot more goings on in the world."

"That's right, look at you and the angels and me, I've always had that gift of being able to see things before they happen. So it's right you're going, just be careful."

"I will Mum. You fancy sitting outside?" I rose, a glass of wine in my hand. It was one of those perfect nights, still, warm and open skies, perfect for chatting outdoors. And that's exactly what we did. We got ourselves some snacks and headed out to the small garden at the back of the house.

"Such a beautiful night Lee, don't you think?"

"Yeah, but what's that Mum?" I said, spotting something in the sky.

"Oh don't Lee!"

"No, look there Mum, in the sky, that pulsating light, do you see it?"

"Is it a plane?"

"No, it's just stuck there, it can't be."

"Look Lee it's orange now, oh Lee!"

"It's all right Mum, it won't do you any harm, I've seen them before."

"You have?"

"Yes."

"You think it's one of them UFOs? Oh look how its pulsing!"

"Could be. Remember that book Dad read me, Chariots of the Gods."

"I do remember, oh I hope it doesn't come down."

"It won't Mum. It could be a spaceship."

"Oh Lee don't. Do you think so?"

"Well, if people believe in angels then why not other beings? And if you think about it, if there are other beings then wouldn't the angels be involved with them too, I mean if they are involved with us?"

"I suppose, it's all a matter of belief isn't it. Shouldn't we get a camera or something?"

"Probably be gone by the time we'd get back."

" Look Lee! It's going." And with that, the pulsating light shot up at lightning speed before disappearing.

Isn't it amazing how we can witness logic-defying events one moment and the next go straight back to the business of life as we know it? Such duality, and yet we allow ourselves to slip back to the comfort of the rational mind. Who knows, maybe it's meant to be that way. Maybe it is our subconscious that registers these strange events firstly allowing a gradual absorption into the conscious mind. Perhaps this is a fail-safe to prevent us from losing all touch with the reality, whatever reality truly was. The only thing I knew was the more I came to experience the more reality became open for interpretation.

With all thoughts of the wonders of the strange pulsating lights cleared from my mind, I instead filled it with thoughts of the wonders of Egypt, specifically that of Luxor, my magical destination.

"It soon became obvious we were on the threshold of the discovery. It was a sight surpassing all precedent, and one we never dreamed of seeing. I was struck dumb with amazement. It was all I could do to get out the words. Yes, wonderful things." I read these words on the plane heading for Luxor Airport and I was immediate sucked into the wondrous world of Howard Carter, the English archaeologist and Egyptologist who with the help of his backer, Lord Carnarvon, discovered the tomb of the Boy King, Tutankhamun, for the rest of the world, on the 4th of November 1922 in the magical Valley of the Kings.

Stepping out of the airport and breathing in the exotic sights and sounds of wonderful Egypt, I knew in my heart that I was at the start of my own great adventure. I narrowed my eyes, scanning for a taxi. The light seemed stronger here, brilliant and piercing. I didn't have to wait long before a well-worn Mercedes screeched to a halt beside me and a kind-faced Egyptian jumped out to claim me, saying his name was Rahul. "You come with me, kind sir, Rahul will be glad to look after you," he said.

True to his word, Rahul took me safe and sound to my hotel some 12km from the airport, allowing plenty of time for us to get acquainted. And later, also true to his word, he promptly collected me to accompany me on the first stage of my adventure – quad biking in the Valley of the Queens. When Rahul first suggested this to me, I thought the idea was a little strange, to say the least. But his enthusiasm quickly got the better of me and I found myself readily agreeing to his plan.

En route, we stopped at the famous Luxor Bazaar. The evening was setting in, yet the heat was still formidable, especially, I suppose, for a London boy. Still, once I got amongst the mass of bodies that contributed to the excitement of the bazaar I quickly forgot about such mild discomforts. The feast of the senses swirling all around was like a scene straight out of an Indiana Jones movie – haggling, exotic fruit and animals, nuts and spices spilling over everywhere, fine Egyptian cotton wafting in the scented breeze. When I closed my eyes, I imagined those same scents sailing for time immemorial through these same stone clad streets. It was mesmerising.

I loved everything about the taste of Egypt I had sampled so far; the magical bazaar, the vibrancy of the people, the trees spilling over with delicious abundance, dates, bananas - how could anyone not be enthralled by such wonderful sights and sounds. And then there was the most wonderful treasure, in my opinion, the majestic blue Nile with her brilliant white sailing boats traversing her length in the most romantic of ways. The Nile was wonderful and beautiful and majestic and romantic. She was the rushing blood in the veins of this enchanting land.

By the time Rahul and I arrived at our destination in the Valley of the Queens, there was only an hour or so of daylight left. This, I must admit, was more than enough time to be well worn out by the exertion of quad biking over shifting sands in heavy humidity. Still, it was as Rahul had promised, very exhilarating. When it was finished we joined some other guides and tourists for some well-earned chilled beers.

Looking up into the heavens and feeling the warm air embracing me, I felt a sense of contentment and belonging which can usually only be felt in a place called home. I didn't know why, but I felt a very real connection, not only to the land but to the people. I never really considered the notion of past lives before, so I couldn't honestly say if I believed in this possibility or not. The only thing I knew was that through my dreams and subsequent yearning, I felt I was being drawn inexplicably to this land. I would like to say that I asked for a sign to validate everything that was rushing through me, sipping that cool beer and looking out over the golden dunes into the twinkling night, but I didn't and yet there, right there in the skies, directly in our eyeline, was another pulsating light, this time pearly white.

"Look!" I said to Rahul, "tell me you're seeing that."

"Oh yes, we see things like that here all the time. I think they are drawn to this place because of the energies."

"Really, you see them a lot?"

"Oh yes, lots of times I've seen things like this."

"Wow."

"Told you I was the best guide. So tomorrow we go to Karnak, yes?"

Of course it was yes, and the next evening, after a long lounge at the pool, I was yet again out adventuring with Rahul.

"You will not believe the wonders here Lee, it is a most wondrous place, very holy, very special to my people, to me. Very busy though, you bring plenty of water, yes?"

"Plenty," I said, tapping my rucksack.

"Good, trust me my friend, you will need it. I will not spoil it for you, but you will see, the light show is thrilling."

By now, Rahul was indeed like a friend, and if he said it would be thrilling then I expected nothing less. Rahul had kind of taken stewardship of me, and that was perfectly fine with me. He had a pride and passion for his homeland, and my stay was enriched by it. And as a token of our new friendship, he had added, on the way to Karnak, an invitation to dinner with his friends and family to my itinerary. Having the good fortune to be invited into Rahul's home was something I cherished. I told him this in no small measure, which pleased him no end.

In Karnak, I said my goodbyes to Rahul and joined the throngs of tourists funnelling into the Temple. Inside, I could see that there were visitors from all over the planet, all drawn to what I can only describe as the otherworldliness of this ancient temple city. Closing my eyes, as I had taken to doing, I could easily imagine the royal court, jewelled by the mighty Pharaoh, sitting upon mighty thrones, cooled by rippling ostrich feathers. Dating from around 2050 BC, and known by the ancient Egyptians as the "most select of places", it's easy to see how one could instantly be swept up in the fantasy. Covering almost 200 acres, this awe-inspiring sacred complex, built by generations of Pharaohs spanning some two thousand years, was a place of pilgrimage for the Egyptian people, dedicated to their Gods Amun-Ra, his wife, Goddess Mut, and their son, Khonsu. Wandering through the temple complex, you're bound to catch your breath for a moment.

As I went deeper into the mighty structure I felt the strongest sense of connection. As I ran my fingers over the very stones I had months earlier dreamt of, it was almost as if I was once more walking through the very same dream. And then to my utter amazement, as I walked into one of the temples I found myself standing in-front of a pillar with a hieroglyph of an eye on it – the very same hieroglyph I had seen in my dream. My imagination, my intuition perhaps, was now in overdrive. The more I tried to convince myself that it was all a flight of fancy, the more the feeling haunted me. I knew I was in some way connected to this place. It got me thinking that maybe there was something to reincarnation after all.

After a thrilling light show, I met Rahul at our agreed meeting point.

"Well Lee, was it thrilling?"

"Awesome!"

"Ah Awesome, I like that word too. You see everything you wished?"

"And then some."

"Can you imagine this place in all its splendour? I don't think anyone would have such a gift of imagination."

"I don't think so either. You know Rahul, I saw this hieroglyph..."

"Here, you draw it for me," he said passing me a small pad.

"It's something like this," I said, passing it back.

"Ah this is easy, even my son could tell you this. That, my friend, is Wadjet. You never heard of this, no?"

"No, I haven't, I thought it was the Eye of Horus." I was considering letting Rahul in on my secret, but then I thought better of it. I liked him and I wasn't sure he wouldn't throw me out for being offensive or mad.

"All Seeing Eye, Eye of Ra, Eye of Horus many names, but here it's Wadjet. We believe it to be a symbol of royal protection, given by the God of the Sky, Horus, to Pharaoh on his passage to the afterlife."

"So it symbolised guidance?"

"Yes guidance, protection on the journey to the afterlife."

"Do you think it could symbolise spiritual awakening?"

"Yes, from sleep into the great awakening, I would believe so."

As soon as I returned to the hotel, I jumped on my computer and read everything I could find about the Eye of Horus. I had read a lot before, but now I was on a mission to really understand its meaning. I went on to discover that our very own Eye of Horus located in all of us was considered by many ancient cultures to be the seat of the soul. I was fascinated by one theory, which suggested that the pineal gland remains closed until a certain level of spiritual awakening or spiritual vibrations has been reached. Once opened or activated, it is said that the formerly dormant psychic abilities which aid our communications beyond the veil are reactivated.

After an hour or so, I got up from my laptop to stretch my legs. I went to the balcony and stared out at the shimmering Nile. Staring into the mysterious waters, I couldn't help wonder whether I had been brought to this wonder to awaken something dormant in me.

Up to this point, I had considered all the angelic guidance I had been given as support for my physical transformation, but now I had to wonder whether perhaps my physical transformation was the main act.

I woke up the next morning with a brand new perspective on my life. Had everything in my life happened for a reason, even my gender-body mismatch? Had all roads being leading me to this realisation? It was the first time I truly believed, without a single doubt, that I was on a spiritual journey. I didn't have an itinerary nor a clear destination, but I knew I was heading somewhere.

After a truly amazing trip, I left Egypt filled with a renewed sense of purpose, a purpose still unknown, but a purpose nonetheless.

On the plane home, I sat back and thought about everything that had happened over the last few years. Suddenly, it all came together and it all made sense. Whilst before, my interest in spirituality had taken third place behind my transformation and my studies, now, as if by magic, it was firmly placed at the top of my priorities. It was now the single most important thing in my life. And this was, as it turned out, the very reason for me journeying to Egypt. Aren't the ways of the divine spectacular?

Returning from Egypt anew, it was only a matter of days later that I found myself back upon the swings and roundabouts of university. I now wondered what was the real purpose behind my studies for a degree in International Tourism. Was it about building my self-esteem? Was it about opening up the world for myself? I wasn't exactly sure. Before a spiritual volcano had gone off in my life, my world had been very insular. I did, largely, what everyone else around me did. My culture and my upbringing kept me by and large within very well-defined walls, invisible as they may have been.

A secondary effect of my trip to Egypt was my growing connection to not only Mother Earth but also to my fellow man. Whilst before I had blindly seen the separation between cultures, between religions, between countries, now my awakening consciousness was bringing everyone much closer together.

With my flourishing interest in the wider world, I was keen to arrange my placement. As soon as I started back in university I talked to my tutors about the placement and in no time a place was arranged for me in a Canadian town called Hamilton, which was only a half an hour from Niagara Falls. The plan was that I would fly out in October and stay until the following spring.

It was in the midst of preparation for this that I got word that The Sun had decided to run my story. When I eventually got hold of a copy, I was very nervous to see it had been handled. I won't say that the story really did a job on me, because it didn't. But what it did do was to question the legitimacy of having gender realignment operations paid for on the NHS. I guess being controversial sells. And I guess taking out my spiritual awakening and the trauma I had suffered because of my gender really didn't leave too much else. I was happy that the issue of gender realignment was out in the open, but I was concerned that the whole legitimacy of the treatment was being questioned. In the end, I concluded that any debate that brought gender identity into the mainstream ultimately had to be a good thing.

With that minor distraction out of the way, I got the chance to deal with another. With only days to go to my operation, I found that the documentary had been shelved. What will be, will be, I thought, trying to save myself the disappointment. Did I really need the added burden? Perhaps it was a godsend, I told myself. I had been so sure that the media thing would finally happen, but there again, what did I know?

I turned my mind once more to my operation and the wonderful opportunity to go to Canada in the New Year. My plan had been refined to spending the spring in Canada, coming back for my final operation and then flying back out to Canada, a month or so after, to finish the year off in work-placement.

Canada was a great distraction. It allowed my mind to stay well clear of the details of my next operation. I was so looking forward to the experience that I took to doing quite the amount of daydreaming. And it was in this activity that I was fully occupied one evening, looking out of my bedroom window, only a couple of days before my operation. The night sky was so clear you could easily have mistaken it for a gentle summer's night, but when I opened my window I found it had a bite to it. "Wow, that's cold," I said, closing the window tightly. I dug for a lighter, as the thought to pray to Archangel Michael had suddenly popped into my head.   I lit a small tea-light candle and said the few words I had composed to cover my safety during the operations and my guidance along the ever-twisting spiritual path I had found myself upon. Then I blew out the candle, but as I turned to leave something in the sky caught my attention. I turned back fully and opened the window again to get the clearest view, and in no time locked onto a bright shooting light cutting a pathway back and forth across the sky.

Whatever it was, it certainly wasn't man-made, it was going far too fast. And it wasn't a shooting star, because what star moves horizontally in a co-ordinated fashion? And then to my utter amazement, what looked like a glowing star suddenly got a whole lot like a disc. "Okay, I'm actually seeing a UFO," I told myself as my eyes stayed glued to the strange sight. And then, just when I thought things couldn't get any stranger, a second disc arrived. It joined the first in formation and then they both moved off together. I thought they were leaving, but instead they stuck around to complete an awesome air display that any Red Arrows pilot would give his wings to complete. Absolutely transfixed by it all, I watched their aerobatics for, what I thought, was ten or fifteen minutes. In fact, when it finally ended, I was shocked to discover that nearly an hour had passed.

After they had gone, I sat on my bed waiting for my brain to take in all that had just happened. It was by far the most extraordinary thing I had ever witnessed.

Seeing the spaceships had a tremendous impact on my belief structure. From then on I would no longer wonder whether there was life away from our tiny blue planet, because I had seen with my own two eyes that there clearly was. Yes, our world had become a hell of a lot smaller, and I was just itching to find out anything I could about these visitors. I suspected a lot more people must have seen the same thing that night. I suspected people all over the world were seeing similar things on a regular basis. I wondered whether these sightings were increasing to allow mankind to gradually absorb the truth about life amongst the stars. I also wondered when this soft-soaping would cease and the "coming out party" would occur. I don't know why, I just found myself with a deep knowing that these visitors traversing our night-skies were of the most friendly kind. I had a sense beyond that - that they were in fact acting like guardians or big brothers, if you will, just waiting for the little ones to come to age so they could tell them all about the facts of life.

I pondered my experience for some time after, and it brought me back to the morning in Sarah's house, when she recounted her own extraordinary experience of seeing the lights in the sky, and asked me: "How do you know the aliens aren't the angels?"

I now wondered how it all fitted together; how the aliens and the angels occupied the same universe. I wondered how they all got on together, because presumably they would all have to get on somehow. I wondered why films like 'Star Wars' were so fantastical. Maybe there was a divine council of sorts running the show. Unlike my world, my questions had just got a whole lot bigger.

CHAPTER 19

—⬥—

Although I was still none the wiser about the answers to any of these mighty questions, at least my inquisitiveness had taken my mind off the next major hurdle in my physical transformation. In no time at all, October the 3rd arrived and I found myself in hospital again, back under the surgeon's knife. This time around, I was having more work done on my urinary system, what was left of my vagina was being removed and a set of testicles was being created. All in all, the surgery was expected to last around two hours. Which it did, as everything went well.

I woke up afterwards to find the area around my penis criss-crossed with stitches. Even the slightest movement caused unbearable pain. Still, I gathered myself together, determined to just grin and bear it. This wasn't something that had been thrust on me, it was something I wanted. After all, it was a small price to pay for the freedom of being myself.

I considered myself extremely fortunate, not only in having the opportunity to make the change, but also in having such tremendous support, not only from my mother and the countless others I encountered on a day-to-day basis but from the spiritual support that was making itself known a little more each day. I had no doubt of their guidance and of their love. And with all that support, who could not bear a little discomfort? Okay, a lot of discomfort, but the point is the same.

The tunnel had got wider and a distinctive light could be seen. I was now seeing the finishing post, at least with regard to my physical transformation. I had only one more operation to go, thank God, scheduled to take place in the spring. As for my spiritual finishing line, I guessed, and I'm still guessing, that question has someone chuckling quite loudly up above!

Recovery from my penultimate operation brought me to Christmas 2011. Once again the baubles, the lights, the merry-go-round that everyone jumped upon touched my heart. Christmas had been restored for me, as had my relationship with my family, especially my mother. She and I had worked hard together to establish a bond, and we had succeeded spectacularly. My transformation into the man I had longed to be allowed us to let go of the past and forge anew the love between mother and son. She was now the most important person in the world to me – my rock.

Another constant companion of my heart was of course Jamie. The long-distance relationship we had established had continued, and although neither of us would admit it openly, there was always the hint of something more than friendship on the horizon.

I had by now accumulated quite a collection of cards and letters from her. I would from time to time open the box which housed them, I suppose to reminisce on what could have been, but also to remind myself just how much Jamie must still feel for me. To be honest, I still held a tiny smidgeon of hope that faith would sort it all out nicely for me one day and allow us to somehow find our way back together. It really hadn't helped my cause of moving on from Jamie that Candy had once told me that we were soulmates. I had really taken these words to heart, as I had so wanted it to be true. Romantic fool, I know, but hey someone has to don the mantle!

Christmas came and went, taking with it all of the pain from my most recent operation. I was fighting fit by the time the New Year rang in and then, two weeks later, I was boarding a plane to Canada. I was truly flying high in both senses of the word, and it felt wonderful. I was a child again, gawping out of the window, chatting with the stewardesses, lying back and imagining in full colour the wonderful adventures that lay ahead. It was wonderful, and I was so excited. I might have sprouted wings there and then, if I had thought it would have got me to Canada any faster.

As it turned out the plane was efficient enough and we touched down on schedule. I looked out at my first view of Canada and the electricity started again. I couldn't wait to jump into my Canadian adventure. If I could have jumped the queue and run straight out of the airport, I probably would have, but instead I decided to remember that I was an adult and follow protocol.

One by one we filed through the customs checkpoint. I looked ahead; only one more to go before me, a small elderly woman. She gathered her papers, then turned to me and smiled, acknowledging it was my turn. I walked up to the desk, passport and documents in hand, and smiled at the official-looking female customs officer.

"Hello," I chirped, handing over everything.

"Good morning sir, what is the nature of your visit to Canada?"

"I'm a student. I'm studying in Hamilton at the university, it's all there."

The other officer, a man, got a whole lot more official, checking every inch of my documentation.

"Can you stand aside for a moment?" he finally said, rising from his seat.

"Is something wrong?" I said, suddenly feeling a wall building around him.

"Just stand over there sir, I'll be back in a moment."

And with that, he was gone. I moved to the end of the counter, to the spot he had indicated. I could feel the eyes of my fellow passengers following me as I walked. I smiled over at the friendly English grandmother who had sat beside me on the plane. Like me, she disliked flying, but was making the trip to see her new grandson.

"Just checking with the university," I said to her, as I had filled her in on all the details during the flight. I smiled at her, making light of it.

Then two burly security guards emerged out the doors, followed by the male officer who had attended to me. The officer returned quickly to his desk and beckoned the next passenger. The two giants – well, compared to me that's what they were - approached me and stood on either side of them.

"Is everything all right?" I said, looking up at them.

"Mr Carter, you'll have to come with us."

"Why what's wrong?"

"You'll have to come with us."

"No, not until you tell me what's going on."

"Sir, you've been requested to come with us, are you refusing?"

"Hold on a moment..."

"Come this way," the guard insisted, putting his hand on my arm for good measure.

"What's going on?" I cried, as they led me toward the door. "You can't handle him like that!" shouted the kind English grandmother.

"This way," the guard said, almost lifting me through the door. I could hear behind me the protests of my fellow passengers, but beyond the doors now, I was in security land.

"There must be some mistake," I pleaded, as I was efficiently lead into a small holding room.

"Sit down there, someone will be with you," was all I got from the tower who looked down at me. The other guard had waited by the door and was now looking down the corridor.

"You're treating me like I'm a criminal," I protested, about to burst into tears.

"Someone will be with you," the guard said, as he walked away to join his colleague in the hallway. After a whispered word between them, the guard who had done all the talking closed the door. A moment later I heard a lock turn. And once more I found myself incarcerated. It was just like my criminal days, except that this time I wasn't a criminal.

I looked around the little holding room and thoughts flooded my mind in an effort to make some sense out of it all. Did they think I was someone else? Had they found drugs and mixed up the luggage? My head reeled and my stomach churned. I gulped deep breaths, terrified that all the emotional healing that had freed me of my panic attacks would be undone.

The doors opened and another officer, this time a more

senior-looking male, sallow and fifty-something, walked in, the two security guards taking up the rear. I had worked hard to keep all the shadow aspects of my personality at bay, but my frustration and my fear were starting to weigh in on me. I really was starting to dislike the sight of those two.

"Mr Carter," said the slim officer, "It appears that there are some discrepancies with your paperwork. We understand you have previous convictions in the United Kingdom."

"That's right, for theft and fraud. I was in a dark place. Anyway I told all this to the visa agency. That was all done by them. I paid them a lot of money to make sure everything was in order. They said everything was fine."

"That may well be, but it doesn't change the fact that we have a discrepancy. What's on the forms doesn't match the official record we have for you."

"I don't know how that is. I told them everything. I've nothing to hide. I was in a bad place at the time, like I said. I'm not the same person. I'm in college now, turning my life around."

"I'm sure, however at this time I'm sorry to advise you that your legitimacy in this country is being revoked."

"Revoked?"

"You will not be allowed to enter the country, at this time. There is a plane flying back to London in eight hours, and we will make the necessary arrangements."

"Please, this can't be. Can't you ring the university..."

"The decision at this stage is irreversible. You will be retained here until boarding."

"Won't I ever be allowed into Canada?"

"Not for another two years. You may apply again in 2014."

"2014?"

"Apply then," he said, turning to leave.

"Can I at least make a phone call or get my phone? I stored it with my luggage," I said, stopping him at the door.

"Your luggage will be placed on board the British Airways flight. I don't have the authority to allow you to use the phone."

So without even a phone call, I was detained in the small grey room for eight hours, with not even a drink or a bite to eat. When the two officers, who by now I had seriously come to dislike, arrived to escort me to the plane they took hold of me, one either side. I was brought like this out of customs, past the boarding area and onto the plane, handled like a criminal, for all to see. I was devastated.

My deportation from Canada left me shaken for a couple of days. I just couldn't fathom, when everything was going so well, how something so awful could happen. I wondered if perhaps I had done something wrong to lose favour so spectacularly with the angels. It wasn't that I blamed them or anything, of course I didn't. I just wasn't sure why they didn't have my back on this occasion.

I wallowed in my gloomy disposition for a couple of days and then, deciding it wasn't getting me anywhere, I got onto the visa agency. In the end they accept full blame and sent out a full refund, which was something of a positive.

Back at university, they quickly set about finding me an alternative, which was a major positive. This time they arranged a six-month work placement in New York. New York – Jamie! It was perfect. As soon as I heard the news, all memories of Canada fell away. I quickly made a mental note to always, from herein, trust in the workings of the divine. This would all happen immediately after my final operation in April. It was perfect; I would travel to the United States whole and complete, the man every fibre of me longed to be.

Happy as a camper once again, I wrote to Jamie telling her of my plans. It seemed I was not the only one who was happy with the news. Almost instantly, we were planning the things we could do together. Jamie was out of a relationship, as I was. Both of us were free and single, so anything could happen. I just couldn't wait for the date of my operation to arrive.

And then finally it was here - April 8th, 2012. I walked into the St John's Wood hospital and went up to Ward 33, the place where I had started my story, and was wheeled into theatre. Seven, six, five... I felt myself going under and under, and then everything went blank.

I woke up with everything in place. I had a second testicle. I had a pump installed in my penis which allowed me to have erections. I turned over and let a tear flow down my cheek. It was the most amazing feeling ever. I was complete. I was finally me.

My 44th birthday was little more than a week away. Forty-four years old and a virgin, I joked with the doctor when he told me I would have to wait six months before having intercourse. My head swirled; it was beyond my dreams.

I left the hospital a couple of days later sore, bandaged and bruised, but walking on air. My inside and outside finally matched, and nothing in the world had ever felt so wonderful.

The 16th of April, my 44th birthday arrived, and I took a trip to the US Embassy to apply for my visa. The thought of being in New York, with Jamie, in my new ready-to-go manly body was more than my happiness meter could endure. I'm sure people wondered why I couldn't stop smiling, but hey, what did I care? I mean seriously, after forty-four years in the wrong body, you could have steamrollered me to the ground and I would have got up with a smile on my face.

A couple of weeks later an official-looking envelope landed on my doormat, and I raced to retrieve it. "Here we go," I murmured, tearing opening the envelope and unfolding the letter.

"Visa denied... no, this can't be!" I groaned, feeling my insides spill out. I grabbed the phone and dialled my lawyer.

"Hello, this is Lee Carter, I just received my letter from the US embassy and it says here they've denied my application."

"We hoped they wouldn't refuse you on the basis of your criminal record, it appears they have. As we said to you, this was always possible."

"You said not to worry, that we wouldn't have the same issues?"

"Yes, normally that would be the case, but given the heightened security situation in the US there was always that possibility, remote as it was."

"But hold on, I'm not a criminal and I've been to the US since I was in prison."

"Yes, but you see the US authorities always had the power to refuse you entry, given your record, and now it appears they have decided to do exactly that. I know it is disappointing, but the next time you apply the outcome may be favourable. That's just the way it is. We'll just have to see."

I won't lie, the conversation with the lawyer knocked the stuffing out of me. It took me a couple of days to get up off the floor, but off the floor I got and went back to university.

The summer wasn't long coming, nor were my exams, nor was the extra work I was doing, half-heartedly, in the university in the absence of a summer placement.

It was on one of these nondescript days that I got called out of the library by one of my lecturers.

"Hello," I said, picking the phone up.

"Hello Lee, it's your mum."

"Oh hello Mum."

"Oh Lee, I have some bad news. It's your father. He's passed away."

I don't remember my exact words. Isn't it true that words simply fail you in such circumstances? I don't remember what I said to my mum. All I remember is going back to the library and gathering my belongings. I was heartbroken. My father, regardless of everything, was still my father, and I loved him dearly.

I got through the days leading up to his funeral by fixing my mind on the happy times, those salad days of my childhood. Skipping large portions of my adult life, I also focused in on our last meeting.

"I'll have five operations in all Dad, and then that will be that," I said, explaining the full details of my transformation.

"Well Lee, you have my full support as your father. It's a brave thing you're doing to be in the right skin."

"Thanks Dad."

"No, I'm proud of you. Like I said, it's a brave thing."

Hearing my father say he was proud of me sliced away the remaining thorns in our relationship. Almost instantly, all the love I had once felt bloomed back to life. All I had ever wanted from my father was his love and admiration, so to finally receive it was such a wonderful healing for me.

My father's funeral took place on the 29th of June 2012,

exactly two years to the day from my first operation. Arriving ten minutes late, I sat at the back of the crematorium. In the seats in front of me, scattered relatives and friends gathered. It was a small funeral by any standards.

In the front rows I spotted my sister and brother. I wondered if they would even recognise me, as neither had seen me since I'd started the hormone treatment, and neither had really got on board with my transformation. I didn't blame them for that. Of course I understand that their affections were for Lisa, their big sister, and it wouldn't be easy for them to let go of Lisa and welcome Lee into the family. I guess the leap of faith needed to see that Lisa had always been Lee was just a little hard for them.

After the service, Gavin did all he could to avoid me. I respected his wishes and stayed away. We didn't speak then, and to this day we still haven't managed to bridge the void between us. Karen did acknowledge me, by calling me Lee, which meant a lot to me.

It wasn't easy feeling the pain of separation from my siblings. It wasn't easy saying goodbye to my father. And it wasn't easy standing up in front of everyone at the small service and speaking about him. There wasn't one person in the room who knew me as Lee; everyone was accustomed to Lisa. How strange it must have been for all of them.

Of course people I knew, past, present and future would have a hard time getting their heads around it, but none of this mattered to me because just now I only cared about one person's opinion in the whole wide world, and that person was me. My passion had been about experiencing life through a male identify, and my gift, through compassion, to myself was the transformation. What I did I did for myself, for the love of myself and no other. So you see, it didn't matter what other people thought of me. I was free from opinion. I was free.

After my father's funeral I decided to give the US another go. And by September another refusal was in my hands. By now, my need to get away was so great that I had taken the wise course of having a backup plan.

And so, on the 29th of September, I flew from London to Spain, from Spain to El Salvador, from El Salvador to Mexico City and from Mexico City to Guadalajara. From there, three more hours by car took me to my Mexican placement in Colima, on the Pacific Coast.

* * *

By the time I arrived at Campamento Tecoman, the base for my conservation placement, my body felt like it had travelled half the world. Despite the sweaty exhaustion that came with the midday sun, I sank down into the wooden bunk in the volunteers' dormitory feeling nothing but immense relief that I had finally made it to a foreign work placement.

I stayed three months in Tecoman, working in sea turtle hatcheries. I never imagined I would feel so alive working with the animals, doing something that was actually making a difference. I worked no more than five hours a day, which left plenty of time for leisure and contemplation. And as the weeks progressed, I started to feel a greater connection to nature and all her wonderful treasures.

Soon, with my physical transformation at an end, I started to notice an inner stirring. In addition to feeling closer to nature, I felt closer to my fellow man. Working alongside me were volunteers from all over the planet. I don't know exactly how it happened, but the differences in nationality, religion, you know all those little quirks that seem to cause so much separation, started to fade, and before long they were completely gone.

I remember one night going out to protect the turtles when on the way back I looked up at the stars in the heavens and thought, how the hell had I got so lucky? I thanked the angels, because at last I realised that the apparent disappointments of Canada and America had all happened to place me exactly where I was meant to be.

Many do say that the ocean is good for the soul, and I'm certainly not one to argue with that. I really couldn't have imagined a more beautiful and spiritual location, and it was right on my doorstep. My morning meditations seemed to take me to far greater levels of contentment than I had ever experienced.

For the first time since my Asda awakening, I felt a strong connection to a benevolent higher force, and for me that force was God. I felt connected to God, to Source or to whatever you wish to call the divine hand that is the great glue for everything. I truly felt the connection to everything and everyone around and above me and it lifted my very soul.

Speaking once around a camp-fire to one of the project managers, I was introduced to the topic of 'Ascension'. I had not up to this time heard of Ascension or the many physical symptoms that were associated with it. According to the locals, Ascension was when the consciousness of an individual or collective rises up. I was especially interested in what they had to say on the subject, because I had started to have some peculiar aches and pains of my own, which up to this point, I had been putting down to the change in my environment.

As the discussion spread to the rest of the small group

gathered around the flames, I was dumbfounded to find out how spiritual they all were. I spoke about the pressure I was experiencing at the top of my crown and I got back the intriguing explanation that it was probably due to the increased amount of spiritual energy bathing the earth ahead of the auspicious end of the Mayan Calendar.

Again, I had not known a whole lot about the Mayan Calendar up to this moment. Yes, I had heard all the rubbish about the end of the world, but I had chosen not to feed into the hype. I was amazed to find that it was the December Equinox, the 21st, and not New Year's Eve that marked the end of the current cycle, which had lasted some 5,125 years. As the conversation progressed I learnt about the Mayan Elders and their deep-rooted reverence for life.

The whole experience of that night sparked something inside me. I was hooked. I wanted to hear everything there was to hear about this ancient culture. I wanted to meet as many people as I could. And above all, I wanted to be somewhere sacred amid the Mayan Elders on the Equinox. No, it was more than wanting, I needed to be among them. Like Egypt, I now knew my whole purpose for coming to Mexico, for going to university even, was so that I could fulfil this need. I had to go.

"But Lee, to go to Cancún is 1,000 kilometers, in a bus that is not so good and on roads that are not so good," said a sceptical camp administrator.

"I don't mind, I have to go," I stated determinedly.

According to Mayan tradition, the equinox and solstice are the times when the veil between this world and the next is thinnest, so these are times when clarity about oneself and the wider world is gifted. I had for some time now felt at odds with the systems and structures handed down to us at birth. To be frank, nothing I had been told about the world made any sense. I didn't get why the whole world seemed so willing to stay on a treadmill that promised everything and delivered nothing, except to the ones who had carefully installed the treadmill. I didn't get why we had been told the only way to God was through pain and sacrifice, when I knew the exact opposite was the case – God is love and there is nothing else. And I didn't buy into the mass media and the hellish world that they seemed so hell-bent on portraying. I had changed more in the three months in Mexico than at any other time in my life. I was growing and I was opening. I was seeing with new eyes a new tender-hearted world, and it felt like home.

Over the past three months I had experienced so much good fortune, so much synchronicity that I was sure the universe was by now talking back to me, telling me I was on the right path. I was certain I was meant to go. I had to go.

And so, despite the reservations from about everyone I spoke with, I found myself standing at the bus station waiting to catch the "not-so-good" bus that would take me on the mammoth 36-hour journey to Cancún.

Seeing the bus coming, I hitched up my luggage and to my delight saw the bus was numbered 11:11. I laughed out loud – it was yet another sign telling me loud and clear to get on the bus. It was my time. My destiny. It was my purpose. You see one of the biggest internet buzzes at the time, apart from the ending of the world of course, was the 11:11 phenomenon. Apparently, in the months leading up to the Equinox, people all across the world were experiencing that number flashing in front of them. Many people believed, including myself, that it signified the great awakening of humanity – the great clarion call from above. Time to wake up. I was so ready, and what better place for me to do just that than in the midst of ceremonies at an ancient Mayan Temple.

And so, still smiling, I took my seat on a bus that wasn't so bad as it turned out. About me there seemed to be representatives from every nation. I don't know if it was my excitement spilling over, but I could have sworn that everyone on the bus wore a similar smile. Had they all been drawn to this place for the same reason as me? I certainly began to think so, because the atmosphere in the bus was exhilarating, electrifying. There we were, strangers all, embarking on the same thrilling journey.

Whilst my physical transformation was a solo journey, the spiritual journey I was now on, was every inch a shared experience. And although the bus ride was both long and arduous, I arrived in Cancún with the exact same ball of excitement I had held upon our departure. And just like Egypt, the moment I arrived I could feel the energies of the place swirling about me.

By the time we had arrived the sun had already set. I didn't realise just how tired I was until I felt the softness of the mattress under me and fell straight off to sleep.

In the morning, a tour bus took a large group of us to the great Mayan centre Chichen Itzu. Seeing so many different nationalities glowing with joy really touched me. It was humanity at its best, everyone happy, everyone friendly, everyone eager to share the collective experience.

Gathering at the foot of the seventy-five-foot Kukulkan Pyramid with my fellow tourists, I had the great fortune to strike up a conversation with a Maya Elder called Alejandro.

"Today we celebrate the beginning of a new era, a time of great personal and planetary transformation," he said.

"You feel these energies both inside and outside, in your body, in your mind and in your heart."

"I've been feeling a lot of physical changes, aches and pains, changes in my diet, that sort of thing."

"We all feel it in our own way."

"I felt drawn here, and I had the same feeling about Egypt."

"Then you are meant to be here, to celebrate the dawn of the new age."

"Are you talking about Ascension?"

"What we celebrate is called many things, but it is all the same, we all must rise with our Mother Earth. She has taken care of us all for so long and now it is time for us all, everyone, to start once more to take care of her. It is for her. It is all for her. She rises, we all must rise, for nothing can stop this momentum."

As more of his people started to gather in all their exquisite ceremonial finery, Alejandro pointed out the various Elders, Grand Elders, Spiritual Guides and High Priests. Living in the Western world I might have, in my foolery, at one time considered these people to be a step behind the rest of the world. However, listening to Alejandro explain the ways of his people, it quickly became obvious to me that I was but a child preparing for my first day at school. I had walked through the gates in Egypt and now here in Cancún I was taking my seat looking on in awe as the teachers entered the classroom.

My experience in Mexico was simply life-altering. I arrived back in the UK knowing full well that thanks to the mighty help of a whole host of angels, I was finally ready, physically and emotionally, to sit in the great spiritual classroom, and this was grade one, day one. I had changed not only my physical body but my emotional and mental state.

I knew a whole new set of lessons awaited me, and I knew this time I wasn't alone. I knew millions of others, all around the world, were taking the exact same lessons. I knew that after them, millions of others would walk into the same classroom, and so on and so on, up a grade and up a grade until everyone walking upon this earth had graduated. It was just as Alejandro had said: we are all rising up and nothing can stop this momentum.

And like little birds on the newly-ploughed field, a few will take to the heaven first, then a mass will follow and take up the remainder, then all will rise high together. *Namaste.*